THE ULTIMATE GUIDE TO SPORTS MARKETING

Second Edition

Stedman Graham
Lisa Delpy Neirotti
Joe Jeff Goldblatt

McGraw-Hill
New York Chicago San Francisco
Lisbon London Madrid Mexico City
Milan New Delhi San Juan Seoul
Singapore Sydney Toronto

Library of Congress Cataloging-in-Publication Data

Graham, Stedman.
The ultimate guide to sports marketing / by
 Stedman Graham, Lisa Delpy Neirotti, and Joe Jeff Goldblatt.
2nd ed.
New York : McGraw-Hill, 2001
p. cm.
GV713.G62 2001
Rev. ed. of: The ultimate guide to sport event
 management and marketing. c1995.
Includes bibliographical references and index.
Sports administration.
Sports—Marketing.
 Neirotti, Lisa Delpy,
 Goldblatt, Joe Jeff.
Graham, Stedman. Ultimate guide to sport event
 management and marketing.
12211483

2 3 4 5 6 7 8 9 0 DOC/DOC 0 9 8 7 6 5 4 3

ISBN 0-07-136124-3

This book was set in Palatino by Patricia Wallenburg.

Printed and bound by R.R. Donnelley & Sons Company.

McGraw-Hill books are available at special quantity discounts to use as premiums and sales promotions, or for use in corporate training programs. For more information, please write to the Director of Special Sales, Professional Publishing, McGraw-Hill, Two Penn Plaza, New York, NY 10121-2298. Or contact your local bookstore.

This book was printed on recycled, acid-free paper containing a minimum of 50% recycled, de-inked fiber.

This book is dedicated to you—the sport and event professionals, the managers and marketers, students, athletes, fans, spectators, and others who join us in the further development of this exciting profession.

CONTENTS

PART 2 PRACTICAL METHODS FOR ACHIEVING SUCCESS

PART 3 APPENDIXES

FOREWORD

THE SPORT EVENT MANAGEMENT AND MARKETING FIELD is *big business* and has grown enormously during the last two decades. From small participatory events to the mega hallmark events seen by millions, this industry had mirrored the explosive growth of media, entertainment, and tourism.

This worthy volume has arrived at a critical time in the development of this growing profession. I am certain that this text will provide useful information for a wide range of sport event management and marketing enthusiasts: from those considering entering the profession to those with extensive professional experience. The broad information covered in the text will prove invaluable to those with a variety of professional experiences who are rapidly ascending to organize and produce effective sport events.

There are very few books of this kind in the marketplace because the profession is so new. My experience in television and in the "big event" business has reinforced my appreciation for well-executed events. Trial and error produce costly mistakes, so having a blueprint and reference materials are essential. The numerous checklists and the extensive appendixes contained in this volume will make this a resource book for your entire career. For those who are learning about this exciting profession, this book is a must.

Dick Ebersol, President
NBC Sports

PREFACE

IN MY EARLY YEARS OF HIGH SCHOOL, I was determined to live my life beyond the basketball court. Fortunately, I had mentors to assist me in my journey. My mother and father; my high school coach, John Roberson; and my third-grade Sunday school teacher, Inez Edmonds—all encouraged me to be my best on the court and off. Throughout these pages, Lisa, Joe, and I will provide you with a similar guide to becoming the best professional you can be in the exciting field of sport event management and marketing.

Stedman Graham

BACKGROUND

Over the past decade, the sport industry has dramatically grown and is now estimated at over $500 billion. New York City alone claims that the economic impact of the sport industry is $6.9 billion, which includes sports-related media, organizations, and events. Furthermore, the International Events Group in Chicago reports that the amount spent on sport sponsorship continues to increase. It reached $5.9 billion in 2000. This growth has no end in sight, as the sport and entertainment fields grow closer together and event marketing continues to receive a greater percentage of corporate marketing budgets.

The purpose of this book is to help you capitalize on the opportunities associated with the sport industry by becoming acquainted with the history and evolution of this dynamic field, as well as by learning the skills necessary to succeed in it. The three authors view this book as a guide for anyone interested in the field, regardless of race, sex, or experience. Use this book and the information it presents as the key to opening doors and breaking through glass ceilings. For industry veterans, read this book as a reminder of why you selected the profession and as a way to refresh your skills and imagination.

DEFINING SPORT EVENT MANAGEMENT AND MARKETING

The term *sport event management and marketing* includes the organization, marketing, implementation, and evaluation of any type of event related to sport. Examples are from local school and community sport events, not-for-profit and corporate events, intercollegiate sport programs, and amateur and professional league activities such as the Olympic Games and Super Bowl.

WHO SHOULD READ THIS BOOK?

The Ultimate Guide to Sports Marketing is for anyone interested in breaking into the sport event profession or for those who have incidentally found themselves challenged with the task of producing a sport event for any organization, profit or nonprofit. In other words, whether you are a corporate event planner, the local charity fundraiser, a volunteer, the director of a high school sport championship game and award banquet, a league official, or someone looking for a new and exciting career, this book is for you.

WHY YOU SHOULD READ THIS BOOK

The materials provided on the subject, the professional vocabulary and background, the pertinent checklists, and the creative ideas in this book are certain to assist you in achieving the professionalism, excitement, exposure, profit, and other critical objectives necessary for success.

To better understand the professional field of sport event management and marketing, we will take you behind the scenes to comprehend how special events in sport can be effective and profitable. You will meet dozens of seasoned professionals who have helped establish and shape this growing field. Their experiences will help you avoid many of the pitfalls and failures that have befallen them.

Use the coach-player metaphor as a guide to developing your own ideas for effective sport event programs. A winning coach often serves as a mentor to his or her players. World-renowned coaches such as Vincent Lombardi, Lou Holtz, Eddie Robinson, and John Wooden understand that in order to win with people, coaches must capitalize on the assets of each player and blend them to build a consistently successful organization.

We encourage you to evaluate the assets you bring to this profession (e.g., creativity, persistence, detail orientation) and to look for mentors who can help you further develop your talents. The examples that are provided in this volume will certainly enhance, and perhaps accelerate, your achievement. Your rate of accomplishment, however, will largely depend on your ability to identify mentors and adopt and adapt their advice to your own needs.

If you are using this book to develop sport events for the organization you represent, remember that each event is a distinctly personal representation of the culture of the individual sponsor or presenter. Do not use the examples we have given as a final plan but as a catalyst to your thinking process. Once again, however, the role of a good mentor cannot be overemphasized. After reading this book thoroughly, continue your research by interviewing successful individuals in the field and developing an apprentice relationship with an organization or professional that you respect and admire. This experience will bring an even greater meaning to your reading, and the practical experience will greatly enhance your chances of finding a position in this highly competitive field.

A formal education in sport event management and marketing will also assist you in your professional development and career search. See Appendix 2-A for more information on potential career opportunities.

HOW TO OBTAIN THE MOST BENEFIT FROM THIS BOOK

We recommend that you read this book in sequential order to gain the maximum benefit. To assist you with retention and understanding, we have used several techniques to serve as anchors for your thinking process.

Each chapter begins with a thought-provoking question. Pause and contemplate this question before reading the chapter. Often, more can be learned from a well-constructed question than from the answer that follows. We try to provide our own answers for each question, but ask yourself whether other answers might be more relevant to your own interests. Also ask yourself where you can find more information to help you better understand the answers to the questions.

Each chapter concludes with a checklist of key points presented under the heading of "Game Highlights." Be sure you review these key points before continuing. Overall, we have organized the book in a skill-building style; you should master one set of skills before venturing to the next chapter.

The authors recognize the difficulty of capturing the entire body of sport event management and marketing knowledge in one book but have tried to provide suggestions and examples that are universal in nature and can be applied to any type or size event. It is our desire that you not only read the chapters but also continue to return to them for further study and reference. This book is meant to be equal parts of inspiration, motivation, and education.

The word *education* is derived from a Latin word meaning "to extract." If this book is to fulfill its mission of serving as an educational tool for you, your level of accomplishment will be determined directly by your desire to extract information. We can only open the door for you to this new profession. Your desire and hunger to succeed, coupled with experience and mentoring, will ultimately draw you through this entrance and determine the height to which you rise. We challenge each of you to not only dream big dreams and aim high, but also through your efforts to write a new chapter in this dynamic profession. Always remember, the successful event manager and marketer share the same discipline, instinctive talent, and tenacity of the best athletes. The distance you reach will be determined by the effort you expend. So...on your mark, get set, go!

Stedman Graham
Lisa Delpy Neirotti
Joe Jeff Goldblatt

ACKNOWLEDGMENTS

THE METAPHOR OF A SUCCESSFUL TEAM describes many effective organizations. Indeed, excellent teamwork is the most efficient and productive process for achieving goals and objectives.

The authors of this book certainly understand this team concept. Without the committed, generous, and talented team of sport event professionals, we could not have amassed so much valuable information.

Therefore, we must acknowledge those teammates who believe as we do that successful sport programs are special events. These individuals and organizations comprise the most successful team of all. They are responsible for the remarkable achievement of helping sport find a mass audience through reinventing itself as a special event medium. Pioneers all, their early and long labors have given the audiences of today and tomorrow the opportunity to enjoy special events in sports.

Therefore, the authors gratefully acknowledge the following individuals. We apologize for any oversight or omission on this list.

Deborah Abel
Scott Allen
Dylan Aramian
Carl Bach
Monica Barrett
Shmuel Ben-Gad
Ron Bergin
Alexander Berlonghi
Jim Birrell
Dewey Blanton
Charles Brotman
Michael Buczkowski
Peter Caparis
Hill Carrow
Alice Conway
Terry Cooksey
Lee Coorigan
Jim Dalrymple
Mary Ann Davies
Frank Deford
Jim Downs
Sue Ann Drobbin

Jennifer Duncan
Mike Dyer
Dick Ebersol
Jim Elias
Ed Eynon
David Falk
Douglas Frechtling, Ph.D.
Gil Fried
Kenny Fried
Dennis Gann
Barry Glassman
Mark Goldman
Marty Grabijas
Anita Graham
Wendy Graham
Bill Gray
Chris Green
Bill Hall
Dennis Harp
Donald E. Hawkins, Ed.D.
Denise Hitchcock, APR
John Hodges
Ed Hula
Connie Israel
Clyde Jacobs
Jeff Jacobs
Mamie Jacobs
Chris Janson
Jack Kelly
James Kemper
Phil Knight
Jill Kriser
Susan Lacz
Andre Lanier
Glen Lietzke
Jennifer Jordan-Lock
Dan Levy
Deborah Levy
Barnett Lipton
Jimmy Lynn
Andrew Marsh
Mark McCullers
Gianni Merlo
Melissa Minker
LeConte Moore
Jan Moxley
Jessica Muskey
John Naisbitt
Suzanne O'Connor
Susan O'Malley
Richard B. Perelman
Barbara Perry
Tom Peters
Brenta Pitts
Gerald M. Plessner, CFRE
Dick Pound
Emilio Pozzi
Karen Pritzer
Robert Rinehart
Susan Roane
Carol Rogala
Mary Ann Rose
Jeff Ruday
Beth Ruggiero
Steve Schanwald
Tim Schneider
Jean-Claude Schupp
Josephine Sherfy
Barry Silverman
Dr. Valene Smith
Ky Snyder
Sheryl Spivack, Ph.D.
Jim Steeg
Howard Stupp
Frank Supovitz
Tom Swanson

Jeanne Taylor
Michele Tennery
Ron Thomas
Stephen Joel Trachtenberg
Jim Tunney
Peter Ueberroth
Osmund Ueland
Lesa Ukman
Jim Vandak
Hugh Wakeham
Clay Walker
Tommy Walker
Neville Water
Bob Waterman
Armstrong Williams
Oprah Winfrey
Dan Witkowski
Virginia Wolf
Larry Yu, Ph.D.
and the sport and event management students at The George Washington University

We hope that you, the reader, will come to share our appreciation for these team players as you explore this field. Perhaps one day you will have the opportunity to meet some of these outstanding sport all-stars in person and thank them for their contributions that enabled us to provide you with their secret plays.

THE ROLE AND SCOPE OF SPORT EVENTS

The oldest standing building in Rome is the Colosseum.

Red Smith, announcer,
on the role of sports in society

1 CHAPTER

Understanding the Sport Industry, the Players, and Opportunities

It comes down to a very simple saying: There is a right way and a wrong way to do things. You can practice shooting eight hours a day, but if your technique is wrong, then all you become is very good at shooting the wrong way.

Get the fundamentals down and the level of everything you do will rise.

Michael Jordan

WHY IS SPORT EVENT MANAGEMENT and marketing a growing industry, and how can you increase your chances for rapid success?

Sport is a universal phenomenon that crosses all social, religious, and language barriers. It is a common denominator that appeals to the masses and is thus a very attractive and competitive career path. Large sport marketing firms like SFX report receiving over 5,000 résumés annually, while Nike, the shoe company, receives over 35,000 unsolicited résumés for everything from secretarial to sales to administrative positions.

Within the sport industry, one can pursue a number of different career opportunities, including managing and marketing athletes, sports organizations, products, facilities, and events. Although challenging to break into, sport job opportunities continue to grow in number, thanks to the seemingly insatiable appetite for sport entertainment. More than 14,000 companies and 29,000 executives are currently listed in the *Sports Market Place Directory*, a national sport register. Although an exact number of sport-related jobs is difficult to calculate, estimates are as high as 5 million. Not all sports jobs are glamorous, however. Many have tasks that are similar to other industries (sales, accounting, clerical), and the pay may be low. Nonetheless, the demand for these positions remains high because applicants want to work in an exciting and challenging profession. Many have remarked, "I get paid for doing what is essentially my hobby!"

While the focus of this book is primarily on the management and marketing of sport events, much of the information applies to any position in the sports industry. Some of the responsibilities of a sport event professional are understanding the goals and objectives of the event and its host(s); conducting research and designing an appropriate plan; budgeting; marketing to all constituents (participants, spectators, sponsors, media); hiring, training, and coordinating staff and volunteers; selecting and supervising contractors and concessionaires; implementing the plan; and evaluating results.

Preparing for a sport event is similar to preparing for a sport competition. Winning coaches spend hours reviewing tapes and conducting research to determine the best game plan. They scout and aggressively recruit the top players for their team and then train and coordinate these players on the field to win. After the game, the coach evaluates each of the player's performance, as well as the team as a whole. In addition, the outcome of a sport competition and a sport event is unpredictable. Yet in both, success is more likely with training, planning, and practice. A sport event manager may assemble as few as 20 or as many as hundreds of vendors, suppliers, and professionals, but all must work together to form a winning team.

There will be no second chance. Championships are won one game at a time. The sociologist William Graham Summer once wrote, "The sport establishment is a system of antagonistic cooperation." Each vendor or player may have a private and personal agenda that must be suppressed for the sake of team victory. The only goal, shared by all, is to triumph with each sport event.

APPRECIATING THE HISTORY AND VARIETY OF SPORT EVENTS

Although historical accounts credit alternatively the Greeks, Chinese, or Egyptians as the originators of sport, we know from the first written account of sport, Homer's *Iliad*, that athletic competition from the beginning was part of a larger festival—in this case, the funeral games from Patroclus. Drawings found on the walls of prehistoric caves show that men and women have always enjoyed leisure, recreation, and sport, and that these activities were often coupled with celebratory or special event activities. The organizing committee for the 1994 Winter Olympic Games in Lillehammer, Norway, patterned the Game's logo, sport pictograms, and merchandising line after 4,000-year-old Norwegian rock carvings and elements of ancient Norwegian culture (see Figure 1-1).

Today, thousands of sport events take place each year, from grassroot tournaments such as a youth volleyball or soccer tournament to fund-raisers like the Susan G. Komen "Race for the Cure" to megaevents the size of the Olympic Games and World Cup Soccer. Collegiate and professional sport competitions are also categorized as events, especially as the emphasis moves more toward the entertainment of fans. (See Figure 1-2.) Each of these sport events is organized by one or more of the following entities: national sport governing bodies, sport venues/clubs/teams, sport commissions, educational institutions, corporations, and private entrepreneurs.

Events can further be classified as spectator-driven or participant-driven. Most hallmark events such as the Olympic Games are spectator-driven, while grassroot tournaments are participant-driven.

Upon further evaluation, it is common to find a myriad of events within one event. A football game, for example, offers tailgate parties; a pregame, halftime, and postgame show; corporate hospitality tents

Figure 1-1 *Official Sport Pictograms for the 1994 Winter Olympic Games*

Utfor
Downhill
Descente

Super G
Super G
Super G

Storslalåm
Giant Slalom
Slalom géant

Slalåm
Slaom
Slalom

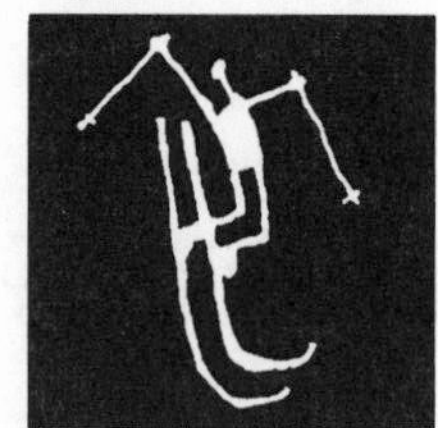

Freestyle kulekjøring
Freestyle Moguls
Ski artistique Bosses

Langrenn
Cross-country skiing
Ski de fond

Hopp
Ski jumping
Saut

Skiskyting
Biathlon
Biathlon

Ishockey
Ice hockey
Hockey sur glace

Kunstløp
Figure skating
Patinage artistique

Hurtigløp
Speed skating
Patinage de vitesse

Kortbaneløp
Short-track speed skating
Patinage de vitesse sur piste courte

Bob
Bob
Bobsleigh

Aking
Luge
Luge

Figure 1-2

Types of Sport Events

National Governing Body (NGB) Sanctioned Events
Disabled Sport Events
Professional Sport Events
High School and Collegiate Athletics
Grassroot and Youth Events
Unique/Proprietary Sport Events
Business Meetings, Conventions, and Clinics for All Sport Organizations

and suites; and game-day promotions and giveaways. While the main event takes place, each of these auxiliary events adds value to the spectator and sponsors. To help attract crowds, many teams are now mimicking the marketing and operational slogan of the Buffalo Bisons, a triple A baseball team: "Every Game's an Event" (see Figure 1-3).

Figure 1-3

1999 Buffalo Bisons
Home Promotional Schedule

April 8	OMAHA	1:05 p.m.	Opening Day
April 9	OMAHA	7:05 p.m.	fridaynightbash!
April 10	OMAHA	2:05 p.m.	Hippity Hop Egg Hunt
April 11	IOWA	6:05 p.m.	Easter Parade
April 12	IOWA	7:05 p.m.	Molson Monday/Dyngus Day
April 13	IOWA	1:05 p.m.	Two for Tuesday
April 21	NEW ORLEANS	7:05 p.m.	Business Person's Day/Secretary's Day Celebration
April 22	NEW ORLEANS	7:05 p.m.	Pizza Hut Pop-up Thursday
April 23	OKLAHOMA CITY	7:05 p.m.	fridaynightbash!
April 24	OKLAHOMA CITY	2:05 p.m.	Earth Day Celebration
April 25	OKLAHOMA CITY	2:05 p.m.	TBA
May 3	LOUISVILLE	7:05 p.m.	Molson Monday

continued on next page

Figure 1-3 *continued*

May 4	LOUISVILLE	11:05 p.m.	Two for Tuesday/Buffalo Public School Days
May 5	LOUISVILLE	1:05 p.m.	Business Person's Day
May 6	PITTSBURGH	4:05 p.m.	Exhibition Game, Presented by Old Vienna
May 12	NASHVILLE	7:05 p.m.	Business Person's Day
May 13	NASHVILLE	11:05 p.m.	Pizza Hut Pop-up Thursday/Catholic School Day
May 14	INDIANAPOLIS	7:05 p.m.	Carnival Weekend/ fridaynightbash!
May 15	INDIANAPOLIS	2:05 p.m.	Carnival Weekend/Darien Lake Day
May 16	INDIANAPOLIS	2:05 p.m.	Carnival Weekend/100 Club Day
May 17	INDIANAPOLIS	7:05 p.m.	Molson Monday/German Festival Night
May 28	NEW ORLEANS	7:05 p.m.	fridaynightbash!
May 29	NEW ORLEANS	7:05 p.m.	Jubilee Little League Weekend/Summer Safety Day
May 30	NEW ORLEANS	7:05 p.m.	Jubilee Little League Weekend
May 31	NEW ORLEANS	7:05 p.m.	Molson Monday/Memorial Day Picnic
June 6	NASHVILLE	6:05 p.m.	TBA
June 7	NASHVILLE	7:05 p.m.	Molson Monday
June 8	NASHVILLE	7:05 p.m.	Two for Tuesday
June 9	NASHVILLE	1:05 p.m.	Business Person's Day
June 10	LOUISVILLE	7:05 p.m.	Pizza Hut Pop-up Thursday
June 11	LOUISVILLE	7:05 p.m.	fridaynightbash!
June 12	LOUISVILLE	7:05 p.m.	TBA
June 13	LOUISVILLE	12:05 p.m.	TBA
June 14	INDIANAPOLIS	7:05 p.m.	Molson Monday
June 15	INDIANAPOLIS	7:05 p.m.	Two for Tuesday/Italian Festival night
June 25	NEW ORLEANS	7:05 p.m.	fridaynightbash!
June 26	NEW ORLEANS	7:05 p.m.	Donruss Baseball Card Day

continued on next page

Figure 1-3 *continued*

June 27	NEW ORLEANS	2:05 p.m.	TBA
June 28	OKLAHOMA CITY	7:05 p.m.	Molson Monday
June 29	OKLAHOMA CITY	7:05 p.m.	Two for Tuesday
June 30	OKLAHOMA CITY	1:05 p.m.	Business Person's Day
July 4	LOUISVILLE	7:05 p.m.	Independence Day Celebration
July 5	LOUISVILLE	7:05 p.m.	Molson Monday/Polaroid Team Photo Day
July 6	INDIANAPOLIS	7:05 p.m.	Two for Tuesday/Irish Festival Night
July 7	INDIANAPOLIS	1:05 p.m.	Business Person's Day
July 8	INDIANAPOLIS	7:05 p.m.	Pizza Hut Pop-up Thursday
July 9	OMAHA	7:05 p.m.	fridaynightbash!
July 10	OMAHA	7:05 p.m.	Wheaties Day of Champions
July 11	IOWA	6:05 p.m.	Surf & Snuggle Tee Shirt Day
July 12	IOWA	7:05 p.m.	Molson Monday featuring "The Blues Brothers Act"
July 22	NASHVILLE	7:05 p.m.	Pizza Hut Pop-up Thursday
July 23	NASHVILLE	7:05 p.m.	fridaynightbash!
July 24	OKLAHOMA CITY	7:05 p.m.	TBA
July 25	OKLAHOMA CITY	7:05 p.m.	Turn Back the Clock Day/Buffalo Baseball Hall of Fame
July 26	OKLAHOMA CITY	7:05 p.m.	Molson Monday
August 5	LOUISVILLE	7:05 p.m.	Pizza Hut Pop-up Thursday/Upper Deck Card Album Giveaway
August 6	LOUISVILLE	7:05 p.m.	fridaynightbash!
August 7	LOUISVILLE	7:05 p.m.	TBA
August 8	INDIANAPOLIS	6:05 p.m.	TBA
August 9	INDIANAPOLIS	7:05 p.m.	Molson Monday
August 10	INDIANAPOLIS	7:05 p.m.	Two for Tuesday
August 22	OMAHA	6:05 p.m.	TBA
August 23	OMAHA	7:05 p.m.	Molson Monday
August 24	OMAHA	7:05 p.m.	Two for Tuesday
August 25	OMAHA	1:05 p.m.	Business Person's Day

continued on next page

Figure 1-3 *continued*

August 26	IOWA	7:05 p.m.	Pizza Hut Pop-up Thursday/Polish Festival Night
August 27	IOWA	7:05 p.m.	fridaynightbash!
August 28	IOWA	2:05 p.m.	TBA
August 29	IOWA	2:05 p.m.	TBA
September 3	NASHVILLE	7:05 p.m.	fridaynightbash!
September 4	NASHVILLE	7:05 p.m.	Back to School Day
September 5	NASHVILLE	7:05 p.m.	TBA
September 6	NASHVILLE	7:05 p.m.	Fan Appreciation Day

Made-for-television events are yet another type of sport event that deserves attention. With the increase in television rights fees, the introduction of cable television, and the need for more sport programming, made-for-television sport events have grown in popularity. These events include the Goodwill Games, X Games, and Gravity Games, and although they usually attract fewer on-site spectators, most of the logistical elements remain the same. Historically, ABC's Roone Arledge was the first television producer to recognize sport as a special-event medium and was determined that the television audience would enjoy the event regardless of the outcome of the competition.

To achieve this goal, Arledge used cranes, blimps, and even helicopters to obtain dramatic views of the stadium, the campus, and the surrounding countryside at an event. With handheld cameras for close-up pictures of the spectators and players, and rifle-type microphones to pick up local sounds, Arledge made the fans an integral part of the sport event. Once the fans perceived themselves as potential performers, they began to display banners, run onto the field, and engage in numerous other attention-getting and scene-stealing activities.

Other sport-related businesses such as health clubs and sporting good companies also utilize special events as a means to attract and retain members and to sell merchandise. Regardless of the type of event, the goal remains to meet customers' needs and to ultimately retain or increase the patronage of the sport event and the corporate sponsors.

To remain viable, each generation of sport event marketers must produce creative geniuses, such as the father of major league baseball promotions, Bill Veeck; impresario George Preston Marshall; the "Barnum of the Bushes" of minor league fame, Joe Engel; or master Olympic marketer Peter Ueberroth. Gone are the days when teams simply opened their gates and hoped that spectators would enter. For teams in a slump, it is important to divert attention form a poor season by developing sport as a special event so that the score becomes incidental to the overall entertainment value the fan receives.

For megaevents, large corporate sponsors such as Coca-Cola and M&M Mars invest heavily in research to attain the greatest return on their investment. Coca-Cola's marketing strategy typically includes painting the town red and white with ads, billboards, umbrellas, and chairs, whereas M&M Mars lights up the surrounding landscape with its product colors of orange, green, yellow, and brown. The planning takes years, not days, of careful preparation on signage placement; media buys; local, national, and international retail promotions; sales incentive contests; on-site hospitality; travel; accommodations; and ticketing to ensure success.

Research conducted by Professor Robert Rinehart, affiliated with California State University at San Bernardino, states that the Super Bowl is a "modern ritual of pilgrimage in which people attend to reunite with their friends and experience the event in concert with others of similar interest." In fact, Rinehart found that individuals attend the game "to be seen, to enjoy the hoopla, to support the team, and to continue a ritual." Similar research conducted by Lisa Delpy Neirotti on the Olympic Games identified the "party atmosphere" as a strong motivator to attend the Games. For many, this sport event experience is a recurring life-shaping experience.

Sport event producers, in conjunction with their corporate sponsors, are beginning to create all-day interactive programming for consumers. The ATP Tour Fan-Feast, for example, is an all-day sideshow that consumers participate in before, during, and after the main event. Each activity is designed to highlight a sponsor's product or service in a playful environment. Kodak, therefore, hosts the Kodak Korner where fans get pictures taken with cutouts of tour players, Sega premieres its "Electronic Tennis" video game, and Rolex times fans' tennis serves. As planning proceeds for these events, the organizer must segment each market to meet consumer and sponsor needs and to achieve specific outcomes. This process requires research and knowledge about the lifestyles of the guests and potential trends that may be incorporated to encourage participation.

THE STARTING BLOCKS

The first step is perhaps the most difficult and challenging of any career search or transition. While it is extremely difficult to enter the sports industry at top-level positions, it is not impossible. The secret is to create a plan and then work your plan until the time is right for your career opportunity. If you are working full-time, seek opportunities to volunteer at events during the weekends. Find out what events your company may be sponsoring, and express interest in helping out. Contact not-for-profit organizations, schools, clubs, and professional event management firms. Ask them if you can volunteer to help with a forthcoming sport event. Sport events such as professional All-Star games, championships, and golf and tennis tournaments create a number of temporary positions. These events will not only provide you with valuable experience but also assist you in developing relationships that can lead to a career in sports. Unfortunate but true, building a Rolodex is almost as important as experience and education.

According to Stedman Graham:

> Volunteering and learning from experts is your quickest way to the top. We are not reinventing the wheel. The work that we are doing and that is being accomplished has been done before. Trial and error is the most dangerous and expensive form of learning. You should consider interning or apprenticing with an experienced professional prior to attempting to produce your own sport events independently. A mentor can give you the advice and guidance until you have the right skills and training to go off on your own. These are essential to building a strong base that will enable you to understand the business and build a successful future for yourself and your family.

It is important, however, to select a mentoring organization carefully. To establish your relationship with the organization, send a letter of inquiry similar to that shown in Figure 1-4. Be sure to do your homework prior to sending any correspondence. Find out who is directly responsible for coordinating volunteers or for organizing the overall event. Jennifer Jordan-Lock, who served as the director of Press Operations for the 1998 Goodwill Games and many other events, suggests that you do not call the individual before you send the letter but make your follow-up call on the date that you indicated in the letter. This demonstrates your integrity and organizational skills.

Do not be disappointed if you are referred to someone else or even turned down. Be persistent and continue searching for opportunities until you establish the critical relationships necessary to succeed. Never wait for the phone to ring; it is up to you to pick up and dial.

Figure 1-4 *Sample Query Letter*

Your Address
City, State, ZIP
Telephone
Facsimile
Date

Name
Title
Organization Name
Address
City, State, ZIP

Dear (Mr./Ms.):

Your forthcoming sport event is of great interest to me. I am writing to volunteer my services to assist you with any aspect of this activity where I might be of use.

My résumé is included for your review. I am particularly interested in [X], but am willing to help you in any area.

Good luck with this event. I will call you next Tuesday to discuss my possible involvement.

Sincerely,

Name

Title

Although experience is one way to learn a skill, another is thorough formal study. Over 140 colleges offer programs in sport management. A combination of both experience and formal study is ideal.

PERSONALITY, LIFESTYLE, AND WORK STYLE CHARACTERISTICS YOU WILL NEED

With your letter, attach a résumé listing your direct or related experience to sport event projects. Sport promoter Charles Brotman says, "Send me your résumé and it will be read. We never know when we might need someone with your exact skills." Although special skill sets such as computer technology and graphic design are always in demand, sport event professionals typically share several common traits (see Figure 1-5). Use this figure only as a guide. It is not applicable to every sport because each sport is different and therefore requires unique skills.

Another trait common to many sport event managers is that they are highly competitive. Some, though not all, were professional athletes and understand the spirit of competition and good sportsmanship. All, however, understand the importance of competition in raising the benchmark of quality with each event. The competitor they face is themselves. Each time they accept a new sport event challenge, they seek to improve their chances of success and to refine their performance.

EXPECTATIONS

Because of the high demand for sport-related jobs, starting salaries are often low and most positions require internship or other experience. Refer to Figures 1-6 and 1-7. SFX, the world's largest live sport and entertainment company, currently offers two internship programs: one for college students earning course credits toward a degree and another for people looking to break into the sport/entertainment industry on a full-time basis. The first stage of the full-time training program lasts five months, during which time the candidate is paid an hourly wage in accordance with the federal minimum wage, up to a maximum of 40 hours per week. No benefits are offered at this time. At the end of this period, the candidate is reviewed. If

Figure 1-5

Common Traits of Sport Event Managers

1. Comfortable with preparing and managing a checklist of activities
2. Projects a positive attitude
3. Can work independently or as a member of a team
4. Accurate and quick at details
5. Articulate on the telephone and in written and oral communication
6. Creative, flexible
7. Capable of working under extreme pressure for long hours
8. Good at working with all levels of people including volunteers
9. Effective at balancing multiple projects simultaneously
10. Excellent time manager
11. Effective negotiator
12. Finance- and budget-conscious
13. Possesses good typing, word processing, and other office skills
14. Leadership ability
15. Quick problem solver
16. Good motivator
17. Desire to learn and grow

acceptable, he or she progresses to the second stage, where for the next seven months, the candidate earns $12.50 per hour up to 40 hours per week, plus full-time employee benefits. At the end of the year, if the candidate's work is positively assessed and there is a need, a permanent position will be offered. Salary is negotiable, but an average starting base is between $30,000 and 35,000.

Regardless of the starting salary, each of these positions can serve as a catalyst for management to notice you quickly, thus accelerating the possibility of your promotion. The successful sport event manager often possesses strategic planning and management skills that owners and supervisors seek when considering employees for advancement. Do not be afraid to make suggestions for improvements or take on additional responsibilities that will demonstrate your competencies.

When searching for a sport event job, you may often find that these jobs are hidden within traditional career titles or job descriptions (e.g., assistant athletic director or assistant director of commu-

Figure 1-6

Sport Event Salary Guide

Salary Level	Potential Annual Salary*
Entry level	0 to $18,000
University sport program	$30,000
Minor league management	$40,000
Major league management	$100,000
Sales and marketing managers	$50,000 and higher
Entrepreneurs (gross revenue)	$500,000 and higher

*These figures may be adjusted upward with the addition of sales commissions, bonuses, and other incentives.

Figure 1-7 *Job Advertisements*

DIVISION I UNIVERSITY

Position: Athletics Promotions/Home Events Manager

Duties: Develop and implement an ongoing promotional campaign for intercollegiate athletics. Responsible for coordinating all aspects of home event management including setup, staffing, game operations, game-day promotional activities, and ticket consignment.

Requirements: Bachelor's degree required. Experience in athletics promotions/marketing at the collegiate level preferred. Excellent communication skills and ability to work closely with constituent groups required.

Salary: Commensurate with experience ($25 to $35K). Send letter of application, résumé, and names and phone numbers of references to...

2002 WINTER OLYMPICS—SPORTS PRODUCTION PROFESSIONALS NEEDED

The Salt Lake Organizing Committee for the 2002 Olympic & Paralympic Winter Games is currently seeking sport production professionals to manage and/or assist venue teams, producing 78 live sporting events across 10 indoor and outdoor venues.

Lead Producer/Management positions require a minimum of 3–5 years strong sport event production. Coordinator positions require 2–3 years of sport production/entertainment or events experience.

Salaries for the Sport Producer positions range from $50–65K and Coordinator positions range $30–45K.

Please submit one résumé per position, including a cover letter explaining your qualifications to...

nity relations). The Baltimore Orioles baseball team management includes special events as a multidisciplinary activity that utilizes the skills of not only the public affairs department but also group sales and stadium operations. The title of sport events coordinator, manager, or director is relatively new. Therefore, you may need to inquire within a variety of departments regarding which group has direct responsibility for special event planning and management and then identify the salary range for this position.

The marketing side of sport event management is more lucrative. If you can bring in money for an organization through sponsorships, advertisements, or ticket sales, you will be compensated accordingly. Alan Rider, author of "The Mobile Stockbroker" (published in the January 1993 issue of *Home Office Computing*), states that events-oriented marketing professionals can earn more than $100,000 a year and freelance planners can earn from $1,800 to $30,000 in fees for each project. These entrepreneurs may bill a flat fee for all of their services or a percentage of the overall cost (usually from 10 to 20 percent) for larger, more complex events. The sport event planner becomes a general contractor, a position similar to a homebuilder. Be forewarned, however; since most sport events take place after normal working hours, you will be required to spend nights and weekends on the job.

Now that you recognize the opportunities that are rapidly emerging in sport events, you are ready to begin the critical process of planning events. In Chapter 2, you will master the principles of planning to further ensure the success of your sport event.

GAME HIGHLIGHTS

- Realize that the production of sport events is big business and that there are a number of career opportunities available.
- Seek professional employment in this field by identifying mentors and preparing yourself through formal education as well as practical experiences.
- Recognize that sport events are part of tourism and have a large economic impact in the United States.
- Understand the demands of working in the sport event field and the need for creativity, organization, and flexibility.

Critical Planning to Master the Game

Beware of the big play: The 80-yard drive is better than the 80-yard pass.

Fran Tarkenton

How does the practice of developing winning plays affect the outcome of the game, and how can you use this same strategy to win with sport events?

Former Secretary of Defense Donald Rumsfeld said, "Plan backwards. Set your objectives and trace back to see how to achieve them, even through you may discover there is no way to get there and you will have to adjust the objectives."

A wise business executive once advised, "Innovate or evaporate." The same is true for the emerging field of sport events. Successful innovation hinges on the ability to create solutions for strategic challenges using the best available information.

Successful coaches invest significant time researching the competition so that they can best prepare their players for the game. Furthermore, the best coaching professionals recognize the strengths and weaknesses of their players and team organization in order to design winning strategies.

In this section, we will present a model for analyzing an event's strengths, weaknesses, opportunities, and threats to help you design a winning game plan for your event.

SWOT: THE STRENGTHS, WEAKNESSES, OPPORTUNITIES, AND THREATS ANALYSIS

A crucial first step in preparing a game plan for a sport event is to conduct a strengths, weaknesses, opportunities, and threats (SWOT) analysis. The SWOT analysis is a detailed examination that helps you look at internal aspects of your organization and sport event, along with external variables that may affect your overall success.

The strengths and weaknesses part of the analysis allows you to look at the internal resources available in planning your sport event. Opportunities and threats provide you with crucial information for assessing external situations, such as political issues that may directly or indirectly affect the plans you formulate.

Prior to conducting a SWOT analysis, you must be familiar with every detail of the sport event, including budget, personnel, volunteers, time, date, location, target audience, and population size of the community where the event takes place.

We will use a 5K road race scheduled for a Saturday morning in April on the Mall in Washington, D.C., to examine the SWOT analysis. Organized by the George Washington University Sport and Event Management Forum, the event expects between 500 to 750 runners from the metropolitan area. Proceeds will benefit the Forum scholarship fund.

Strengths

What distinct competencies do you as a professional bring to the event? What additional competencies can you identify within your own organization? What other resources within the organization and community can you identify that will strengthen your position in planning this event?

Even if you do not have any specific sport event experience or formal training, consider skills you have developed in previous positions or the experience of organizing and managing a family. The combination of skills, along with a knowledge and interest in sport, certainly provides you with strengths that can help you to succeed in producing your sport event.

Forum Strengths

- The Forum will provide plenty of experienced sport event managers to work at the event and marketers to sell the event.
- The Federal Park Service will provide the security for a fee. They are experienced in crowd control on the Mall and have worked at various fun runs and rallies.
- Tents donated by a Forum board member will be erected to protect runners before and after the race from the sun or rain.
- Internal and external written communications are facilitated through the use of e-mail and faxes. All promotional materials are produced in-house with a university desktop publishing system and a Web site created and hosted on a university server.

Use Figure 2-1 to identify the practical skills and abilities that you or others in your organization may possess. Although your interpretation of these strengths is not an empirical science, the overall SWOT analysis will help you to identify the strong traits your organization possesses. Keep in mind that every sport event is distinct and may require a varying amount of strengths to ensure success.

Weaknesses

Analyzing weaknesses as well as strengths is extremely important, as these internal aspects can easily become a burden to your sport event program. Convene a brief meeting among key staff and volunteers to determine any weaknesses. Ask them to suggest internal areas that are critically inadequate, that may be controlled and corrected by training, or that require elimination before their weakness erodes your entire organization. Elimination may mean that key staff or volunteers must be reassigned or even released. Remember, the list of weaknesses can be as long as the list of strengths, but they must be recognized and dealt with efficiently.

Figure 2-1

Strengths Analysis Checklist

Assess each skill by writing the term **strong, average**, or **weak** in the Assessment column.

Skill	Assessment
Financial Planning Budgeting, accounting, management	
Human Resource Management Recruiting, training, supervising, motivating staff and volunteers	
Safety, Security, Risk Management Admissions, venue grounds, spectators, players, personnel	
Hospitality Invitation design and production, amenities, coordination of logistics, hosting activities	
Food and Beverage Negotiations, quality, quantity, contract and price	
Sales and Marketing Prospecting, selling, closing, servicing	
Writing Correspondence, promotional copy, internal memoranda, newsletters, trade publication articles, media releases, follow-ups	
Leadership Ability Persuasion, motivation, listening, problem-solving skills	
Other skills or strengths:	

Forum Weaknesses

- The Forum does not have any start-up capital, so it must rely on in-kind donations until cash is raised from sponsorships.
- Staff time is limited for this project, so the organization is heavily based on volunteers.
- The race course is on federal land. Since no financial transactions can take place on federal land, no on-site registrations can be accepted. An alternative site must be arranged for the day of registration.

- No concessions can be sold because the event is held on federal land.

Use Figure 2-2 to identify the weaknesses that you or others in your organization may possess.

By concentrating on strengths and weaknesses, you are shoring up your organization to best handle the opportunities and threats from external variables. Getting your ship in tip-top shape at the planning stage is critical to survival on the restless seas ahead.

The external variables that may affect your sport event include both opportunities (positive elements that need to be exploited and searched out) and threats (negatives that should be confronted or avoided). Less controllable than internal variables, opportunities and threats nevertheless require careful analysis to ensure a successfully planned sport event.

Opportunities

The opportunities that present themselves may increase your revenues, generate greater positive public relations, and provide other benefits for your organization.

Figure 2-2

Weaknesses Analysis Checklist

Assess each weakness by writing the term **critical**, **controllable**, or **eliminate** in the assessment column.

Weakness	**Assessment**
Disagreements among key staff and/or volunteers	
Personality conflicts among staff and/or volunteers	
Lack of trained, experienced personnel and/or volunteers	
Short planning time	
Funding problems	
Facility shortage or inadequacies	
Other weaknesses:	

Forum Opportunities

- A large registration is expected at this early time of the year because athletes want to participate in this short-distance 5K race as a warm-up for longer-distance races later in the season.
- Washington, D.C., has a strong base of recreational runners who will support the event.
- The event is held during a busy tourist weekend, so many people will be near the mall area, creating the high visibility that sponsors find attractive.
- The president of the university has agreed to be the honorary chair for the event and run in the race.
- Students have a stake in the proceeds, so they will register and encourage their peers to run as well.

Use Figure 2-3 to identify the opportunities for your event. Characterize these opportunities as probable if there is sufficient evidence to determine they are likely to occur. Define them as developable if an opportunity, such as media coverage, is not yet firm but highly likely to occur. Finally, determine whether an opportunity requires control. If the

Figure 2-3

Opportunities Analysis Checklist

Assess each opportunity for its value by writing the term **probable**, **developable**, or **requires control** in the assessment column.

Opportunity	Assessment
Historical activity—centennial, sesquicentennial, bicentennial, quincentennial	
Prospective partners or volunteers	
Prospective sponsors	
Other major events prior to or following yours. Activities that could increase your attendance	
Tourism activities in the area of your event. Scenic, historical, or cultural attractions	
Friendly business community	
Friendly governmental agencies	
Other opportunities:	

opportunity you have identified supports your goals and objectives, develop it. However, if it does not entirely support your end result, determine ways to control it. For example, a tourist-related activity such as a major music festival may be scheduled on the same date as your event. Control this activity to the best of your ability. Otherwise, this scheduling conflict could shift from an opportunity to a threat. A solution is to hold your event prior to the music festival so your participants also can enjoy the festival. Sponsors will get a bonus as well.

Threats

From political unrest to inclement weather, threats are real occurrences that may jeopardize the overall success of your sport event. Football coaches have long preached that "a good offense is your best defense." By recognizing as many potential threats as possible, you increase your chances for success by identifying any factors that may impede that success.

To determine the universe of threats that surrounds your sport event, bring together managers from various parts of your event-planning process. This includes risk management, volunteers, marketing, transportation, ticketing, concessions, and all other critical departments. Ask all managers to list any potential threats within their department and to identify any threats that may affect the event as a whole.

Forum Threats

- Inclement weather is probable at this time of year.
- A bicycle race scheduled on the same day may attract athletes away from the 5K race.
- Students have threatened to rally at the event in protest of tuition increases.
- Local police, fire, and rescue teams may not have enough human resources for both your event and a competing one.
- A new ordinance is being discussed within the city council that will require all events to pay for police services.

Figure 2-4 is an assessment guide to help you identify potential threats and assess your vulnerability. All threats that are listed in Figure 2-4

Figure 2-4

Threats Analysis Checklist

Assess each threat by writing the term **serious, monitor further**, or **requires coverage** in the assessment column.

Threat	Assessment
Political unrest	
Economic recession	
Negative environmental impact	
Advocacy group protest	
Violence	
Crime	
Trade union disagreements or strikes	
Acts of God	
Weather or other uncontrollable occurrences	
Other threat:	

can be potentially controlled. However, it is essential that you assess the vulnerability of your sport event within its context. For example, political unrest may be potentially serious but requires further monitoring. Acts of God cannot be controlled, but they can be monitored and should be covered by insurance to reduce your financial exposure.

CREATING AND WORKING YOUR PLAN

Too many organizations spend countless hours developing plans that are then filed away for posterity. Successful sport event management and marketing professionals use their plans as a critical tool to sculpt their success.

A variety of event-related software packages are available to assist in project management, financial and data analysis, development of diagrams, site plans, and tournament scheduling. Tournament Builders by SportsMVP.com, for example, not only facilitates the scheduling of tournaments offline but allows users to post the schedule and update results online so that participants, significant others, and media can remain current from anywhere anytime. According to Jan Moxley, author and publisher of *The A C [Advance Coordination] Manual* (Interactive Communications, 1996), "The problem with most of the existing software is that it lacks detail and the ability to integrate a number of events and activities, forcing organizers to use a variety of programs."

Most of the larger sports events and organizations have created proprietary programs such as the one described by Jim Birrell, vice president of Operations for Turner Sports and the Goodwill Games:

> With the 2001 Games being held in Brisbane, Australia, and 900 freelance broadcast personnel required to produce 45 hours of coverage, it is not feasible to bring all the broadcasters over there. Therefore, an international talent search and database management system has been created through the Internet, whereupon once a freelance broadcaster has been identified and terms agreed upon, he or she completes an extensive form that is posted on the Web. Besides personal contact information, questions included in the form include departure and arrival dates and locations, hotel selection, current employment status. With a click of a button, this information is automatically shared with all affected departments. The housing coordinator knows that one less room is in her block for the Holiday Inn; the travel agent knows to book a certain flight, which is then electronically ticketed, which triggers the flight itinerary to be posted on the Web site for the employee to check; the personnel office sees that this person is not an employee of Turner and sends the appropriate forms or contract through e-mail, which are then resubmitted via the Internet with an authorized electronic signature. This not only saves time but thousands of dollars in overnight international shipping.

The Salt Lake Olympic Organizing Committee is using a similar system for volunteer registration, while Primavera project management software is being used by the Organizing Committee to track the 46 functional areas, 288 projects, and 4,343 activities that need to be completed to stage the Olympic and Paralympic Winter Games. Some of the commercial companies entering this field are View Point Technology in Canada, MSL in Spain, and Eurotech in France.

Furthermore, Frank Supovitz, group vice president, Events and Entertainment, for the National Hockey League, explains the system he uses to organize the many events for which he is responsible:

> Each event is completely different and therefore requires a separate strategic plan. However, for multi-events occurring within the same time period (such as the NHL All-Star Game that includes a Heroes of Hockey [Alumni] Game, a skills competition, various receptions, and the All-Star Game itself, I create individual production schedules and then incorporate them into a master planning document to create synergy between each project.

A practical approach to organization is to keep your master plan in a three-ring binder. You will see how useful this becomes when you begin to accumulate schedules, contacts, logistics, and other important information. The binder keeps them in one place where the information can be updated easily. As the event draws near and schedules become final, this binder becomes your event operations book. Copies of your plan book or portions of it should be given to everyone involved with the sport event to keep them apprised of the most current information.

Regardless of what system you use, the components in Figure 2-5 should be part of any sport event plan.

Figure 2-5

Sport Event Plan
Developing a Sport Event Checklist

1. Determine your projected revenues based on venue capacity and historical data. Then develop the budget and an expense plan utilizing these projections. Working realistically within this budget will cause much less stress.
2. Determine the time frame for preproduction, production, and postproduction activities. Do not be overanxious and do things that require redoing later or additional work and expense. For example, ticket sales are accompanied by advertisements and promotions. If you start your campaign too early, before the public is ready to purchase tickets, you will be expending energy unnecessarily. In addition, order brochures and promotional materials in adequate quantities. Reprinting may double the original cost.
3. Organize your time by first determining what tasks must be performed in sequential order, specifying the time and date. This is essential when licenses and permits are required. Special application deadlines and

continued on next page

Figure 2-5 *continued*

procedures may be imposed. Solicitation of corporate and foundation money is also sensitive to time considerations because of budget cycles. Do your homework and learn when companies develop their budgets, when their fiscal year ends, and when foundations consider proposals.

4. Plan backward. List each task that needs to be done and decide on deadline dates. Figure out the steps required to complete each task and the time needed. If you want people to respond to your invitation by a certain date, calculate the time for invitation design and printing, labeling, mailing, receipt, and response. Subtract this time from your deadline date and you know when to begin this task.
5. Allow for extra time (by providing sufficient padding to your schedule) to handle unforeseeable delays.
6. Confirm and verify your plans with everyone involved in the activity such as vendors, key staff, volunteer leaders, and officials. We recommend a weekly meeting with all staff and a monthly meeting with everyone involved. Mailing an internal newsletter leading up to the event is not only informative but also keeps everyone motivated and on track.
7. Determine what protocol is required that may affect your timing and sequence of events. The International Olympic Committee (IOC) requires that invitations to the Olympic Games be mailed exactly one year prior to the competition.
8. Determine and incorporate into your planning any specific league or federation protocols or regulations. The National Collegiate Athletic Association (NCAA), for example, allows only a limited amount of alcohol-related advertising. Professional leagues dictate a specific time frame for television commercials in pregame, halftime, and postgame shows. Regulations on the number, size, and type of venue signage is also common.
9. List all activities for which each department is responsible in a separate schedule of events. Then incorporate these individual activities into the master plan. Coca-Cola developed a comprehensive project management computer program that listed and tracked progress on all activities associated with and leading to the 1996 Olympic Games in Atlanta, Georgia.
10. Include in your plan book a master contact form listing the names and other critical numbers (work, home, e-mail, fax, mobile telephone, beeper) of each member of your sport event management team.
11. Allow for contingency decision making in your plan. If the event is called because of rain, how does this affect your plan? Downhill skiing is always programmed on the first day of the Winter Olympic Games in case of weather delays.
12. Make your plan in the smallest workable increment. Use a maximum time window of 15 minutes. You must plan televised sport events in second-by-second increments (see Chapter 8).

PLAN FOR UNIQUENESS

When Mike Dyer, vice president of New Development for the NBA, was working as the executive director of the 1994 St. Louis Olympic Sports Festival, he realized the importance of thinking outside the box:

> Traditionally, organizing committees held elaborate, high-priced opening ceremonies in stadiums that cost thousands of dollars to produce, resulting in little or no profit. Considering our limited budget and the need to spearhead the Festival in the community, we decided to hold the opening ceremony under the famed St. Louis arch and invited the public to attend for free. We ended up attracting 80,000 people, and the excitement from this opening event was contagious, resulting in thousands of ticket sales for the remainder of events.

As expressed by Dyer, "Although it is important to evaluate previous events, don't be afraid to do things differently. Every event can evolve and change." It is also important not to let an event go stale. For example, the NBA decided to give the All-Star "slam dunk" contest a rest for two years. When they brought it back, both the players and audience were more enthusiastic.

Another example of bucking tradition is the idea of the Amateur Athletic Union to hold the opening ceremonies of the Junior Olympics in the middle of the Games when the majority of participants are attending the event, rather at the beginning.

INTERNATIONAL EVENT PLANNING

Two of the major challenges of organizing events abroad are distance and communication. "You cannot just jump on the next plane and conduct a site visit in Japan like you can do if the event is in the United States," explains Mike Dyer, former vice president of the NBA Events and Attractions Group. If you are traveling thousands of miles, you better make plans to visit every hotel and venue and to meet with all the essential people. You must rely heavily on the people on the ground to assist with these visits and meetings. It is also essential to understand how business is done in the country where the event will take place. In Asia, for example, the people are very efficient and detail-oriented. Expect to attend meeting after meeting. In other countries a "mañana" attitude may be more prevalent. With the three-hour lunches in Spain, you may feel like nothing will get done.

Regardless of the cultural differences, it is vital to follow up every meeting in writing and to make sure documents are signed and exchanged so each party is fully aware of respective responsibilities. If someone in Asia says "we'll check," beware. Since it is culturally rude to say "no," most likely "we'll check" means "no." Upon written confirmation, you may find that your foreign colleagues agreed with very little of what you thought they agreed with.

The issues of gender and seniority may also create problems for events organizers. Even high-level females may find it difficult working with men in some countries. Knowing simple protocol such as how to greet people will go a long way when building relationships in foreign countries.

It is also important for sport event managers to realize that most arenas overseas are not like those in the United States. They typically do not have concession areas and locker rooms, and if they do, they are small. Few arenas are air-conditioned or have video scoreboards, and smoking is also still permitted.

CONDUCTING YOUR PLANNING MEETINGS

When planning meetings with staff, volunteers, sponsors, or service providers, always remember that everyone's time is valuable and that the more efficiently the meeting is run, the more likely that people will participate and the outcome will be a success. One of the most often heard concerns expressed by volunteers is that the organizers are wasting their time by having them just sit around and do nothing. If you call a volunteer meeting or training session, make sure that you begin on time and that the material is ready and presented in an orderly fashion. Use Figure 2-6 as a guide to meeting planning.

CELEBRATING SUCCESS AND CONTROLLING STRESS

To keep the motivation and spirits high among your event staff, build into your planning cycle a series of miniature benchmark celebrations that allow you to recognize the accomplishments of your

Figure 2-6

How to Win a Gold Medal at Your Team Meeting

Step 1: Announce the meeting well in advance to allow each team member to prepare properly. Request that all team members submit with their attendance confirmation forms any agenda items they want to cover. Circulate an agenda before the meeting.

Step 2: Post a welcome message with directions to the appropriate meeting room. Whenever possible provide light refreshments to offer hospitality and energize the participants.

Step 3: Use a flip chart, and appoint a scribe to stand by the flip chart and write down the key points covered during the meeting.

Step 4: Always start the meeting on time even if all the participants have not arrived. Latecomers will probably be on time for the next meeting.

Step 5: Review the agenda, ask for any additional items, and then ask that the agenda be approved.

Step 6: Allow each member to contribute to the discussion and encourage not only agreement but also positive dissonance.

Step 7: Keep the meeting on schedule. Ask individual team members how much time they will need to present their agenda item. Record their response and use it as a benchmark to keep the meeting on schedule.

Step 8: Alert your team members when only 15 minutes remain until the end of the scheduled meeting. Give them the option of ending on time, continuing the discussion at the next meeting, or postponing the discussion until needed.

Step 9: End the meeting precisely on time but first recognize the participants for their productivity. Your team members will appreciate your promptness and work even harder next time to help you facilitate the meeting when they know that you respect their time.

Step 10: Analyze the positive and negative aspects of the meeting by asking your team members to list what was successful and what could be improved upon in the future.

team members (e.g., the signing of the first sponsor, the groundbreaking for venue construction, 100 days to the event). Every successful plan will include many opportunities to celebrate the achievements you and your team have worked hard to attain. Those who worked on the 1984 Los Angeles Olympic Games remember how Peter Ueberoth constantly rallied the troops. When spirits started to sag, he found reasons to celebrate, and this certainly contributed to the success of the Games. Similarly, the Atlanta Olympic

Committee scheduled brown-bag lunches for employees on the first Friday of every month up to the beginning of the Games and invited guest speakers to the lunches, including many former Olympians who shared their memories of Olympic participation.

To absolutely guarantee your success in planning your sport event, use the simple formula given in Figure 2-7 to stay on schedule and to remain focused on the goal.

A meeting planner once remarked that more than 3,000 separate decisions are made about any meeting from the beginning of the planning cycle through the management of the event. In the sport event field, this number could easily triple because of the complexity of combining protocols, expectations of different customers (sponsors, event owner, participants, media, spectators), multiple venue sites, various ethnic cultures and populations, and your own creativity.

Indeed, both the left side and right side of the brain receive a tremendous workout as you plan your sport event. The creative as well as the logical side is essential to your success. Therefore, details, your ability to communicate accurately and freely, and your willingness to gain access to expert advice will certainly increase your chance for success as you plan your sport event.

It is natural to feel tension and stress when embarking on a new mission. However, allowing your natural tension to turn into stress will be extremely counterproductive to your goal. When feeling stress, try to identify what part of the planning process is causing the stress. You may find that you are not adequately prepared to handle a specialized area such as protocol or financial management.

Once you have identified the cause of your stress, you can remedy this discomfort by delegating the task to an expert on your team or source it out. Remember that stress is not productive to long-term achievement of your goal. Deal with it quickly and efficiently so you can get on with planning your successful sport event. Keeping a sense of humor is also vital.

Figure 2-7

The Not-So-Secret Sport Event Formula for Success

Details + Communication + Expert Input − Stress = Success

PLANNING FOR CONTINGENCIES

Despite your most careful planning, an act of God or other catastrophic event may occur. If you have planned correctly and professionally, you will be able to handle these developments with a minimum amount of concern from your guests. The following are four examples of potential challenges to your planning program and the contingencies you might develop to deal with them.

Loss of Key Personnel

The loss of a senior official in your organization could be devastating to operations and staff morale. One way to plan for this contingency is to encourage your team to job share.

Request that employees learn each others' jobs and set aside a specific time each week to train one another. During the 1990 Goodwill Games in Seattle, a number of key personnel left at a crucial time in the competition. Several volunteers who had demonstrated leadership potential in the early stages of the games were promoted to senior management positions. Their previous cross-training enabled them to finish the project successfully.

The 2002 Salt Lake Olympic Organizing Committee has implemented an eight-point retention and reward program that motivates their employees to stay throughout the Games. This includes a compensation package that continues to pay out for a certain period of time after the completion of the Games based on the number of years employed. This transition pay is only paid to those individuals who remain with the organization until their end date, as stipulated in the hiring letter.

Similarly, plans need to be made to retain volunteers throughout an event. Based on the experience of Jeannine Hunte, a sport management consultant, only volunteers who have worked three matches before the semifinals are allowed to work the final match at the Legg Mason Tennis Classic in Washington, D.C.

Weather Emergency

Your corporate golf tournament in Kawaii is canceled because of a hurricane. A snow emergency prevents your 70,000 spectators from traveling to your championship basketball tournament. Flooding pollutes the city water system, and health officials close all public venues, forcing you to cancel or postpone your gymnastic meet. Advance planning is important in handling these crises. Did you purchase cancellation insurance to protect your investment? Did you have a strategy to notify the participants of an alternative plan that is equal to or exceeds the value of the scheduled tournament? Playing the "what if?" game can help you plan contingencies and prepare for unexpected disasters.

Damage Control: Pool Cooling System Fails

According to Jack Kelly, former executive director of the 1986 U.S. Olympic Festival in Houston, Texas, and current executive director of Bowling Proprietors Association of America, "I remember when, two hours before the swim competition in Houston was to begin, I received word that the pool cooling system was not functioning." Thinking quickly, Kelly called every ice company in the area to contribute ice blocks to cool down the pool so the meet could start on time.

Power Outage

A D.C. United Major League Soccer Game had to be called at halftime when the lights would not turn on at RFK Stadium in Washington, D.C. Once the stadium was evacuated and the power turned off, the lights were fixed in 10 minutes. An electrical storm knocked a fuse out, but electricity could not be cut to check the problem while people were in the stadium. Now it is standard operating procedure to turn the lights on before any event even though this costs money.

SPORT EVENT PLANNING: SUMMARY

As Yogi Berra once said "It ain't over 'til it's over." Berra was not only a championship baseball player but also a great strategic thinker. He understood that planning has neither a beginning nor an end; it is a continuous series of event itself.

As a professional sport event planner, you must constantly be planning to improve your events through a thorough evaluation process. This process begins with your first meeting and continues long after the event has concluded and you begin to plan the next event.

By analyzing strengths, weaknesses, opportunities, and threats (SWOT), you can take a critical look at the universe within the your organization and around your event.

As you develop your plan, you will achieve success through a series of team meetings. If these meetings are organized for maximum effectiveness, you will move efficiently toward your strategic sport event goal. And if you celebrate even small successes, you will raise the self-confidence of your team and keep spirits high.

Most important, there is no challenge that cannot be overcome with proper contingency planning. Practice damage control as you develop your plan to ensure that small problems do not have overwhelming consequence. Like sport itself, practice makes perfect—or at least minimizes risks and injuries.

The famous architect Mies van der Rohe reportedly said, "God is in the details," and so it is with this first critical process of producing a successful sport event. Attend to the most minute detail, communicate freely, insist on expert input, and resist stress to achieve the sport event for which you have planned.

Planning successful sport events is equal parts art and science. In Chapter 3, you will find that designing, planning, and controlling event logistics is a not-so-precise science that will greatly influence the outcome of the artwork for your sport event.

GAME HIGHLIGHTS

- Conduct a SWOT analysis to determine the internal and external variable that may affect your event.
- Organize your meetings to reflect the success you plan to achieve with your event. After all, a good meeting is an event.
- Identify opportunities to celebrate success that will motivate staff and reduce stress.
- Plan for every possible contingency and practice damage control to prevent a minor problem from becoming a major catastrophe.

RESOURCES FOR EVENT PLANNING SOFTWARE

Event Command by Actis Inc. (www.actisinc.com)

Event Planner Plus by Certain Software (www.certain.com)

Meeting Pro by Peopleware (www.peopleware.com)

Summit Pro and Summit Light by MIE Software (www.miesoftware.com)

Room Viewer by TimeSaver Software (www.timesaver.com)

Tournament Builder by SportsMVP.com (www.sportsMVP.com)

Advance Coordination Manual and CD-ROM by Zone Interactive (www.zoneinteractive.com)

Microsoft Project 2000 (www.microsoft.com)

Primavera Software (www.primavera.com)

Designing, Planning, and Controlling Event Logistics

You can't think and hit at the same time.

Yogi Berra

WHY IS ATTENTION TO THE MOST MINUTE detail critical to your success in planning sport events, and how can you make certain that every aspect of your event is carefully designed to satisfy the needs of every constituency group?

ASKING THE RIGHT QUESTIONS

Barry Silberman, former president of Entertainment and Development for Washington Sports and Entertainment and currently president/CEO of Estadios Panamericanos, offers this important advice in producing a sport event: "Gather as much information as possible. You can never ask too many questions, and if you assume that you know what your client is talking about, you may find yourself in big trouble." Silberman, for example, assumed that the soil used for bull riding and tractor pulls at the USAir Arena would be suitable for the Spanish Riding School of Vienna. Unfortunately, he did not find out until the last minute that a different loam quality or pebble content was required for this horse event. The only solution was for staff members to scramble and pick pebbles from the soil.

Likewise, event organizers should be aware that there is special salt-free sand used for indoor beach volleyball events held in arenas sometimes used for hockey and skating events. The salt in regular sand could affect the ice-making ability of the venue.

Silberman also emphasizes the need to ask the right questions. For indoor tractor pulls, it is important to find out the weight and amount of vibration that will be placed on the floor and investigate whether it will ruin any ice-making equipment under the floor. When you are asked to produce an event that you have not done before, the first thing you should do is call someone who has. You can also ask the appropriate sport governing body for recommendations.

LOGISTICS

Of the many different sport events that Barry Silberman has produced, he believes that events that attract a great many teams, extensive media, and on-site hospitality, such as the NCAA Basketball Tournament, are the most complex to host. Silberman considered the NCAA to be a "great client," however, because it knew what it wanted and had specific guidelines to achieve this. Throughout the event, everyone knew what they had to do, and people from the NCAA monitored all activities. In all sport events, logistics are a critical consideration and a determining factor in the success of the sport event.

Often the most brilliant idea has gone sour owing to poor logistical planning. How many times have you attended a function with a magnificently displayed buffet only to stand in line for what seemed like hours because only one line was prepared rather than two? A good rule of thumb is one food or beverage line for every 75 to 100 people.

The term *logistics* is derived from the Greek *logistikos* (the science of calculating) and *logos*, which means reason. Logistics, in modern usage, also means handling the details of any operation. To combine the two, we might ask the question, can the sport event manager direct his or her creativity into a reasonable path that will produce an effective event? The answer should be yes if you are to ensure safety, respect the public trust placed in you, and meet the goals and objectives established for the event.

One way to prepare for success is to create a logistical plan. The level of logistical planning is directly influenced by the conditions surrounding the event (e.g., number of different sports and venues, level of competition).

In this chapter, we examine all dimensions of logistical planning for sport events. Appendix 2 has samples of a production schedule and a master plan showing how logistics function within the framework of your sport event.

Figure 3-1 offers a checklist of some of the conditions that must first be determined before you can begin your logistical planning. Use this checklist as a reminder during your planning.

Figure 3-1

Sport Event Logistical Conditions Checklist

_____ What is the purpose of the event—raise money, generate media attention, product marketing, customer entertainment?

_____ How large is the event—number of participants, spectators, media, and VIPs?

_____ What is the budget?

_____ Will the event be held indoors, outdoors, or both?

_____ How many venues will be used and how far apart are they?

_____ Are outside vendors required? If so, which ones and how will they be selected?

_____ What are the requirements of the facility and do they meet Americans with Disabilities Act (ADA) and health department standards?

_____ Is there a need to build or renovate the venue?

_____ How much time is required for setup and takedown of the sport event?

_____ Will food and beverages be served, and if so, what permits are required?

_____ What type of food is appropriate to serve?

_____ Will food and beverage be dispensed free, paid by prepurchased ticket, or paid with cash at the event?

continued on next page

Figure 3-1 *continued*

_____ How many guests do you guarantee for?
_____ What type of entertainment, if any, will be provided?
_____ Are ceremonies scheduled?
_____ Will the athletes, spectators, and media arrive and depart by private automobile, private motorcoach, or public transportation (type of transportation, itinerary, and special needs)?
_____ How will staff and volunteers arrive and depart from their assigned locations?
_____ What housing requirements are needed for athletes, media, VIPs, and spectators?
_____ Is enough housing available to accommodate all contingencies?
_____ What are the sanitation needs (portable toilets guideline: 1 per 100 to 200 people)?
_____ Will the audience include a large segment requiring special accommodation (e.g., disabled, senior citizens, multilingual speakers)?
_____ Will the spectators pay to attend, receive free admission, or have a combination of admissions?
_____ What is the appropriate entrance or registration fee?
_____ How will the tickets be sold and distributed?
_____ What is the seating configuration—stadium, thrust (3/4 round wherein the audience sits on three sides of the stage), auditorium, or a combination of seating designs?
_____ Is general, reserved, or festival seating ordered for the event?
_____ How many staff and/or volunteers does your event require? (Warning: Experience event managers say that 20 percent of volunteers typically do not appear the day of the event.)
_____ What additional training will be required for staff and volunteers?
_____ Should special outfitting be ordered for event staff and volunteers?
_____ How will uniforms be distributed?
_____ How much storage area is required (equipment, merchandise, etc.)?
_____ Does the event have a high-risk factor (e.g., a pyrotechnics show) and is the audience involved in the performance in any way?
_____ Has the necessary insurance been purchased?
_____ What are first aid, police, and crowd control requirements?
_____ Is increased security needed (e.g., teams with intense rivalry, hot weather, etc.)?
_____ How will the program be promoted? Is this an annual event or a hallmark (usually a nonrecurring, historical milestone) event?

continued on next page

Figure 3-1 *continued*

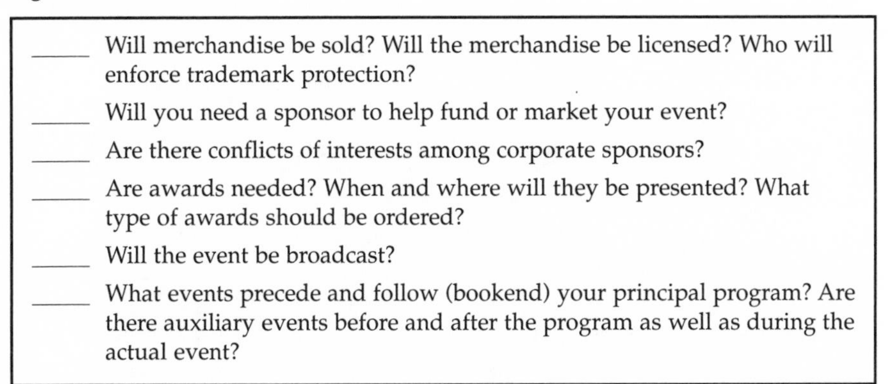

_____ Will merchandise be sold? Will the merchandise be licensed? Who will enforce trademark protection?

_____ Will you need a sponsor to help fund or market your event?

_____ Are there conflicts of interests among corporate sponsors?

_____ Are awards needed? When and where will they be presented? What type of awards should be ordered?

_____ Will the event be broadcast?

_____ What events precede and follow (bookend) your principal program? Are there auxiliary events before and after the program as well as during the actual event?

Once you have answered these questions, you will have a better idea of your logistical and operational requirements and can begin to develop an organizational structure. An organizational structure identifies the direct order of report so you can effectively plan and manage all the details of your event. Key positions and external contacts should also be identified to support the organizational structure (see Figures 3-2 and 3-3). Dennis Gann, executive director of the Sioux City Convention Center and Auditorium Tourism Bureau, recommends that when you organize your sport event committee, no more than three people should have final decision-making power. A good mix is to have one person responsible for legal and government entities, one for finance, and another for logistics. The purpose of the event also determines the level of logistics. For instance, charity sport events are typically more concerned with the bottom line and do not plan for as many amenities as the high-profile sport event geared to attract media attention.

Depending on the results of your SWOT analysis and the scope of your event, outsourcing certain responsibilities may be a prudent decision.

WORKING WITH VENDORS

As a sport event spectator, do you ever notice who provided the tents, portable toilets, grandstands, and electricity, or who printed the programs, manufactured the volunteer uniforms, removed the trash, and

Figure 3-2

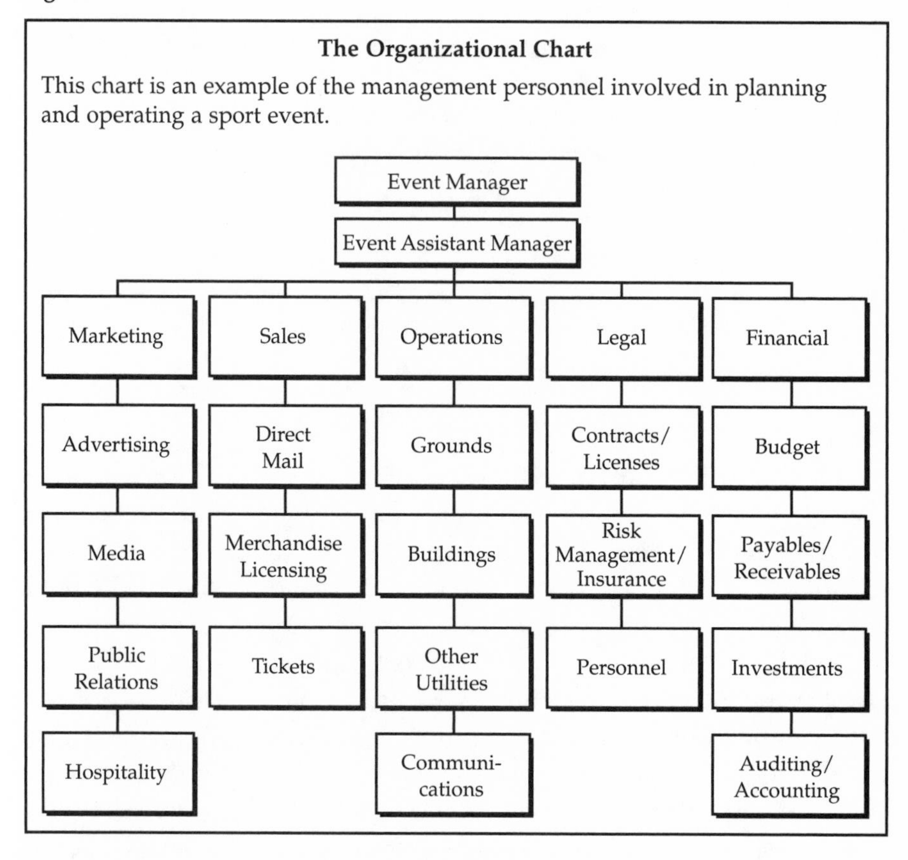

secured the grounds? For the majority of people, the answer to this question is no. As a sport event manager, however, these are some of the most critical decisions that often determine the overall success of an event.

The first step in the vendor selection process is to determine the various categories of goods and services required for each event. According to Jeanne Taylor, championship director for the 2000 U.S. Senior Open and numerous other golf championships, over 30 separate vendor categories are required to produce a professional golf tournament. In addition to the products and services listed above, events frequently contract out for graphic designers, concessionaires, office furniture, signs, courtesy cars, scoring system, tent caterer, hotels, generators/air conditioning, trailers, photography, copiers,

Figure 3-3

Key Personnel and Important Contacts

Each person in charge is a critical link to the future cohesion of your entire event.

- Admission supervisor
- Athletic trainers
- Box office supervisor
- Buildings supervisor
- Catering manager
- Civic, municipal, and federal officials
- Communications manager (public address, radios, scoreboard, internal-wireless, and external-public telephones)
- Convention and Visitors Bureau director
- Delegation leaders
- Emergency services supervisor
- Entertainment coordinator
- Fire marshal
- Grounds supervisor
- Housing coordinator
- HVAC (heating, ventilation, air-conditioning) supervisor
- International officials
- Marketing director
- Media center director
- Medical supervisor
- Military leadership
- Parking supervisor
- Police
- Protocol expert
- Public relations director
- Public safety (signage, nonmarketing) supervisor
- Sanitation supervisor
- Security supervisor
- Television producer
- Transportation supervisor
- Utilities supervisors (electric, water, gas)
- Volunteer coordinator

towing, landscape, badges/credentials, tickets/parking passes, table/chairs, parking attendants, car wash attendants, communication radios, fencing, fuel, and shuttle buses.

After identifying each of the required vendor categories, a request for proposal (RFP) must be developed for each service area and distributed to appropriate vendors, who, if interested, will respond with a bid proposal. Most importantly, RFPs should include an overview of the event, with specifics about the scope of responsibilities of both the vendor and host organization.

The list of responsibilities for a caterer may include providing all food and beverage service personnel, as well as equipment for corporate tents and kitchen commissary areas; contracting with the selected tent, trailer, electrical, and waste management vendors to provide the necessary facilities and services required to perform operations; arranging for a florist and a decorating company to furnish all the floral and interior decorating or theme displays; securing all the necessary permits and licenses required for the food service operations; procuring certificates of insurance; and serving meals to the volunteers and players for free. An RFP for a caterer may also ask for a general description and layout of the main catering compound, operational plans, sample menus with pricing, and any minimum guarantees that a corporate client would need to fulfill for various meals.

The host organization's responsibilities for catering would typically include providing the corporate tents with adjoining service areas; the space necessary for the catering compound and access to service roads; admission and parking credentials for all employees; at least 2 two-way radios on the host organization's operational frequency; fencing and security for the kitchen compound, corporate village, and all other facilities; public and employee restroom facilities; and in-kind food and beverage provided by sponsors for use in preparing volunteer and player meals.

Frequently, a number of different vendor categories are included under one RFP. This typically occurs in RFPs for tent companies, where they will be asked to not only provide tentage but flooring, carpeting, a hospitality village boardwalk (a deck connecting all tents), electrical/air conditioning (or heating), lighting/ceiling fans, lightning rod/fire protection, television stands, furniture, cleaning service, and decor packages.

To fulfill such a request, the tent company usually must hire subcontractors. The primary benefit of a comprehensive RFP is that one general contractor, the tent company, and not the event manager, handle the coordination of all these details. And, according to Tom Cipu, sales executive of Classic Tents in Silver Spring, Maryland, the tent company can usually deliver a better price since the subcontractors already know the tent company and can trust that tasks will be done in an efficient manner.

In addition to vendor and host responsibilities, RFPs should list specific requirements regarding the type of product to be used and/or the way in which services are to be delivered. For example, in an RFP for a tent vendor, the following statement may be included: "AstroTurf carpeting to be of upgraded quality that has not been used prior to the event, and the carpet shall be tacked down and not taped."

Additional information requests about the vending company, including years in business, experience, size, current and previous clients, as well as the price for each of the items listed in the scope of responsibilities and the time required to perform the service, should also be specified in the RFP. Often, the minimization of setup and teardown time is extremely important to a host organization.

The number of on-site staff that the vendor plans to scheduled for your event is another important question to address. This is especially true for categories such as tenting and lighting. Dave Pavelko, operations manager for the Correl Champions, quickly learned the importance of hiring a local lighting company with on-site staffing when high winds tipped over most of the event's stadium lights. Because of liability issues, it was extremely difficult to then find a local company who would touch the problem. Unfortunately, the number of on-site staff often increases the cost of service, so be careful of what you request.

Evaluation criteria is yet another area to include in an RFP. The criteria for graphic design service may include proposed method of approach, experience in comprehensive project design and production, expertise and experience of personnel, and competitiveness of overall pricing. Whenever possible, Jeanne Taylor prefers to visit different events and witness the work of potential vendors firsthand before making a vendor selection. When selecting a communication vendor, it is important to check how many frequency channels are available on the radios; if the equipment works between hotel floors, in the arena, and at the airport; and that the channels do not bleed over.

As expected, experience and price tend to be the most important criteria across all vendor categories.

Although most RFPs are specific to one event, the duration of the contract should always be stated in the RFP. Some organizations that produce multiple events of similar type (e.g., PGA, NFL) sign 3- to 4-year national vendor agreements. Overall, long-term agreements are typically more efficient for both the host and vendor. One, the time and energy involved in the vendor selection process is eliminated, and two, the vendors have time to develop a close working relationship, which allows them the opportunity to assist one another wherever needed. Certain vendor categories such as landscape and printing will almost always remain local for obvious reasons.

Finally, vendors should be offered the opportunity to visit the event site prior to submitting their proposals and asked to add any features that they feel may be missing from the RFP. This helps avoid any hidden costs entering into the project.

As you can see, before an event manager can write an RFP, he or she must be extremely familiar with the event. In the words of Tom Cipu, "The more detailed the RFP, the more accurate and helpful a bid proposal will be. Without knowing the exact number, type, or style of tents, as well as the physical layout of the grounds, it is difficult for any tent company to appropriately respond to an RFP."

Another frustrating point for many vendors, as expressed by Susan Lacz, principal of Ridgewell's Caterers in Bethesda, Maryland, is an RFP that asks for the world without offering much in exchange. If a host organization demands a large catering commission as well as high-quality, reasonably priced food, they should consider ways in which to work with the caterer versus nickel and diming them to death. For example, if a caterer is charged for everything they need to work, including the space required to set up their operation, that fee will simply be reflected in the menu pricing. And in the end, the higher the price of the catered food, the less satisfied the corporate owner might feel about the event.

To avoid this problem, some vendors suggest that event managers with minimal experience in writing RFPs include more "what if" or "how" questions. For example, a RFP for a caterer would ask "What commission would you offer if trash, space, and access were provided?" and "What commission would you offer if you were charged for trash, space, and access?" Or, "How would you set up your kitchen and service area given the specific space dimensions?" Some event managers, such as Jennifer Jordan-Lock, actually prefer this approach to selecting vendors. According to Jordan-Lock, "By asking open-ended questions, it allows you to better judge how vendors think on their feet—a critical characteristic of anyone involved in events industry."

Irrespective of how the information is collected, the final step in the vendor selection process is to actually review and compare all the bid proposals received based on the stated criteria. Ultimately, the highest ranked organization is selected and a contract is signed. Although Chapter 5 covers contracts more thoroughly, for now, just remember to read carefully and make sure all possible event scenarios are covered through various clauses such as *force majeure*.

In conclusion, a sport event vendor RFP should include as many details about the event as possible, as well as the specific roles and responsibilities of both the vendor and host organization. The most important consideration to remember is to feel comfortable and confident with your vendors, as they are your true partners in an event.

SELECTING A WEB PARTNER

In today's high-tech world, an additional event vendor may be a Web developer or Internet company. If electing to outsource Internet development or to work with an existing Web company to help market and administer your event, be sure to follow these recommendations:

1. Make sure that the Internet company actually has the technical capacity to do what they are claiming they can do and that they can provide all the functions you want them to do (e.g., online registrations, database management, page skimming, e-commerce, chat rooms, tournament draws, security, outbound e-mail, easy use and maintenance of schedules, news, statistics). Many dot coms will come with a fancy laptop presentation demonstrating their capabilities, but they may not be able to actually implement them. Ask to see a site that has been developed by this company and that is up and running on a server. If one is not available, ask how long they expect before they will have the service ready to demonstrate. Find out what version of software is being used—is the company in beta testing or are they on the third version? Obviously, you may not want to be the guinea pig. Also, inquire about the load capacity, how much information can be put on the site (e.g., digital photos), and how much business they can handle.
2. Gather information on the people running the company, along with their past experiences. It is often helpful to work with people who not only have the technical expertise but who also have some experience working in the sports industry so that they

understand the needs of all constituents, as well as the politics of amateur and professional sports. Find out how many staff members the company has and how many are working in the field helping local sport coaches and teams utilize the Internet. What type of service or training does the company provide? Is there a service desk open 24/7? Also, how many people do they have selling advertisements and sponsorships? Be leery of those sites quoting large amounts of money that your organization will receive from ad revenue if they do not have an advertising sales force. Also, how many other sports organizations, teams, athletes, or events are working with the Internet company? Ask for references.

3. Request to see records of the company's funding or financial status. Many dot coms may be running on a shoestring hoping that by signing your organization or event, they will be able to secure angels and venture capital financing. Once they sign your organization, they may also be too busy signing other organizations or looking for money to actually develop and grow your Internet site. Unless this company has something very unique to offer, you may be better off going with a group that has venture capital money already in place. Another factor to consider, however, is how close a company is to going public. Often, once a company issues an IPO, the founders and people that have developed the company will depart soon after their golden handcuffs have expired, leaving you with a new and often skeletal staff.
4. Find out what type of revenue opportunities the company is offering. Some companies offer a flat fee and/or stock options in exchange for total control and exclusivity over your site. This includes all revenue potential. Such fees are negotiated based on the leverage of the party (e.g., the number and demographics of members and/or fans, the prestige of the sport, the amount of content). Aside from losing some identity, a concern with this model is that the Internet company may sign an advertiser or sponsor that conflicts with one of your organization's existing sponsors.

Other Internet companies work on a revenue split model where your organization keeps a larger percent of any advertisement or sponsorship revenue that it brings in, and vice versa, the Internet company keeps a larger percent of those advertisers or sponsors that they sign. For merchandise sold on the Web site, if the merchandise is specific to your organization (e.g., it bears your name or logo), you should receive a greater percent of the profit. Percentages range from 5 to 30 percent depending on the type of product.

Still other Internet companies designate areas on the Web site in which your organization can sell local advertisements and keep 100 percent of the revenue, along with other areas for national advertisements that the Internet company sells and keeps the revenue. In addition to these revenue models, you may also want to negotiate bonus clauses for reaching a certain number of visitors, for an increased percent of page views, or if the company is purchased or goes public.

5. As far as identity, ask how the site will be structured. Will your organization be able to keep its own brand identity and its own URL, or will visitors need to type in the URL of the Internet company? Will your Web site keep the look and feel of your organization and/or your current Web site, or will your Web site be similar to other organizations that have signed up with the Internet company—in a cookie-cutter format. Will the Internet company be able to put advertisements wherever they like, or are there specific locations on the site designated for advertisements?
6. Considering that the Internet is still a new phenomenon, your organization may prefer to hedge its bet and work with a few companies. You could hire a Web developer to simply design your site, find another company to host (i.e., provide the server) for the site, and then maintain it internally by hiring a Web master. Or, you could have one company design, host, and maintain your main site and have other companies develop and host subsites, such as a kids' club site, alumni site, community site, or e-commerce site, that are all linked to the main site.
7. When negotiating a contract, it is advised to ask for a nonexclusive short-term agreement or designate exclusive rights for only specific services. Do not offer blanket rights, as you do not know what technology may be coming in the near future or what the

value of your rights may be in the future. For example, if you offer full Internet rights and broadband width grows dramatically, the Internet company could possibly start video streaming your events online, limiting your ability to maximize television rights fees. Other contract terms should include (a) prior approval of all design work to make sure the image of your organization is portrayed appropriately; (b) a list of product categories that the Internet company is prohibited from associating with your Internet site; (c) the minimum amount of revenue the organization will receive per year, with specific percentages outlined for all revenue streams such as sponsorships, advertisements, and merchandise; (d) milestone dates that the company must meet if new technologies were promised; (e) the right to review and approve any mergers and acquisitions that involve the transfer of your rights from one Internet company to another with an out-clause if the terms of the contract change (this is very important in case the new Internet company is applying a different business model than the one you originally agreed to); (f) bonus clause that offers your organization a financial incentive if the company you are currently associated with gets purchased or goes public; and (g) approval of any links that will be placed on your site with a reciprocal link required (typically you only want to link with sites that draw an equal number or more visitors to their site).

VOLUNTEERS

Sport events typically require intensive volunteer participation. According to Jeff Ruday, chief operating officer and director of Finance for the Hoop Dreams Scholarship Fund:

> A three-on-three basketball tournament with 800 to 1,000 participants will require approximately 500 volunteers to serve as court monitors per court per day, plus others to handle refreshments, registration, score table, and so forth, not to mention setup and breakdown of equipment.

Recruitment and training of volunteers is important in all sports events. A charity or sponsor associated with an event is a good source for volunteers. Another successful way to recruit volunteers is to mention the need for volunteers in your promotional materials. Popular event such as the Cherry Blossom Run in Washington, D.C., which requires a lottery drawing to enter, offers volunteers an automatic registration for the following year. Megaevents such as World Cup Soccer require a very structured volunteer recruitment and training program. The number of volunteers required to host the Summer Olympic Games is approximately 75,000, while 1,000 to 1,200 are required for professional All-Star events and golf tournaments. A volunteer coordinator is typically hired to develop and oversee such programs. When possible, identify volunteer leaders for specific tasks and ask that each of these people recruit the number of additional volunteers that they will need to complete their assignment. Volunteers are more likely to show up if they are reporting to a friend or family member. This is often referred to as "herding volunteers" versus a "cattle call for volunteers."

Budget considerations should also come into play when discussing volunteers. Although the term *volunteer* is used, the cost of recruiting, outfitting, feeding, and transporting volunteers range from $10 to $250.

Training programs typically include a basic educational component followed by specific department training. Simulation exercises should be included in these sessions where potential scenarios are played out as close to reality as possible. Volunteers with radios in hand should sit around a table while the problem is posed. They should then simulate what they would say and do to rectify the problem.

Once the day of the event arrives, let the volunteers take charge. Tell them to do what they have to do (get more ice, water, call emergency services, and so on) to make the event enjoyable and safe for participants. Make sure your volunteers understand that the customer is always right and to show respect.

Whether volunteers or paid employees, you should appoint troubleshooters to supervise the setup of the event, the flow of people, and the breakdown of the event.

UNIFORM DESIGN AND DISTRIBUTION

Have you ever wondered why certain sport event volunteers and staff members are dressed the way they are? Have you ever considered the planning it takes to design, manufacture, and ultimately distribute all those outfits? According to Andrew Marsh, a veteran sport event manager and a uniform distribution coordinator for World Cup USA 1994, this is one of the most challenging yet important pre-event logistics. The uniforms of the staff and volunteers and perhaps even the contractors and vendors should reflect the "look" of the event. Not only will uniforms provide a means of identification and authority for the staff, but they bring class to the event.

Well before the event begins, the style, color, and fabric of the uniforms are selected for specific reasons. For example, the executive staff, interpreters, administrators, and hosts and hostesses may be outfitted in a blazer and slacks or skirts and blouses, since it is likely that they will interact with the media, sponsor representatives, or public officials. To avoid confusion among the patrons and to build team spirit, each division within the management team should have a unique uniform color and style. The admissions or public information staff may wear a blue polo shirt and matching shorts or pants, while the ushers wear a red T-shirt or windbreaker. The operations and support staff members are outfitted in more casual attire, such as shorts and a T-shirt, that does not affect their work—namely, setting up equipment. The uniforms for security and medical staff must be readily identifiable yet not threatening to the spectator. The security guards for the World Cup wore a khaki uniform complete with purple berets reflecting the international and peaceful flavor of the games. The medical personnel wore white jackets with an internationally recognized green cross on front and back. The uniform fabric must be selected with consideration for the weather and temperature. Obviously, you do not want wool uniforms for a summertime event or shorts in the winter.

Depending on the number of staff involved, the style (e.g., elastic waist or button) and number of pieces in the uniform, sizing and distribution could be problematic. It is very important that the staff, particularly the volunteers, get the correct uniform and that it fits well. An ill-fitting uniform reflects poorly on the event and for a volunteer with shorts three times too big, make it doubtful that he or she will enjoy helping you out. It is important to consider these points when selecting uniforms:

- Sizing
- Ordering in time for manufacture
- In-kind sponsorship of uniform parts
- Simple distribution
- Exchanges/return policy
- Alteration of executive uniforms

When Lisa Delpy Neirotti volunteered for the 1988 Seoul Olympic Games, she first reported to a warehouse where she was measured for her uniform and provided a shoe coupon. This coupon was redeemable at certain stores throughout the city that carried the official uniform shoe. Lisa later returned to retrieve her uniform, at which time her credential was scanned and she was checked off as receiving all pieces of the uniform.

FACILITIES

Venue selection is extremely important but may be limited by the type of sport event availability within your region. Each sport governing body provides guidelines on required venue dimensions and amenities in order for an event to be officially sanctioned. The number and type of permits and restrictions demanded by a venue, such as unions or signage restrictions, may also influence your decision. In addition, you must consider the expected size of the crowd. You do not want to hold your event in a 15,000-seat arena if only 2,000 people will attend.

Access to public transportation is another critical factor. Again, one of the most efficient ways of handling these challenges is to find out what others have done in similar situations. If at all possible, select a venue with a suitable area for hospitality. The Reston Town Center in Virginia, where the Muscular Dystrophy Association (MDA) Tour de Bud bicycle event took place, has a public pavilion equipped for food service. Such amenities reduce the overhead of tents and trailers.

A sport event that requires a great deal of equipment (e.g., skiing, cycling) will need a storage facility. Each cross-country team at the 1998 Winter Olympic Games brought approximately 30 pairs of skis. That meant that between 40 to 70 tons of sport equipment needed to be secured and stored during the games.

Ask athletes for course ideas in sports such as cycling and running. Try to keep participants off the main roads and avoid traffic lights and turns; if the course is straight, you need fewer directional signs and police officers. Although volunteers should be posted at major intersections for safety and directional purposes, most cities also require and charge for police officers to work the event.

WEATHER

Scheduling of the actual event as well as timing of rehearsals is just one consideration under weather conditions. The number of staff and volunteers required for an event also depends on the weather. More people will be needed to shovel snow and prepare grounds in bad weather. Inclement weather, or merely the threat of it, can clog highways or reduce audience size. Have standby crews in place in the event of inclement weather.

The *Farmer's Almanac* is a useful tool in predicting likely weather conditions; however, as the date of the event approaches, the National Weather Service is a better gauge of rapidly changing meteorological activity. Still another source of weather information is the Federal Aviation Agency located at your local airport. Ask the agency for recommendations on weather conditions and your future activities.

Whether you hire a personal meteorologist or merely raise your index finger to check the wind direction, paying attention to the weather is a major logistical consideration before, during, and immediately after your event.

TRAFFIC FLOW: KEEP THINGS MOVING

According to a survey conducted by the George Washington University, the most common logistical problem at events is traffic control. Effectively moving large number of cars and people in and out of events requires a solid transportation plan and cooperation from local law enforcement and transportation departments, as well as event organizers and volunteers. Police should be located at strategic positions (traffic lights, stop signs) on all routes leading to and from the venue in order to keep traffic moving in a continuous flow.

Directional signage should be located on highways as well as on all tributary roads, alerting travelers to event traffic and suggesting appropriate exits and parking options. Likewise, if a shuttle system is used, satellite parking lots need to be conveniently accessed with an adequate number of parking spaces and appropriate signage to inform people where to park and pick up the shuttle. A parking lot at a large shopping mall is often selected, as there tends to be plenty of parking. In addition, stores often welcome this idea because it may drive visitors to shop before or after the event.

Another strategy to keep traffic flowing is to prohibit or restrict pedestrian crossing by setting up blockades or positioning pedestrian police. In Atlanta, pedestrians increased traffic congestion by freely crossing busy lanes of traffic. If necessary, temporary pedestrian over-crossings should be built.

At venues where public transportation is available, be sure to implement a crowd control plan. During the 1998 World Cup in Paris, France, police set up a blockage outside the metro/train station limiting the number of people entering the station to avoid overcrowding on the platforms, which could lead to injuries.

Furthermore, bus drivers need to be trained and provided specific directions with contingency routes in the case of traffic or accidents. Grave lessons were learned from the 1996 Olympic Games in Atlanta when bus drivers were recruited from outside Atlanta and the budget did not provide enough funds to bring the drivers to Atlanta before the event for training. The result was drivers who continually got lost and one who actually stopped her bus and left it when she realized that she was heading down a ramp for a highway claiming that she has never driven on a highway and could not do it. In New York for the 1998 Goodwill Games, a bus taking media to a figure skating competition on Long Island drove in circles for 30 minutes in New York City rush-hour traffic before Lisa Delpy Neirotti finally approached the driver and asked him to radio in for directions. To simplify training, a schedule should be created so that bus drivers are assigned to a limited number of venues reducing the need to learn directions to all venues. In Nagano, Japan, bus drivers for the 1998 Winter Olympic Games actually had onboard navigational systems in the vehicles providing specific directions.

TRANSPORTATION

Spectator Arrivals and Departures

Professional parking lot supervisors use the terms *trickle* and *dump* to describe the rate at which spectators will attend your event.

Trickle means exactly what its image conveys. Your guests will come and go from the sport event throughout a given period of time rather than all arrive and depart at the same time. Dump means the opposite of trickle and describes all the guests arriving and leaving within a narrow window of time, such as 30 minutes prior to the event and within one hour following it.

These arrival and departure activities not only involve public safety but also interact with the entire hospitality experience. A spectator's first impression of your event may be through the automobile windshield upon arrival in your parking lot. The last impression most certainly will be of your parking facility and traffic control.

Determine early on the means by which guests, athletes, spectators, and media will arrive. Then design and control transportation and parking logistics to meet their needs (see Figure 3-4). Do you have a jumper cable service in your lot to assist stranded drivers? Do you have adequate lighting, signage, and parking hosts that make the guest feel secure and at the same time help reduce the likelihood of crime? Should you provide a parking shuttle from the satellite parking lot to the front gate to assist your guests and reduce parking congestion? Should you work closely with a municipal transportation agency to encourage spectators to use mass transit by offering an incentive such as a discount admission or a sponsored ad gift specialty? To avoid a large rush of traffic to the opening ceremonies of the

Figure 3-4

Traffic Patterns to Consider in Planning

1. Athlete housing – practice field – competition area – media center – cultural/social activities
2. Media housing – media center – practice field – competition area – cultural/social activities
3. VIP housing – competition areas – special requests
4. Spectator pickup points – competition areas

1988 Calgary Olympic Games, Maxwell House hosted a community breakfast that attracted many people to the stadium early. Likewise, many events plan fireworks or concerts after an event to avoid a mass exodus. The goal of any successful arrival and departure is to ensure a safe, easy, and fun experience for the spectator.

Athletes, Media, and VIP Guests

Transportation of athletes, VIP guests, media, and other officials needs to be considered for larger events. Depending on the demand, transportation, in some cases, can be contracted out in whole or in part.

Transportation of VIP guests can be as simple as hiring a limousine or as complex as hiring a bus company with hosts and hostesses on each vehicle. When transporting athletes to and from the airport or to competition and practice venues, remember to request the appropriate type of vehicle (e.g., trucks for bicycles or pole vault equipment) or at least provide specialized equipment, such as a bicycle rack for a car.

For media, make sure the transportation system is efficient. At the 1996 Atlanta Summer Olympics, the media were outraged by the "hub" system in which media buses from all venues took passengers to a hub area where they had to transfer buses to go to the media center, to the media village, or to another venue. Lisa Delpy Neirotti remembers the outbreak on the bus returning from the Opening Ceremonies at 11:30 p.m. as the media bus passed the media center heading to the hub 2 miles away. Reporters were trying to jump out the windows so they could get to the center in time to meet their press deadline.

Transportation logistics such as the overlap of beginning and ending times in multisport and venue events are very important. Miscalculation and coordination of buses could cause major traffic congestion. For megaevents such as the Olympic Games, normal traffic patterns are studied and events scheduled accordingly. Local companies are also asked to make arrangements for employees to work from home or take vacations during the period of the Games.

Continual monitoring is necessary to either increase or decrease the number of buses in circulation on each traffic pattern. At the 1998 Winter Games in Nagano, it took a few days before the organizers realized that they should put more than one bus on the route from the media village to the press center between 8 to 9 a.m., as this was peak travel time to make the daily 9 a.m. IOC (International Olympic Committee) press conference.

Large parking areas with clearly marked signage must also be planned close to public transportation and/or for shuttle pickups. In addition, make sure your limousines and buses have a predetermined area to stage.

Organizing the transportation of event entertainment may also become an issue. When Frank Supovitz had to transport over 1,000 halftime show participants to San Diego's Qualcomm Stadium for the Super Bowl, he knew he had to have plan A, B, and possibly C:

> When you are moving large groups into a crowded areas, you must not only work with local police to establish a traffic pattern but also plan for emergencies such as the bus breaking down and other emergencies which require an immediate remedy to keep the schedule on time.

Transportation for high school, collegiate, and professional sport events must also be coordinated and monitored. Schedule your transportation as far out as possible, but the day before each sport event, double-check the exact departure time and the bus driver's name and home number in case of emergency. Professional teams hire travel managers to handle all ticketing, equipment cargo, and local transportation needs. *SportsTravel* magazine is an excellent resource for those involved with event-related travel and logistics.

The checklist in Figure 3-5 will help you keep your schedule running smoothly as you plan and execute your transportation manifest.

When providing transportation, make sure to inform guests of the length of the journey, especially if there are no bathroom facilities on board the vehicle. Also, take advantage of this opportunity to make a first impression by introducing your guests to the area. Ask the transportation host to provide information and interesting details along the journey. Your guests will also appreciate refreshments if the trip is particularly long. Guests arriving from great distances can be irritable, so you can use this initial greeting to promote a happier attitude. A good first impression is particularly important for the media because you always want positive press coverage. Make arrangements beforehand for special media parking, and have a media area or building designated specifically for their use.

Figure 3-5

Transporting Athletes and Participants Smoothly

1. Identify all transportation and parking needs (athletes, VIPs, media, spectators, entertainment).
2. Make certain all riders have proper credentials.
3. Confirm that the bus company has appropriate parking passes, an accurate and current manifest listing all riders, a schedule of pickup and delivery, and routes.
4. Verify that all bus drivers are connected through communications to a central dispatcher who reports to you.
5. Work with local, traffic, and parking officials to produce an accurate map showing the confirmed transportation route, including specific drop-off points, pickup points, and parking designation. Be sure to note if there are any restrictions on the size of vehicle that can access these points. If large buses cannot be accommodated, smaller vans will need to be secured.
6. Prepare with authorities a separate alternate route to be used in case of emergencies (threats, traffic jams).
7. Assign one person to confirm and verify that the entrance gate is accessible to all transportation and that the guard has been briefed.
8. Position one staff person at the transportation arrival area to keep the area clear and to greet riders and direct them to their appropriate entrance.
9. Confirm that the bus company has insurance and has named your organization as an additional insured party.
10. Do not identify buses with specific names. This attracts attention. Instead, use a simple numbering system and give each rider a pass with the same number.
11. Know the phone number for a 24-hour towing service in case any bus requires assistance. Arrange with the operator of the tow truck to be on standby during the transportation period. Always have a spare bus ready to go in case stranded riders must be transferred.
12. Arrange for a security escort if protocol requires it.
13. Provide a rest area with refreshments for the bus and limousine drivers during the event.

SPECIAL ACCOMMODATIONS

With the passing of the American's with Disabilities Act (ADA)—which mandates that reasonable accommodations be made to provide equal access for persons with disabilities—ramps have been built, handrails have been hung, and infrared listening systems have been installed to allow spectators and athletes with disabilities the opportunity to enjoy and participate in sport events without undue restrictions. As you plan your sport event, be sure to survey the needs of your various constituency groups. Perhaps your groups sales department has sold a block of tickets to a group with disabilities and you may need to make special arrangements. Most sport events today often schedule a sign language interpreter to assist hearing-impaired guests. Sports events such as the Paralympic Games obviously will have a much higher number of individuals with disabilities in attendance than other events.

As a producer of a sport event for athletes with disabilities, you need to identify all venue limitations and remove barriers for people who are visually, auditorially, and physically impaired. Since the ADA applies strictly to public facilities, you may need to build temporary ramps with plywood or remove stall doors in private venues. Changing rooms with seats should also be available for athletes who need to remove artificial limbs prior to competition. The disabled parking plan is also critical for temporary venues. Make certain you determine how many spaces are required by local ordinance and that you assign them in the correct location with appropriate signage.

Kirk Bauer, executive director of Disabled Sports USA, also suggests assigning volunteers as facilitators to help people who are blind adjust to unfamiliar territory, aid wheelchair athletes up steep grades not built to code, or help in the transfer from the wheelchair into sport equipment or into the pool. This last responsibility requires the volunteer to have some knowledge of appropriate and safe transfer procedures.

Another unique logistical consideration when producing sports events for athletes with disabilities is the various categories that must be included. The National Amputee Summer Games have classifications such as wheelchair, stand up, and blind so that athletes compete on an equal playing field. In addition, there are three levels of visual impairment. In disabled ski competitions, there are 15 different physically and visually impaired classifications. If a wheelchair category is included in a regular run, special consideration of the terrain should be made. Avoid steep and windy hills, and try to select hard concrete surfaces over gravel surfaces.

FOOD AND BEVERAGE

Susan Lacz of Ridgewell's, a catering firm in Bethesda, Maryland, first became involved with sport event hospitality in 1988 and has since developed a profitable niche for the 72-year-old catering company. She has truly witnessed sport hospitality escalate and transform into big business. To illustrate the rapid growth, Susan mentioned that "16 years ago there were 6 tents at the U.S. Open and in 2000 there were over 50. A tent that cost $12,500 at the Preakness in 1988 would today cost approximately $80,000 plus." Of course, the demand and cost for hospitality varies in different demographic regions.

The tradition of food at sport events started during the era of folk games and continues as a strong influence today. At games like the NFL Super Bowl, the per capita expenditure on food and beverage may climb to $50 or more per person. Food and beverage is not only big business in sport events, it is also a serious logistical concern for a variety of interrelated reasons. Although Chapter 4 covers hospitality in detail, a few of the logistical considerations are described in the following sections.

Licenses and Permits

Not the least of these concerns is liquor liability. In this era of mass litigation, concessionaires are rightly concerned about the pouring laws in their jurisdiction and are investing heavily in training programs for their staffs to make certain that the dispensing of alcoholic beverages is in accordance with the law. One major logistical consideration is who will hold the liquor license for the event. Determine whether beer, wine, or liquor will be dispensed free or sold. If the venue "clubhouse" has a liquor license, you may not need to apply for a separate license.

The health department will also require your sport event to obtain a license or permit to dispense food that needs to be heated or cooked. Nonalcoholic beverages, fruit, prepackaged, or prebaked food such as muffins and bagels do not require a permit.

A host of regulations will be required to obtain this license, including in some jurisdictions running water for each food stand and netting to protect food from foreign substances. Some jurisdictions may require food handlers to have individual licenses and to wear specific clothing such as protective headgear. The sponsor, manager, host, or concessionaire dispensing the food or beverage has a responsibility to know the law and comply accordingly. Therefore, before you handle any food or beverage, make sure you learn what is required in order to feed the multitudes that come to your event. This information can be obtained directly through the health department in the appropriate geographical jurisdiction.

Purchasing, Inventory, and Distribution of Goods

Purchasing, inventory, and distribution of goods, as well as the design of the service counter are other logistical concerns regarding food and beverage. You must consider the type of event (number of stops in play), the time of the event (meal time or snack time), the capacity of the venue, the amount of tickets sold, and the weather, particularly if food or beverage is sold outdoors. Historical records are also helpful in determining the appropriate quantity of food to purchase. And you must know where the food and beverage will be warehoused, how it will be transferred, and who is accountable. Placement and design of service stands should also be considered in terms of space allocation for maximum efficiency and spectator access. Quality can only be maintained through continual evaluation of needs and the distribution service.

Determining Final Guarantees

A final guarantee on the number of guests or amount of food is usually required 36 to 72 hours in advance of the event. This guaranteed date and time is critical. If you miss it, you may be obliged to pay for the number of guests you estimated in the original contract. When determining the final guarantee, consider that if the event is free, it is typically safe to guarantee for 15 percent under the actual number of confirmed reservations. (See Chapter 4 for more information.)

Food Concessions

For the general public, be sure to have ample supply of food and beverage and staff to keep the concession lines to a minimum. Train employees to prepare for busy times (e.g., halftime, breaks) and to know what food sells the best. At the MCI Center in Washington, D.C., the "chicken in the basket" is the most popular food item and lines back up while people wait for their order to be filled. New technology may relieve some concession congestion by allowing attendees to pre-order, prepurchase food orders via the Internet, and even specify the time that they would like to pick up their food or have their food delivered to their seat! At the venue, attendees go to an express line and present a team debit card or coupons that shows their pre-order.

TICKETING AND ADMISSIONS

The sale of tickets is a logistical challenge that can determine the financial success or the doom of your sport event. Your first major decision should concern the distribution network. Will you print and distribute your own tickets? Options include selecting a company such as Ticketmaster or Tickets.com that prints, sells, and accounts for all tickets for an added premium, doing it in-house, or choosing some combination of the two. In selecting an outside ticketing agency to distribute your tickets, find out how extensive the distribution channels are in your area, whether they offer online ticketing, and if they require exclusive rights. Once you have identified the company, negotiate royalties and service charges. Ticket service charges can vary depending on the price of the ticket and the event itself. High-end boxing tickets of $400 or more increase the distributor's risk; thus, a service charge of $10 may be added. As the host organizer, you should remain in control of the computer setup and reserve certain sections of seats or earmark seats with obstructed views. For online ticketing, check to see if names and contact information can be collected on visitors to the site and if customers are able to select a specific seat or simply assigned a seat.

Mark McCullers, general manager of Columbus Crew stadium, states:

> Communication is the key to success in sport events. If all advanced specifications are not accurate, ticketing becomes a problem. An example is a pole that was said to be 20-feet tall and turns out to be 40 feet and blocks the view of 15 seats. Or the top lighting shelf of a boxing ring is wider than communicated and blocks the view of spectators in the upper seats. Or ... on the regulation-size field for World Cup Soccer,

the corner of the field is obstructed in the upper-level seats. Since this does not allow spectators to see the corner kick, such seats must be identified as obstructed seats.

Forgery of tickets and scalping are major concerns for sport event management officials. Holograms have been effectively used to identify fake tickets. It is important to know the local law as it relates to scalping and to inform ticket purchasers. The Baltimore Orioles set up a "scalp-free zone" in which ticket holders can sell their tickets at face value.

Security for ticketing and admissions is essential to ensure the safe collection, accounting, and deposit of funds. An experienced accounting firm can assist you with developing certain protocols to reduce the risk of your cash management. Make certain that each ticket booth has police or armed private security supervision and that the transfer of funds is made either by armored truck or with a police escort. Vary the time you transfer funds and alternate your route.

All ticketing and admissions personnel or the principal contractor for this area should be bonded to guarantee your investment. In addition, each ticketing and admissions worker should be trained, supervised, and checked in and out of the operation to ensure fidelity.

Barry Glassman, formerly program coordinator for the Muscular Dystrophy Association, secures his financial intake at sport events by keeping more than one person on each money-collecting and counting position. He advises that "no one person should be in charge of collecting, counting, and depositing money. A series of checks and balances should be in place to protect your assets, including dual signatures on checks."

Many sport event managers have successfully used a secret spectator system to catch dishonest ticketing and admissions personnel committing a felonious act. If these persons are aware that secret spectators are being used, they may think twice before committing a crime. In addition, raised lettering on tickets or boldly printing the date or game number helps to easily identify the ticket and reduces admission losses. Other suggestions are to place plain-clothes observers in front and behind the entrance gates and to rotate ticket supervisors in no particular order—sometimes clockwise every gate, at other times counterclockwise every two gates.

In sport events as in general entertainment, credentialing has grown in importance with increased criminal activity. Make certain that all admissions personnel are thoroughly familiar with the various credentials and test them to make sure they can easily spot counterfeit identification. (See Chapter 6 for specific information on credentials.)

TICKETING AND SEATING VARIATIONS

As we know, each sport event is different. Some require tickets to be purchased that include admission only, while other includes admission and parking. The benefit of including parking is the reduced time it takes to move cars into the lot and the reduced number of parking lot attendants required during the event. Other events are free yet require some form of ticket (this increases the psychological value of the event and assists in managing the numbers of spectators), while others, although rare, just open the gates and let everyone enter. For ticketed events, the selection of seats may include luxury box or suite tickets, reserved seating, general admission, or festival/open seating:

- The luxury boxes are usually leased by corporations, require a catering service, and often have an exclusive entrance in addition to special parking arrangements.
- Reserved seats are typically located in prime locations close to event activities. These seats are often of better physical quality than general admission seats.
- General admission seats are a lower-priced seat usually in a larger section with a more distant view of the sport event.
- Finally, festival seating or open seating allows the spectators to choose his or her seat without prior assignment by ticket number. Venue managers do not look favorably upon this type of seating because major riots, even deaths, have occurred as fans have stampeded for seats. For safety and security reasons, many venues have banned festival seating.

The type of admission and seating plan you select will ultimately determine the level of logistical planning required for your event.

When free festival seating is offered, more security is required to restrain the spectators. If you select paid reserved seating, less security is needed because of the orderly seating system you have planned. However, each event requires a different level of logistical preparation. You can ease your burden by making certain you match the type of ticketing and plan of seating to the audience to assure your guests of a smooth operation.

SEATING DESIGN AND CONTROL

Stadium-style seating is traditional for most sport events. It uses four sides of the stadium for the spectators to view the event. However, with the high-tech, made-for-TV spectaculars planned for the Olympic Games and major bowl games, two other types of seating occur in sport events. Spectators may experience a thrust style where the action "thrusts" into the middle of the audience seated on three sides or an auditorium style where the audience is seated out front and the action takes place on only one side of the athletic field.

As you prepare your logistical plan for the seating configuration of your sport event, remember that the more angles involved in production, the higher the cost. Although the auditorium style is more cost-effective, the stadium style allows spectators greater participation. Consult with your television producer to ensure that your staging and seating will allow the maximization of television viewer involvement.

SAFETY AND EMERGENCY PRECAUTIONS

Whether you are planning a 5K road race or organizing the World Cup of Soccer, care must be taken to ensure for the safety of spectators and participants. Arrangements need to be made for police, fire, and emergency services. Refer to Figure 3-6 for procurement ideas. When organizing international events, particularly soccer events, ticket assignments need to be allocated based on team alliance so that rivals are not sitting next to each other. For the 1998 World Cup in France, venues were designed to prohibit spectators from moving freely around the stadium (ticket holders in one section could not enter another section), and in other soccer venues in Europe, opposing teams are seated in a fenced enclosure.

Figure 3-6

Emergency Care Procurement Ideas

- Local Red Cross may provide emergency care for your sport event in exchange for a small contribution.
- City or county fire and police may be available at no charge, but they can be called away for emergencies. If fees are charged, they may be waived depending on the relationship the event director or organization has with government officials and the amount of profit made.
- Private security and ambulance companies are usually paid by the hour. A typical fee for a private ambulance company is $150 per hour. Be sure that the ambulance service is used not only for transportation but also is capable of emergency care.
- An organization such as the International Association of Fire Fighters or the Radio, Emergency and Communication Team (REACT) may provide free services as a sponsor. REACT is a nationwide disaster relief organization whose members use events to practice their skills. The organization is especially fitting because its members are local and know the area, have medical and communications training, and provide their own medical and communication equipment.

Make certain that any high-risk entertainers or performers (high-wire acts or fireworks companies) name you, the event manager, and your organization as an additional insured party on their insurance policies. Check with your insurance professional to determine the level of risk and then make sure the appropriate insurance is in place. (See Chapter 6 for more details on insurance.)

Without alarming the spectators, post appropriate signage or make frequent announcements alerting them to potential risks. Document these announcements and signage with photography and recordings. Signage such as "Halftime show activities are extremely hazardous. Please remain seated throughout the performance as a safety precaution" or "Pyrotechnic Staging Area, Do Not Enter" may protect you from a future lawsuit.

HALLMARK OR RECURRING EVENTS

A hallmark event—that is, a special event that does not typically occur regularly at the same location or time—presents a particular set of logistical problems because of the erratic nature of the event and the new environment for most of the spectators. A recurring event presents somewhat easier logistical challenges because the audience may be composed of a high percentage of repeat attendees who are familiar with the venue and understand the event process and system in advance of arrival.

When planning logistics for either a hallmark or recurring event, make certain you understand the habits of your spectators in order to plan accordingly. If spectators are likely to arrive early for a hallmark event to avoid parking problems, you must plan for extra staffing at that time. Using the same logic, spectators at a recurring activity may arrive somewhat later and you must staff to meet their arrival patterns.

Keeping precise statistics of the arrival, flow, and departure times of your guests is helpful for both recurring and hallmark events. You can compare and analyze data for the production of your next event of similar size and scope.

AWARD CEREMONIES

The presentation of awards can be as simple as mailing a certificate or ribbon through the mail or as elaborate as an all-participant gala dinner and dance. For outdoor events such as road races, it is advised to have a decorated awards stage in which participants can gather. Entertain them with music prior to the presentation. A dynamic emcee always adds to the overall ambiance.

Awards dinner banquets may be held in a gymnasium or restaurant. Food can be provided either by a caterer or by parents potluck-style in a gym, while restaurants will typically offer a choice of menus from which the organizer will preselect for the entire group.

Preceding the award presentations, a motivational speaker is often invited to address the athletes. Typically a local sport hero or sport reporter is a good, affordable choice. A slide or video show is also fitting during dinner or at the end of the evening after the awards presentations. In addition, you may wish to contact the office of the mayor or governor to see if the mayor or governor, or a representative, can attend. If no one is able to attend, request a letter that can be read during your ceremonies.

If awards (e.g., certificates, trophies) are to be distributed, be sure to bring one or two extras just in case. The setup and testing of audiovisual equipment, especially the microphone and slide/video projector, is an important consideration, particularly when using a facility unfamiliar to you.

NEGOTIATING HOTEL ROOM BLOCKS

The first step in negotiating a hotel room block is to understand the importance and value of what your event brings to a property. Remember, the business of hotels is to first sell beds, then food and beverage, and finally meeting space.

The amount of leverage you have when negotiating arrangements depends primarily upon the size of the group, as well as the time of year. According to Richard Kenah, president of TravelSport, "The magic number is 10 rooms." Once this threshold is hit, the negotiation leverage swings toward the event organizer. Additional leverage is acquired if the room block is reserved during a slow time of year. The coordinator of a golf tournament would receive an excellent price on lodging if the tournament is scheduled in October at a resort near the beach or in a ski area where the weather is still good for golf but not for swimming or skiing. Likewise, if the city that you are traveling to does not have a convention scheduled, the downtown hotels become more flexible in negotiations. In general, weekend room rates are more negotiable.

The opportunity for repeat and dependable business is also very important to hotels. If the hotel knows that your event will return to the property year in and out and that the chance of cancellation or nonpayment is extremely rare, the likelihood of a more favorable contract increases. Room attrition (guests departing earlier than expected) is another factor considered in negotiations. To assist in keeping your hotel record good, event organizers should explain the event/tournament structure (selection and elimination process) and work closely with the hotel to monitor the allocated number of hotel rooms blocked for the event. Within a minimum of 3 months before the event, a specific room block number should be provided to the hotel, and at 30 days before the event, the organizer must decide if they will guarantee any of the unsold rooms or release the block. For events where teams are selected within one or two weeks of the event, this policy will need to be adjusted. Another suggestion is to require a two-night prepaid deposit, nonrefundable one month out. "This drastically reduced the number of double bookings and guarantees at least two nights" exclaims Peggie Knorra, account executive for Quality Hotel & Suites at Courthouse Plaza in Arlington, Virginia.

Naming the hotel as the "host" or "official" hotel also helps in negotiations. To encourage event participants to stay in the "host" hotel, be sure to incorporate hotel information in all collateral material, including the registration brochure, the event's Web site, and in any other direct-mail pieces. An emphasis should be placed on the price and convenience of the host property. Hotel brochures should also be included in the preregistration packet as a stand-alone price and/or mailed to all registered participants as far in advance as possible. For large events, it would be wise for organizers to negotiate with different-priced accommodations in the area so that participants may choose between a high-quality or economic property. This is especially true when a discounted property is located adjacent to the "official" hotel.

If the event is a marquee event and provides high visibility, you should seek an exclusive hotel sponsor. The terms of the sponsorship are such that in exchange for event recognition and associated benefits, the hotel sponsor will provide a specific number of room nights plus a discounted year-round rate for the host organization. This is how Doubletree Hotels became a sponsor of the Champions Tennis Tournament. The amount of complimentary rooms range anywhere from 10 to 500 depending on the value of the sponsorship.

The amount of food and beverage your group requires also plays into the negotiations. Professional sport teams and most collegiate revenue sport teams have at least two full meals during each visit serving up to 100 people. Road races may plan a preevent pasta party at the hotel. Other events may hold an awards banquet.

Similarly, the potential for the hotel to earn additional income from incidental charges is another negotiating point. Obviously, professional athletes have more disposable income to spend on room service, telephone calls, movies, and mini-bars, but many NCAA Division I athletes also receive per diems that are frequently spent within the hotel. This strategy does not work for teams requesting all incidentals be turned off.

Finally, one of the negotiation strategies most frequently recommended is relationship building. Insist on working with only one hotel representative who will handle all your requests from rooms to meals. This not only simplifies your life but also forces one person to be responsible and accountable to your group. By developing a close working relationship, this person can also serve as your internal champion should any problems develop.

Now that you have your ammunition, the next step is to use it to negotiate favorable contract terms. The items most negotiable include room rates, a suite for the event organizer, early arrival and late checkout, bus parking, cots or roll-a-way beds at no cost, free use of audiovisual equipment and the fitness gym, storage space, and complimentary meals for coaches.

Before ever meeting with a hotel representative, however, do your research. Find out what hotels are in the area, the average rate, availability, and the exact location within the city. If you find out that it is a busy time of year for the hotel, ask why. You may also want to ask what other groups are booked into the hotel at the time of your event. This information may help to determine if you should look elsewhere. The location of the hotel is important—not only to determine the closeness to practice and competition venues but for proximity to food and entertainment.

For those who prefer to outsource this responsibility of securing hotel accommodations, consider the following options. Most convention and visitors bureaus (CVBs) designate one person to handle hotel requests. All you do is call the local CVB and ask them to issue a hotel lead. These leads are sent to all properties in the area with a description of services required. The CVB will either ask you a series of questions related to your needs or perhaps fax a form to be completed. You can then ask the bureau to collect and package all the names and information about properties interested in hosting your group or request that each hotel contact you directly. This is a no-lose situation for you, since most CVBs do not charge for this service and you retain all negotiating power.

Another option is to use a sports-travel specialist such as Dirk Smith with Sports Destination Network, Inc., and Eddie Bishop, whose job is to negotiate for your team the most favorable hotel contract. These specialists usually have experience in both the sport and travel businesses and have numerous hotel contacts. Most sport representatives are placed on retainer by properties, thus eliminating the possible conflict of interest connected to commission-based compensation. However, it is always wise to inquire how the consultant is being compensated.

Whether negotiating yourself or working with a sports-travel representative, it is important to understand the hotel business and the leverage you bring to the table. Also, always confirm the specifics of your hotel arrangements in writing. This is especially important as personnel may change within the term of the contract.

BOOKENDS AND OTHER CONFLICTS

The events that occur before, during, and following your event—bookend events—have special significance for logistical planning. We have previously discussed the first logistical concern about arrivals, parking, ticketing, and seating. Other events scheduled too closely to the starting time for your event may cause traffic jams and resulting confusion. You need to survey all departments and agencies, including the local convention and visitors bureau, to be aware of all events that will be held near the time of your event.

Another concern with bookend events is housing for your athletes, officials, staff, media, and spectators. When another major event is held in your host city at the same time, there is a risk that this event may consume all available hotel space. Study your hotel agreements carefully to make certain the hotel or hotels are firmly committed to your organization through a specific date and time.

The possibility of a bookend situation for the sport event can also have positive effects. You can purposely select an event to piggyback your event. You may be able not only to boost attendance but also to share promotional expenses with the management of the other event or the local convention and visitors bureau. Research name entertainment that will be in the area during your event. If you decide to book this act, your costs could be substantially reduced.

Furthermore, when creating a bookend situation, you create a greater economic benefit for the local community because visitors are likely to remain in the area for an extended period and spend more money. At the same time, be selective so that the bookend event complements rather than overshadows your event, distracting the media.

These logistical concerns are only a starting part for your overall analysis. Most international and national sport federations have detailed organizational guidelines outlining logistical requirements for hosting their specific events. Refer to Chapter 11 for more sport specific logistical information and Chapter 12 for bid proposal information.

BEGINNING THE LOGISTICAL PLANNING CYCLE

Once you have identified all of the logistical concerns of your specific event, the logistical planning cycle commences. This cycle begins with turning the brainstorm or creative idea into a solid form through a system such as a chart or time line. This has been compared to the difference between a dream and a goal; a goal is only a dream . . . written down. Figure 3-7 lists in sequence some of the steps needed to plan a sport event.

This schedule is incomplete for a number of reasons. First, four months is usually too short a time for a planning period. Missing from this schedule is a date for each activity to both commence and to be completed. You may use "COB" for close of business, provided every-

Figure 3-7

Action Plan

Date	**Activity**	**Person responsible**
1 Oct. 01	Brainstorming meeting	M. Smith & committee
5 Nov. 01	Select date, contract site	Legal
11 Dec. 01	Site inspection	Operations
21 Jan. 02	Contract vendors	Legal
25 Jan. 02	Design marketing campaign	Marketing
5 Feb. 02	Ad campaign commences	Marketing
15 Feb. 02	Interview schedule begins	Marketing, PR
20 Feb. 02	Site setup commences	Operations
21 Feb. 02	Site setup complete, inspect	Operations, legal
22 Feb. 02	Media day at site	Marketing, PR
23 Feb. 02	Event date	Operations
24 Feb. 02	Tear down event site	Operations
25 Feb. 02	Accounting, reconciliation	Financial

one in your organization and vendors agree on the appropriate closing time. Better still, assign a specific time to each activity to ensure a precise and therefore nonconflicting schedule with other activities. For example, the electricity needs to be installed before the caterer arrives and the tents need to be erected before the decorator can begin. When precision planning is implemented, you will find little opportunity for details to slip through cracks in your logistical reasoning.

As the event date draws closer and you begin to layer your organization with new team members who may not know how they fit into the big picture, an event production plan or schedule should be created that provides minute-by-minute directions and helps place everyone in their appropriate roles. Appendix 2 contains a sample production plan for a basketball game halftime show. The Lillehammer case study further illustrates the importance of a well-conceived and well-followed action plan.

Lillehammer Logistical Case Study

The importance of detailed logistical planning can be seen in the opening ceremony at the 1994 Winter Olympic Games in Lillehammer, Norway. Although the performance itself was brilliant, many ticket holders were unable to get to their seats in time to enjoy it, and by the end of the ceremony, 11 spectators were hospitalized with broken bones. The reasons for such complications are multifaceted.

First, all spectators were funneled through one entrance. No direction was given to general standing admission ticket holders and reserved seat ticket holders about their seating location. The result was a mad crush of people in one area not knowing what to do. General admission ticket holders stood in the stadium aisles, blocking the way for reserved ticket holders trying to get to their seats. Everyone in the stadium area, including security and ushers, was wearing a white plastic poncho for television aesthetics, so it was difficult to identify persons with authority. Lisa Delpy Neirotti recognized an official volunteer and asked, "Why aren't you checking tickets?" The reply was, "It won't help anyway." As the rush became more intense, security and ushers simply merged with the spectators.

> Another safety consideration was the steep and icy incline all 40,000 spectators had to climb to reach the stadium. LOOC's environmental efforts precluded putting salt on the grounds. Unfortunately, this left everyone slipping and sliding up and down the mountain. A veteran sport manager, Hill Carrow, recommended that a work crew be assigned to continually spread gravel along the busiest walkways. Although the Norwegians were gracious hosts, they forgot that the rest of the world was not used to such slippery conditions and perhaps not as physically fit to challenge the elements.

Producer Dan Witkowski has summarized the science of logistics into four commandments: "If God gave Moses Ten Commandments to run his life, a successful sport event can be controlled by four key commandments." (See Figure 3-8.) Keep in mind, however, the advice provided by Barry Glassman: "The best way to learn how to produce a sport event is to attend and participate in as many as possible, particularly your competitors. There is no need to reinvent the wheel, just learn how to make it better."

Figure 3-8

Cardinal Rules for Planning Large-Scale Productions for Major Sport Events According to Dan Witkowski

First Commandment: The Show Must Not Upstage the Sport

No matter how great your show may be, the primary reason that people are buying a ticket is to see a sport being played.

Peter Rozelle, the brilliant commissioner of the National Football Leagues and the genius behind the Super Bowl, successfully made the last Sunday in January the unofficial American holiday. (Actually, the Super Bowl is observed by more people than many official holidays.) Rozelle and his staff were careful to have a balanced mix of sport and entertainment to appeal to a huge audience. Even if you are not a football fan, chances are you have attended a Super Bowl party or watched the spectacular pregame or halftime extravaganzas. Keep in mind that while the show is important, people ultimately come to watch a sport event.

Second Commandment: Plan, Plan, Plan

There is no such thing as overplanning. If your event is outdoors, you had better know the exact time of sunrise, sunset, dusk, when the sun will be in the

continued on next page

Figure 3-8 *continued*

spectators' eyes, what direction the wind will be from, and what the average wind speed is in the stadium at that time of year. However, compiling these facts does not mean your event is a sure bet, but it forces you to think of all the contingencies you may have to implement.

Before God got his current job, perhaps he was an event producer. I know of very few sport events that have actually been canceled because of rain. A Super Bowl halftime show has never been rained out. No matter how sophisticated the computer equipment for forecasting weather, we rely on the *Old Farmer's Almanac* more than anything else for scheduling rehearsals and performances. It is also consulted every year before the date of the Academy Awards is decided . . . honest!

By thinking "what if?" during your preproduction process, you can deal with those last-minute crises that bombard you the last few days before the live event. Contingency planning forces you to think things through.

Third Commandment: Overcast Your Cast and Crew

Always overcast 25 to 40 percent more people than you need for your show if you are using volunteers. If your show requires 1,000 people, cast 1,250 to 1,400. No matter how much fun a show sounds like in the beginning, it is a lot of hard work for the volunteers. Respect their time and do not waste it. Do not rehearse more than necessary, and keep people busy when they are scheduled. If you have a thousand people waiting for rehearsal with nothing to do because the props or costumes have not been taken out of storage, that is the equivalent of wasting one-half year of a working person's time!

Even if you are well organized, people will drop out because of conflicts with work, school, transportation, or other social commitments. Make sure you communicate the total rehearsal schedule and time commitment when you recruit volunteers. However, have plenty of understudies ready to step in so you are not caught short.

Fourth Commandment: Use Technology to Improve the Show

The most important tools of a sport event producer are a dictation recorder and a camcorder. The dictation recorder should be used to log all your production notes during the preproduction and rehearsal sage when ideas are coming in so fast you don't have time to write them down.

If you have a secretary or assistant, have this person transcribe the microcassettes or your staff-written notes for you. Then the notes will be ready at your next production meeting, that same night after rehearsal, or the next morning.

The camcorder can serve the same function for rehearsals. It allows choreographers, directors, costume dressers, dancers, and so forth to see the problems on tape. In particular, during a big production of a ceremony or halftime show, choreographers are trying to work out small problems, and they don't often see the big picture. However, a camcorder—set up in the bleachers

continued on next page

Figure 3-8 *continued*

or in the audience and shooting a side, constant picture of the field or stage—will allow the production team to analyze what must be done to make the show attractive from the point of view of the audience or television.

Final Note: Following these rules will not guarantee a successful sport event production, but it will greatly increase your chances of success.

The myriad of details that affect logistical planning often cloud one's overall view of the purpose of the event. In Chapter 4, you will be able once again to see the forest for the trees as you explore the importance of hospitality and protocol.

GAME HIGHLIGHTS

- Remember that the term *logistics* means "what is reasonable."
- Notice the activities before and after your sport event because they will directly affect your planning.
- Identify the key elements for success and logistical personnel necessary to begin your planning. Athlete, VIP, media, and crowd arrival and departure patterns are critical influences on your logistical staffing needs.
- When deciding on your sport event, consider that the location (indoors or out) and the number of public venues will determine scheduling, staffing, and other critical factors.
- Establish an organizational chart of all staff positions to enable communications.
- Develop an action plan that accounts for each sport event task and the person responsible for each.

PROVIDING HOSPITALITY AT SPORT EVENTS

Some of us will do our jobs well and some will not, but we will all be judged by only one thing—the result.

Vince Lombardi

WHAT ARE THE REQUIRED INGREDIENTS to produce an entertaining, profitable, and memorable sport hospitality program?

Regardless of the type of sport event, there will always be a hospitality component involved, whether a simple reception or a multiple-day sponsor village. At sport events, hospitality is most often provided for the media, officials, athletes, and sponsors. The extent and organization of the hospitality program, however, will vary based on the type and size of event, objective of the program, location, and budget. For smaller events, the hospitality program may be detailed to a staff member or volunteer who will arrange for the location, décor, food, beverage, and entertainment. Most of the time, such a hospitality offering will be held in a conference or meeting room within or adjacent to the sport event venue or under a tent if the event is held outdoors. Typically, there will only be one hospitality center for all constituent groups. The food is frequently donated by a local restaurant in exchange for an in-kind sponsorship (refer to Chapter 9 on sponsorship). Similarly, in-kind decorations can be secured through a local florist or garden center, and the entertainment could be as simple as a stereo or television set.

For larger events, a company is outsourced to plan, manage, and sometimes sell the event hospitality program (see Chapter 3 regarding vendors). This is the case for events such as the U.S. Open, Super Bowl, or Olympic Games. Ridgewell Catering, for example, will service over 30 tents and feed close to 10,000 people during the Super Bowl. In such instances, the hospitality vendor will interface with the event organizing committee, as well as with each of the corporate sponsors, concerning individual hospitality needs and preferences.

QUESTIONS AND CONSIDERATIONS WHEN PURCHASING A HOSPITALITY PACKAGE

When purchasing a hospitality package for a sport event, be sure to ask what the package includes. For example, at some events it includes only tickets and parking, and catering and decorations are additional. Since corporate entertaining is a very personal matter, it is important for the hospitality company to offer the flexibility for creating unique packages. Susan Lacz, principal of Ridgewell's Catering, explains that "tents are often sold with a standard level of décor and a laundry list of extras such as ambient lighting, upgraded carpet, ceiling liners, technology centers, and built-in bars. Some clients prefer a no-frills package, while others want food served throughout the event and unique décor specific to the sport or to the company."

The cost of hospitality packages for sport events range from $35,000 to $150,000 depending on the exclusivity of the event and its geographic location. There are also different-priced packages within events depending on the size and location of the tent at the event. Catering charges run from $75 to $150 per guest plus tax and service depending on the type and amount of food ordered. Often there is a minimum catering fee per package, so be sure to ask prior to purchasing. "One of the most efficient and affordable deals around is the Outback Sky Suites," exclaims Lee Coorigan, tournament director of the State Farm Senior Golf Tournament. Outback Steak brings in trucks that fold together to create indoor sky suites that pop right up on the green and come with running water, stereo system, theatre-style seating, and a bar. For the tournament week, corporations could purchase a standard 32- by 22-foot sky suite for $35,000 to $40,000 or the jumbo suite for $50,000 including catering. Compare this to $80,000 for a one-day tent at the Preakness plus $40,000 in catering charges. Michele Tennery, manager of corporate meetings and events for CapitalOne, recommends asking the following questions related to sport event hospitality packages:

- If 200 tickets come with the package, can two-thirds of them be used one day?
- If I want to purchase more tickets, what is the cost and is there a cap on how many I can buy?
- Where is the parking for my guests and how many parking passes do I receive?
- Do I have access to the event logo to produce merchandise for guests or must I purchase from the event supplier.
- What type of signage will identify the tent (dimensions, color, style) and do I have any discretion as to how it looks? If it is a flag on top of the tent, what happens if there is no breeze? Some companies may want a lot of visibility, while others want to be more discreet about their hospitality investment.
- Are there any advertising opportunities included in the package (e.g., an advertisement in the program) or could we purchase at a reduced rate?
- How far in advance do we have to lock in to the event?
- Can we staff the tent with our own people? Will our staff need to use a ticket or how many "staff" passes are included? This is important when wanting to retain a high ratio between staff and client.
- Where will our tent be located? Can we include a clause stating that our tent will not be located in the same area as a competitor's tent or a company known for rowdy parties?

- Are we allowed any clubhouse badges and is it possible to get more?
- Is there anyone special coming through the tent area and can we schedule them to stop in our tent?
- Can we be included in the opening ceremonies or receive invitations to any exclusive events (e.g., VIP cocktail parties)?

At larger events, the hospitality company as part of its vendor contract commonly handles the hospitality for media, athletes, officials, and VIPs. These individual hospitality centers should be located in a convenient and secure location for each group—for example, close to or inside the media center.

À LA CARTE AND INDIVIDUAL HOSPITALITY

Another hospitality option that may be more compatible with the objectives of a company and less expensive than a packaged hospitality program is to organize an à la carte hospitality experience. This is also the way to go for companies that may be locked out of an event that they are not sponsoring. Carl Bach, managing director of Reliance National Insurance (UK), provides an excellent example:

> Together with my secretary, we personally invited 20 of our customers and asked them to meet at the Dug Out sport bar, reserved a table at the establishment which was serving a preset Game meal, [and] hired a luxury bus to pick the group up from the bar, bring to the game, and return at the end of the competition. Team caps were distributed on the way to the game, and once inside the gate, souvenir programs were provided and refreshments offered to all guests. On the return bus ride, results of a football pool contest conducted earlier in the evening were announced and prizes were awarded.

A new option for individuals or companies that want to host just a few guests is to purchase tickets at a higher price that allow access to a more upscale concession area. Two examples include the Pavillion at the Kemper Open in Maryland and the Hunt Club at the Gold Cup in Virginia. These higher-priced tickets allow the holder to enter a special area with comfortable and sheltered seating, an open bar, and private restrooms.

WINNING THE HOSPITALITY GAME: 10 EFFECTIVE HOSPITALITY STRATEGIES

From the invitations through the departure of the guest, there are certain strategies that can ensure success:

1. *Know your guests' needs and expectations.* Determine in advance the appropriate sport event for your target audience. Identify your prospective guests' interests by asking their friends or coworkers or by sending a questionnaire to a random sample of potential attendees. Once an event is selected, the next step is to determine if your guests are participants or spectators. The participants will want to be active and entertained continuously throughout the sport event, while the spectators would prefer to relax and enjoy the action on the field rather than be distracted by other activities. Often, this is a difficult balancing act. Questions regarding alcoholic beverages, smoking, specific forms of entertainment, and foods should also be asked. Ham sandwiches for a Jewish audience are never appreciated, while meatless entrees on Fridays during Lent will be gratefully acknowledged by practicing Catholics. For frequent invitees, create a file listing their educational background, food preferences, social profile, allergies, and medical history, even their golf handicap. If a group has been hosted before, it is especially critical that you find out what worked and what did not. At annual events, each year's activities should build upon those of the previous one.

   Once you know the avocational interests of your guests, you can begin planning for those activities that will not only please them but also drive their actions and feelings toward your predetermined goal. For example, if your survey reveals that your guests are golfers, you may wish to rent a portable miniature golf course and hold a putting contest at your hospitality event. Or perhaps your guests are volleyball fans. Setting up a portable volleyball net with a Nerf volleyball provides not only an interactive activity but may create considerable excitement as the other guests enjoy the food and drink while watching your championship players having fun.

2. *Plan with the understanding of what the sport event is expected to achieve for the guest.* Is the goal networking for business purposes? Is the sport event an incentive award for high sales productivity? A promotional activity to build brand awareness of a new product? A vehicle for entertaining prospective customers or thanking them for previous orders? Or simply a way to create goodwill between the guests and the corporate sponsor?

   By understanding the precise purpose of the sport event, you can develop strategies to achieve specific goals. A program that supports two or more goals may make things more complicated but still possible.

   The host of a hospitality spot event serves at the bonding agent who glues the guests to one another and the entire group to the goal of the event. Station greeters at the entrance to the hospitality event welcome each guest and offer directions to the first of a series of event activities. Each guest is entitled to certain rights when they accept an invitation. Figure 4-1 is a guide to guarantee that each guest will enjoy the sport event.

3. *Understand the arrival patterns of your guests.* Will they trickle in or all arrive in one wave or in several waves? Your staffing for food and beverage must match the arrival time of guests.

4. *Plan according to what has preceded or will follow the guests' arrival.* For example, if the event is scheduled to begin at 6 p.m., it is unlikely that your guests have eaten dinner. Consequently, your planning must allow for food substantial enough to satisfy their hunger yet light enough to keep them from snoring through the event that follows. Make sure that athletes on your guest list understand the schedule and the menu. At the World University Games, athletes invited to the reception at 5:00 p.m. assumed that they would be fed a dinner. Instead, they were served only snacks. When the group returned to the athlete's village, the dining area was closed.

   When planning catering for the media, do not forget that journalists work long hours and that food service should be readily available as long as the press center is open.

Figure 4-1

The Guest's Bill of Rights

By accepting this invitation...

- I am entitled to arrive at and depart from this sport event easily, safely, and efficiently.
- I am entitled to be greeted as soon as I enter the event site.
- I am entitled to be introduced to other guests by the host.
- I am entitled to be comforted with a beverage, food, or other tactile experience within three minutes of my arrival.
- I am entitled to enjoy pleasant surprises to establish a favorable memory of this sport event.

5. *Create appealing invitations.* Nontraditional mailing containers—tubes, boxes, and so on—capture the attention of the prospective guest. The Lower Delaware Chapter of the International Special Events Society (IS) used a brief videotape including messages from the mayor of Philadelphia and the former governor of Delaware to invite guests to a fifth anniversary celebration for the organization. The videotape was labeled "A Personal Message for ______________," with the name of the recipient. From a bottle containing a secret map with the instructions to the regatta, to an embroidered headband with the instruction to the starting line of a 10K run, to an imprinted golf ball with the date and time of your hole-in-one shoot-out, the possibilities for innovation are endless. Avoid loose glitter, scents, or other items that may leave behind an unwanted residue when opened.

   According to award-winning special event designer Sue Ann Drobbin of Washington, D.C., "A successful invitation grabs the prospective guests' attention and also sends a subliminal message that generates positive excitement about the event." An invitation imprinted on a jigsaw puzzle may become the talk of the office as prospective guests seek help in piecing together your message. The more people start talking about your event the greater the potential response. Another creative example is to send a teaser invitation on card stock with the message "Hurry! Call this toll-free number to attend the hottest sport event this month! Operators are standing by with more information. Call now!" The prospective guest who calls will get a recording with the voice of a famous sport personality who invites them to the party, provides them with the necessary details, and asks them to RSVP when they hear the beep. You then mail a second post-card to each confirmed guest with travel directions and other critical information. Perhaps the best advice is to design the invitation so that it becomes a souvenir of the event, a keepsake to remind guests of a wonderful experience for years to come.

Delivering the invitation is often taken for granted as an incidental process and expense, but it is probably the most important step in getting a positive response from prospective guests. Like comedy, timing in invitation delivery is everything. Midweek deliveries are generally better than Mondays so your invitation is less likely to compete with dozens of other mail items. For hand-delivered invitations, early morning is usually best because it is easier to find recipients in their offices then. Private couriers costumed as referees or umpires make a big impact entering the traditional office setting. If you prefer to use overnight delivery services, ask for a volume discount. Fax and e-mail are also becoming popular vehicles to deliver invitations and to gather RSVPs. Washington Sport and Entertainment created a three-dimensional e-mail invitation that when opened resounded of cheering fans. This invitation was mailed to all the high-tech firms in the Washington Metro area, inviting them to a season ticket open house.

Of course, the following components should always be included in an invitation: (a)Who should attend; (b)what is being offered; (c) the date, time, and location of the event; (d) driving or other travel directions; and (e) instructions on how to respond and a deadline to do so.

6. *Understand the protocol for sport events.* Most sport organizations have specific guidelines for the protocol of their individual sport events. Be sure to ask for these guidelines and to inquire about any other traditions the organization may have. Figure 4-2 provides some basic event guidelines as described by Hugh Wakeham, event marketing director for Live Entertainment of Canada, Inc.

Figure 4-2

Protocol Guidelines According to Hugh Wakeham

Entrance of Athletes

- Two teams (e.g., at a football game): guest team enters first, followed by the home team.
- Multiple teams (e.g., at an international game): guest team enters the stadium in alphabetical order according to the language of the home team, followed by the home team. For the Olympic Games, Greece enters first, followed by all other teams in alphabetical order with the exception of the host country, which enters last.

Anthems

- Two teams: guest anthem first, followed by the host anthem.
- International event: official anthem only.

Flag Raising

- Host flag center: guests' flags placed alternately right and left according to precedence of flags.
- Olympic flag (or other international flag) takes the central "host" position, with other flags arranged either alphabetically (the flags of participating nations) or according to precedence (if they are made up of the host country, state, and city).

If a dignitary is invited to attend a sport event, that person's social secretary or someone from the dignitaries office will certainly inform you of proper protocol and security measures. Refer to the reference list at the end of the chapter for additional readings on protocol.

7. *Focus on the first and final impressions; you never have a second chance.* No matter what type of event, it is critical to concentrate your hospitality planning on areas that will have the greatest impact on your guests. The second-greatest impact is the first impression. The greatest impact is the final impression. With this said, consider the following illustration of how to move an event from low-key to high-key effectively. As guests arrive, walk them through a sport time tunnel where, with black-and-white slides and taped voices with music and cheers, they can recall fond memories of a great moment in sports. Then as they exit the other end of the tunnel, have some of the current athletes assembled in living color to sign autographs and pose for photos.

Often, guests arrive in an agitated state because of traffic or some other factor and miss the first impression entirely. Through proper planning, you can turn this around by posting a greeter to assist the guests to ease into the party atmosphere and offer refreshments to help them relax. This is also a good reason to make the final impression more positive and meaningful, the one they go home with. Whether you introduce a surprise sport Hall of Famer as a guest speaker, stage an elaborate aerial fireworks and laser show, or simply present each departing guest with a special souvenir of the occasion, the final impression is an opportunity that should not be missed.

In terms of party favors, the items should mention or reflect the company or group giving the gift and have a useful life well beyond the event itself. Depending on the item, the name or logo of the sponsor may be emblazoned or imprinted (hats or T-shirts) or may be noted by a small insert or tag (crystal or jewelry). Novelties should also be distributed when they have the greatest impact and offer the least burden to the receiver. For example, you could provide hats to guests so that they can wear them during the game, and at the end of the evening, you could award prizes of sweatshirts and jackets that are much bulkier to carry.

For major events such as the Olympic Games or World Cup Soccer, identification badges, limited-edition clothing, and souvenir pins can become sources of great pride for the wearer. Upon arrival at high-profile events, guests of sponsors receive a goody bag filled with specially designed and marked clothing (enough for his or her entire stay), an identity card, and a handful of special-edition pins. For many guests, pin trading is the most exciting event of the Games and an unforgettable memory.

Event organizers must also provide souvenir gifts for the athletes and media. For events with a large number of repeat participants, it is wise to vary the gifts from year to year. This is not always possible, however, as frequently these gifts are provided by the event sponsors.

8. *Don't forget the amenities. These are the extras that matter*. Whether you are managing sport event hospitality for a few friends or thousands of prospective clients, design and manage each guest

experience as though you were hosting a reception for close friends. In addition to the personal assistance at entry and/or parking gates and the special gifts for guests, welcome signs (conforming to local, state, federal ordinances) should be located in airports, train stations, bus depots, city streets and buildings, hotels, and sport and entertainment venues. For the 2001 NBA All-Star Game, host Washington, D.C., went the extra mile and provided special All-Star promotional pins to all hospitality providers (taxicab drivers, hotel and restaurant staff) in order to increase enthusiasm for the event. Information desks should also be posted in the guests' hotel lobby providing event schedules and general information on activities and dining in the city as well as maps and directions.

9. *Make the plan flexible for nonstop fun*. Sport event planners frequently err in planning so rigidly that they cannot satisfy guests' last-minute whims and changes in attitude. For example, if the sponsor's representative asks for the band to play music from a particular era or to speed up the food service, the flexibility of the event planner is that key to success.

   Too often planners are solely concerned with the tools of the event (music, food, and decorations) and ignore the sole purpose of the event, the guests' response. Professional sport event managers should circulate among the guests throughout the event, asking questions such as "How's the music?" "How's the food?" "Having a good time?" This frequent check ensures that they can correct any problem immediately.

   If a complaint is heard, the client should be notified immediately and apologies should be provided to the guest. If possible, offer the guest something extra such as a bottle of wine for his or her table or additional souvenir gifts.

   Continually diagnose attitudinal alterations by standing to the side and observing the body language of guests. Are they straining to hear one another? Do they appear physically restless? When the event requires a new element, use the guidelines for change shown in Figure 4-3.

   Your sport event closet should be filled with ideas like this just in case you have to make a last-minute adjustment to guarantee nonstop excitement, fun, and success. Likewise, don't be

Figure 4-3

Changing the Game Plan

1. When guests appear fidgety, add a physical activity such as dancing, games, a slide or video program, entertainment, or some other activity to engage them.
2. To calm guests, open a room or area where quite conversation can be held.
3. To keep things interesting during a lengthy banquet or seated dinner, have the waiters appear every 15 minutes with a new dessert delicacy to keep the guests interested while they converse with one another.
4. Use a live video camera to provide instant pregame reports from the sport venue. Closed-circuit technology enables you to be sure your guests are on the sidelines right up until game time.
5. Introduce a surprise element such a cheerleading team, high school marching band, or team mascot to liven up the event when the energy level lags.

afraid to cancel a scheduled activity or entertainment that is unsuitable to the current mood of the event.

10. *Seek suggestions for improvement.* Always find out from your guests how you can improve your event to achieve greater success the next time. This can be accomplished through a formal written evaluation, telephone interview, or more informal exit interview. You also should conduct an internal review with your staff.

    Marketing organizations will, of course, take this process several steps further and determine through sales reports whether the sport event contributed to the sponsor's productivity. In addition, an examination of the morale of the sales force and other employees who helped plan and produce the sport event may determine some key information that will be useful in planning future programs.

    Publish the results of your survey and share this information with prospective clients or sponsors and your own staff.

WORKING WITHIN A BUDGET

Although many of the ideas suggested in the preceding section may seem expensive, you can find ways to be creative and put on a first-class hospitality event without overspending. First consider the time of day you plan to host the event. If you want quality but can't afford quantity, schedule the event before or after mealtimes. This timing allows you to serve light, elegant hors d'oeuvres.

If your guest list is extremely long and you want to reduce the number of RSVPs, consider hosting the event at an odd time or inconvenient location. For example, if the sport event ends at 6:00 p.m., start the party at 8:30 p.m. If the sport event is held at the Madison Square Garden, host the reception at the World Financial Center in lower Manhattan. These strategies force the guest to make a conscious decision whether or not to attend.

Richard Perelman, an event management and information services consultant with Perelman, Pioneer & Company in Los Angles, suggests comparison shopping among competitors on price, quality, and service if planning time permits. For larger programs, this involves writing an RFP and going through a bidding process, as discussed in Chapter 3.

Event producers should also be good value engineers. Value engineering means working within a budget to select the quality and quantity of items that best meet the guests' expectations. For example, the requirements for cowboys on vacation at a rodeo are not the same as those for corporate guests attending Wimbledon. If the decision is between swizzle sticks or more food, which would you select for the cowboys? Additional suggestions on ways to reduce a sport event budget are provided in Chapter 9.

A FINAL WORD ON SPORT EVENT HOSPITALITY

Producers of corporate hospitality programs at the Super Bowl and Olympic Games share the same secrets of success with Little League baseball fund-raising dinner organizers of 10K fun-run award ceremony organizers. To achieve success through sport event hospitality, know the needs and expectations of your guests, plan a series of activities or strategies to satisfy these needs and exceed their expectations, and, above all, make your planning flexible enough to allow for last-minute adjustments to ensure that each guest is enjoying a nonstop positive experience.

Whether you are serving hot dogs and beer or prime rib and champagne, the challenge is the same. Plan and deliver a level of hospitality that the guest would not normally experience. Use your imagination and creativity to transform your basic program into a sport special event. Extra services that can make the difference between an ordinary experience and a memorable one do not necessarily require great financial resources. Sometimes, the extra edge lies in working harder to meet the needs of guests beyond their expectation—what is called "sweat equity." Hospitality involves many steps and critical factors. Figure 4-4 is a checklist to assist you in developing the hospitality for your event.

Hospitality and protocol issues are often derived from customs or traditions rather than rules of law. Chapter 5 examines standard contracts and typical negotiations that will further ensure a hospitable sport event for you and your guests.

Figure 4-4

Sport Event Hospitality Checklist

1. Decide whether to produce the hospitality activities internally or externally.
2. If external help is required, create and disseminate a request for proposal (RFP) to qualified vendors. Qualify the vendors by determining their years of experience and the type of events they have produced previously. Most important, find out the typical number of people in attendance at their events. A vendor who is well qualified to provide hospitality for 50 may be ill-equipped to handle 5,000. The reverse is often true as well.
3. Identify your goals and objectives and include these in a position paper with your RFP to circulate to your staff.
4. Produce a detailed plan book or manual of operations.
5. Identify and secure appropriate insurance, paying special attention to host liability coverage.
6. Identify and secure all necessary permits for local municipality, police, fire, or health departments in order to put up temporary structures such as tents and provide food service.
7. Develop a practical budget and amend as needed during the development of the hospitality program.
8. Once you have solicited vendor bids, review them with expert guidance, negotiate fairly, and seek approval from all parties.
9. Select a menu appropriate to the time of the event and the dietary requirements of the guests.

continued on next page

Figure 4-4 *continued*

10. Establish an estimated attendance number and price per person.
11. Determine when the final guarantee will be required by the caterer (usually 36 to 72 hours in advance of the event). Remember, when determining the final guarantee, typically 20 percent of the guests who have confirmed for a free event will not show up. In addition, 10 percent of the guests who did not confirm will arrive at the last minute. Therefore, you are ready to guarantee most agreements, the caterer will automatically provide a 5 percent overage (excess) clause. This means that the caterer will provide enough food to serve 5 percent more guests than you have officially guaranteed. Therefore, guarantee only 15 percent under the actual number of confirmed reservations. Also take into consideration weather, conflicting events, and major world events that night keep guests from attending. Remember, the guarantee means you are guaranteeing payment for a specific number of guests. **Using this formula could save you thousands of dollars.**
12. Identify and contract for appropriate gifts, amenities, advertising specialties, and souvenirs to give to your guests. Depending on the complexity of the design and the location of the manufacturer, allow 6 to 36 weeks to have these items ready for distribution.
13. Create printed materials including invitation, passes, confirmation notices, maps, signs, and programs. Schedule mailing operations.
14. Schedule all transportation needs, confirm insurance coverage, and provide communications for drivers to handle any last-minute changes.

GAME HIGHLIGHTS

- Know the needs and expectations of your guests and develop a plan to satisfy these needs while exceeding their expectations. Use flexibility to continually fine-tune this process.
- Remember that the first impression is not necessarily the most important. However, the final impression is critical to creating a positive memory of the sport event.
- Design and deliver invitations that attract a positive response from the guest. Be creative! Produce a unique product that will capture the guests' imagination and make them want to attend.
- Measure and evaluate your success through regular temperature checks of the guests' "fun quotient" during the sport event and through a more formal process afterward.

REFERENCES FOR PROTOCOL

American Sport Education Program. *Event Management for Sport Directors*. Champaign, IL: Human Kinetics, 1996.

Cagholm, Christopher. *When Business East Meets Business West: The Guide to Practice and Protocol in the Pacific Rim*. New York: John Wiley & Sons, 1991.

Claiborne, Craig. *Elements of Etiquette*. New York: William Morrow, 1992.

Gjovig, Bruce. *Pardon Me, Your Manners Are Showing: Professional Etiquette, Protocol and Diplomacy*. Grand Forks, ND: Center for Innovation, 1992.

Mack, William P. and Royal W. Connell. *Naval Ceremonies, Customs, and Traditions*. Annapolis, MD: Naval Institute Press, 1980.

McCaffrey, Mary Jane and Pauline Innis. *Protocol: The Complete Handbook of Diplomatic, Official and Social Usage*. Poole, Dorset, England: Devon Publishing Company, 1997.

Post, Peggy. *Emily Post's Etiquette*. 16th ed. New York: HarperCollins, 1997.

Post, Peggy and Peter Post. *The Etiquette Advantage in Business: Personal Skills for Professional Success*. New York: Harper Resource, 1999.

Swartz, Oretha D. *Service Etiquette*. Annapolis, MD: Naval Institute Press, 1988.

Tuckerman, Nancy, Nancy Dunnan, and Jackie Aher. *The Amy Vanderbilt Complete Book of Etiquette*. New York: Doubleday, 2000.

5
CHAPTER

NEGOTIATIONS AND CONTRACTS

I ask a player, "Are you happy with this contract?" He'll say, yes, he is. "Fine," I tell him, "I'm happy, too. We're both happy. But I have one provision before we sign this contract. There will not be any renegotiations."

Arnold (Red) Auerbach,
former general manager, Boston Celtics

WHAT IS NEGOTIABLE, whom do you contract, and how do you find your way through the sport event legal maze?

The need for an experienced attorney in sport event management and marketing is especially important for new events where a number of contracts must be drafted and risk management plans designed. These attorneys must possess expertise in many different areas connected with sport events and may be asked to perform tasks that include athlete contract negotiations, financial and tax considerations, venue concessions and merchandising contracts, sponsorship deals, domestic and international television rights, spectator litigation, insurance, and related hospitality matters such as RFPs and vendor contracts.

In each of these categories, early management decisions and philosophy concerning control, size, and goals of the event, and the potential legal and commercial exposure for the organizer of the event, typically determine the number of negotiations conducted and contracts to be drafted and executed by the respective parties. If the event director and management team wish to promote a single event, make a one-time profit, and control all aspects of the event, they may veer away from vendor and subcontractor agreements. On the other hand, a host committee interested in running a well-organized event for athletes, sponsors, spectators, television broadcasters, and the community at large—all within a balanced budget—may subcontract to a number of experts to ensure the success of the event for both short-term and long-term benefits. From a practical viewpoint, most established event promoters now include a variety of professionals on their staff to address issues typically associated with a large-scale event.

The fact remains that when organizing any sport event, some standard negotiations will take place about the responsibilities of the various parties and the corresponding financial considerations and contracts that need to be executed. Always remember that contractual agreements protect the respective interests of all parties involved. This chapter will help guide you through the various terms of a contract that should be negotiated and included in a contract.

OPTION TO RENEW AND RIGHT OF FIRST REFUSAL

According to sponsorship guru Lesa Ukman, whose Chicago-based newsletter—*IEG Sponsorship Report*—tracks the industry: The option to renew gives the existing sponsor the option to extend the sponsorship agreement when the initial term of the contract expires. The right of first refusal requires the event rights-holder to present a new proposal to the existing sponsor and to allow that sponsor to make an offer to retain sponsorship rights. The event producer can accept the sponsor's offer, or if lower than the full asking price, he or she can try to find an offer of greater value. A lower offer cannot be accepted. Likewise, the right of first refusal allows the sponsor to walk away from negotiations with the option to match any competitor's offer. Depending on the length of the initial contract, a specific time frame—usually eight months to one year before a contract expires—should be designated in which a sponsor must notify the sport event owner of intent to continue involvement in the event. This agreement allows the sport event owner ample lead time to secure another sponsor. Some sponsors may also demand an approval clause for certain sponsorship categories. Coca-Cola, for example, may not want Taco Bell or Kentucky Fried Chicken to be a sponsor because of their affiliation with Pepsi.

TERMINATION AND ARBITRATION

All contracts should include provisions for dispute resolution and termination. Make certain your written instruments outline reasonable cause for termination and a time frame after which all terms are null and void and the parties are free to negotiate with others. You should also include dispute-resolution provisions, such as arbitration pursuant to the rules of the American Arbitration Association (AAA), in order to avoid potentially high litigation costs.

RISK MANAGEMENT AND INSURANCE

To limit your liability, your master agreements must incorporate language pertinent to risk management and minimum insurance requirements for all parties (see Figure 5-1). From naming specific parties as additional insurers to providing certificates of insurance by certain dates and times, these important considerations should be spelled out carefully in writing and checked by your attorney and insurance broker for compliance with your current policies. In any sport event, insurance plays a very significant role in ensuring appropriate protection to the promoter, venue, sponsors, television broadcasters, and performers. Examples of typical insurance coverage for an event include general liability insurance, athlete/performer medical insurance, cancellation insurance, television mechanical breakdown insurance, worker's compensation, prize indemnity, and so forth (see Chapter 6 for more information about insurance).

Figure 5-1

Risk Management/Insurance Action Plan

1. Describe the parties' responsibilities requiring safety compliance with federal (e.g., Occupational Safety Health Administration [OSHA]), state, and local codes.
2. Determine the minimum amount of insurance required by each party, the names of the additional insureds, the date and time that certificates are to be delivered to the sport event manager, and other items required by your current insurance coverage. Ensure that your existing policy conforms to any special event you are promoting.
3. Include a clause requiring each party to exercise due care in the administration of duties to ensure the safety of its organization's employees, your personnel, and the public at large.
4. Determine if waivers of indemnity are required as attachments to the agreement.
5. Determine through legal counsel the wisdom of each party indemnifying the other. Always receive indemnification from the other contracting party because you do not want to be responsible for its action or inaction.

SPONSOR AND SUPPLIER AGREEMENTS

The most important item in contracts between sponsors and the sport event organizing committee is exclusivity—the exclusive sponsorship right per product category or service. This matter should also be discussed with potential licensees, television partners, and service subcontractors such as caterers and hospitality providers.

The importance of exclusivity is illustrated in professional basketball. The NBA has certain rights that it sells, and the team, the venue, and broadcasters have specific rights that each can sell. With all these different rights, a sponsor must consider the various possibilities for ambush marketing and close the holes as much as possible. Ambush marketing is the strategy employed by non-rights-holding companies to create an appearance as if they are official event sponsors. Another term for this activity is *parasite marketing*.

Nike employed ambush marketing techniques during the 1996 Summer Olympic Games in Atlanta by erecting a large interactive exposition next to Coca-Cola's Olympic City, while Reebok was the "Official Footwear Supplier" of the Games. At the 1998 Olympic Games in Nagano, Fuji tried to ambush Kodak, the official film of the Winter Olympic Games, by setting up nonofficial photo centers next to the main press center where they distributed and developed Fuji film for free. As part of their sponsorship rights, Kodak offered this service inside the press center but for Kodak film only.

Control over exclusivity is easier for less developed sports where one sanctioning body is largely responsible for the entire show. Another illustration of the difficulties related to exclusivity is the California State High School Associations, which sold an exclusive sponsorship to Reebok for specific state championships, while signage at individual schools and championship venues was purchased directly from Nike. Simply put, exclusivity is difficult to control, but it would be impossible without contractual stipulations.

As a general rule, a sponsor will require exclusivity related to its particular industry category (e.g., sportswear, soft drinks). Be careful, however, to clearly define the product category. Give a specific description of the category, with the names of particular competitors and products. In the fast-food category, for example, McDonald's may want pizza and Pizza Hut or sub sandwiches and Subway to be mentioned to avoid confusion about pizza and subs as a category of fast food.

When approving sponsor promotions, it is also important to be sure that they do not conflict with another sponsor's rights. In 1994, there was a problem between two World Cup Soccer sponsors: MasterCard, who had the international exclusive rights to both debit and credit cards, and Sprint, who had the national exclusive right to local and long-distance telephone. As a promotion, Sprint created World Cup logoed phone cards and MasterCard sued, saying that these cards infringed on their "debit card" rights. The case was arbitrated and settled by allowing Sprint to give away, not sell, the existing phone cards but did not allow them to produce any additional ones.

Another category that often causes confusion is the financial institutions (e.g., Bank of America) category. The description of this category typically does not include credit cards; these are considered to be in a separate category. This means that even if the sponsoring financial institution may produce a credit card, it cannot promote or associate it with the event.

Trademark Rights

Identification parameters and procedural details must be included for event trademark approvals. All promotional and marketing material, including premiums produced by a sponsor, must be examined and approved by a representative within the organization. The purpose of this scrutiny is to control the quality of the trademarks and to avoid possible abuse or infringement of rights. To avoid excessive delays in the approval process, contracts should specify a turnaround time and contingencies if conditions are not met. A design handbook should be provided to each sponsor, with guidelines on appropriate trademark and logo usage. It is important that the guidelines specify promotional time limits on the use of the trademarks and logos and where they can be used. Lisa Delpy Neirotti noticed boxes of M&M candies displaying the Olympic rights on store shelves and Olympic stickers on U.S. Postal Service trucks for months after each of these organizations Olympic contracts expired.

Territorial Rights

This issue is not as important for local events as it is with national and international events. For the Olympic Games or World Cup Soccer, sponsors are solicited at all levels—international, national, and local—so if specific categories and boundaries are not identified and preserved, exclusivity may be lost. International sponsors have the authority to use the sport event trademarks in all countries participating in the event, whereas national sponsors are restricted to using the trademark within the host country. With international contracts, it is important to specify in writing that any fluctuation in the currency exchange rate will not adversely affect the amount due in U.S. dollars.

Territorial restrictions also apply to television and merchandising rights. For example, NBC has paid for the exclusive Olympic broadcast rights to the United States only. Merchandise licensees may have rights to the European or North American market only.

Since the Internet has no boundaries, specific language must be crafted to protect all rights-holders. This could include an Internet rights-holder per language or per sport, or licensing the content rights to various Internet sites. Since the Internet is still a fairly new, unproven entity, no definitive rules have been established. Lisa Delpy Neirotti is keeping abreast of this dynamic issue and working with the International Olympic Committee and others to determine the most appropriate strategy for sport events to pursue with regard to the Internet.

Sponsorship Fees

The sponsorship agreement should clearly define the specific amount of cash and/or in-kind services, and it must be accepted by all parties and include payment schedules and delivery or service dates. Requests for additional contributions are never welcome after contracts have been signed.

As far as the value of in-kind goods and services, be sure to stipulate in the contract the specific amount of product or the exact service to be delivered, as there may be a big difference in what you think a dollar value will purchase and at what price the sponsor may attribute to these goods or services. For many events, sponsorship contracts now require that in addition to the agreed-upon rights fees and services, the sponsor must guarantee a certain amount of dollars be allocated toward marketing the event. This not only helps you promote the event but encourages the company to leverage their sponsorship to maximize returns.

Specific rights and privileges included in the sponsorship fee also should be clearly defined. The opportunity for accommodations, hospitality, signage, and tickets are frequently provided. For smaller, low-profile events, these are frequently included as a benefit in the sponsorship fee.

Typically, a sponsorship fee simply gives the sponsor the right to spend more money on such items. It is important for a sponsor to ask about the type, location, and cost of tickets, as well as accommodations and hospitality. World Cup Soccer sponsors, for example, were not aware that the tickets allocated to them were not premium seats and only discovered later that premium seats could be arranged for at an additional charge. The opportunity for on-site sales, samples, or pouring rights should also be outlined in the contract.

As far as working with other sponsors or licensees, a "best effort" clause is typically included in the contract to encourage the purchase of premiums or goods from official sponsors or licensees. Best effort implies that companies involved in the event will utilize each other's products or services as long as prices are competitive. Visa, for example, uses UPS exclusively for overnight delivery because both companies are sponsors of the Olympics.

TELEVISION

Television negotiations are becoming more complex—and more lucrative—with the increase in cable, satellite, and Internet options and the rapidly increasing international interest in U.S. sport events. Most television contracts include exclusivity and territorial stipulations. The television rights-holder can then opt to sublicense certain amounts of the programming but generally needs written consent of the licensor. For example, the Winter Olympics offered so many hours of programming that CBS granted a license, for an appropriate sum, to TNT that allowed them to broadcast Olympic coverage on specific days at certain hours. Contracts must also include specifications for satellite rights if a rights-holder has the capacity to produce both feeds.

Another common element included in television contracts is the preferential treatment given event sponsors regarding commercial time slots. According to Howard Stupp, director of Legal Affairs for the International Olympic Committee (IOC), "This is especially important for Olympic sponsors, since there are no advertising billboards allowed in the competition areas." The agreement basically offers sponsors right of first refusal at negotiations with the television rights-holder but not necessarily any price discount. Other contract stipulations in a television agreement include the control of "on-screen" or "superimposed" credits during coverage, the location and number of cameras allowed, the basic technical support provided by the host committee, and copyright credit.

The issue of appropriate "news access" for competitors should also be delineated to protect the rights-holder. The IOC established the "3 × 2 × 3" rule whereby Olympic coverage can be aired by non-rights-holders three times per day, in two-minute excerpts, and spaced a minimum of three hours apart.

PERSONNEL

The most important part of a personnel contract is the specific, detailed responsibility of the individual, including when the employee is to begin and end work, payment schedules, tax withholding, reports procedures, and provisions for changes in the contract (e.g., extension or increase responsibilities). All contracts should also specify the state where contract litigation is to be carried out. It is in the best interest of employees to be identified as secured parties, meaning that they will be paid first if the event goes bankrupt. Secured contract employees are typically paid 25 percent up front, 50 percent with satisfactory progress, and the final 25 percent upon completion of the work contracted. A variety of employees are necessary to produce a sport event, including full-time and part-time employees (primarily salaried), hourly or temporary workers, and independent contractors and consultants.

SPORT CELEBRITIES

Chapter 7 discusses the reasons for hiring or including a sport celebrity in your event. However, you need to spell out the details in personnel contracts for sport celebrities. Frequently, a corporation may employ an athlete for a set number of hours—you must delineate how the hours are to be scheduled and accounted for. Does the celebrity have the right to refuse an engagement? How far in advance must the engagement be scheduled? Is there a minimum and maximum amount of time the celebrity must spend at an event? What type of travel and hotel accommodations will be provided? All contracts must include these provisions, as well as a termination clause for immoral behavior. Some contracts also include specific athletic achievements for the contract to remain in full force (e.g., the athlete must remain ranked in the top five in the world).

NOT-FOR-PROFIT BENEFICIARIES

Chapter 13 discusses sport events and not-for-profit charities in detail, but it is important to highlight certain contractual agreements between for-profit event organizers and not-for-profit beneficiaries. Charitable organizations should be careful not to provide services far greater in value than the dollar amount to be received. Be sure to limit the number of volunteers and the number of work hours required. If the contract requests the use of the not-for-profit postage benefit, check whether your organization is also responsible for the packaging of the materials to be mailed. Contract inclusions like this can cause a great inconvenience for not-for-profit organizations and may eat away any potential revenues. Since not-for-profit beneficiaries typically do not have direct control over the management of the event other than providing necessary services, many request minimum guarantees from the sport event producer to protect their interests.

VENUE CONTRACTS

Suppose that the venue has permanent corporate signage, and your organization requires a "clean" venue (i.e., no signs) or wants to host an event sponsored by a competitor company. Then negotiations about covering up existing signage may be necessary or existing contracts renegotiated. Venues can also apply for a variance of contract (wherein the agreement is amended), suspending all other agreements for a specific period of time while the sport event tenant occupies the venue. Current concession and signage agreements often include a certain amount of days or number of events in which a venue can allow a competing company to have a presence in the venue. The lease rate, security responsibility, other personnel responsibility, concessions, and indemnification are the primary provisions to be covered in a venue contract.

LICENSEES

Category exclusivity on licensed goods depends on the size of the market for an event and the amount of income desired from license fees. Obviously, the price for a license will be less if the category is nonexclusive (more than one licensee may purchase this product category), but sometimes the sum of two parts is greater than the one. The Lillehammer Olympic Organizing Committee (LOOC), for example, decided to grant exclusivity because of its small market, whereas the Atlanta Committee for the Olympic Games (ACOG) opted for nonexclusive licensing agreements because of the large demand anticipated for licensed products. Nonexclusive licensees should request that the contract include a limit on the number of licensees per category. A licensee contract should also stipulate the minimum guarantee required and the royalty payments. Guarantees are based on expected sales, and royalties are a percentage of sales that is paid to the owner of the rights (licensor).

Royalty fees typically run between 5 to 15 percent depending on the value of the marks. Royalty payments are applied to the guarantee, but if enough royalties are not earned over the period of the contract, the licensee must pay the guarantee out of pocket. Once the minimum guarantee is reached, additional royalties continue to be paid to the licensor. Many licensees of the 1996 Atlanta Olympic Games were disappointed with the efforts of the Organizing Committee to follow through on marketing promises regarding the Games marks and mascot and claimed that because of this they did not reach their guarantees and should not be responsible for paying the entire guarantee.

Restrictions prohibiting licensees from selling official licensed items to nonevent sponsors are also included in some contracts. This protects sponsors from ambush marketing. Nonevent sponsors like to provide customers with licensed premiums (a prize, bonus, or reward given as an inducement) to associate with the event. Refer to Chapter 10 for more information on merchandising, and see Appendix 1-C for a sample licensing contract.

HOSPITALITY

On-site sport event hospitality may be offered as an exclusive benefit included in the corporate sponsorship package or marketed to companies as an additional revenue stream for the event. Either way, someone must provide the services; an external management company specializing in hospitality either purchases the on-site hospitality rights or is employed as a subcontractor.

Frequently, only sponsors of the event are offered the opportunity to purchase hospitality packages, and site selection is on a first-come, first-served basis or depends on the corporation's tenure as a sponsor of the event. If this is not the case, any company may request information about hospitality packages and their availability. For both the event organizer and the company purchasing a hospitality package, it is important to ensure the right to quality control of the provider. Thus, if either the event organizers or the clients are dissatisfied with the level of service, selection of food, décor, or any other item, they have the option of requesting reasonable changes that, if not fulfilled, entitle them to a refund. (See Figure 5-2 and Chapter 4 for more information on hospitality.)

Figure 5-2

Hospitality Action Plan

- Determine who is responsible for purchasing hospitality services (e.g., event organizer, sponsor, venue).
- Decide what company will provide hospitality services.
- Determine if the hospitality package is comprehensive.
- Make sure the hospitality package is not in conflict with current sponsors (e.g., the hospitality company serves Budweiser while your event sponsor is Miller).
- Include a quality control clause in the contract.

WHEN TO UTILIZE LEGAL COUNSEL

The involvement of an attorney depends entirely on the originality and complexity of the event and, correspondingly, the contract terms. Sample contracts for standard events are available in the International Event Group's *Legal Guide*. Jennifer Jordan-Lock, an attorney who works with sport events, explains:

> Sport events have unique features that require advice and counsel from an attorney trained to identify potential pitfalls and prevent loopholes in your contracts. For example, a standard rental agreement used by convention centers contains language preventing any operation that involves hazardous waste. But if your event will have a photo processing service in this venue, then you have to negotiate the removal of that language from the contract because the chemicals used to process film contain hazardous materials.

Another example illustrating the importance of understanding the unique features and scope of sport events before signing a contract is the agreement Electronic Data Systems (EDS) of Dallas, Texas, made to produce all the results of the 1992 Barcelona Olympic Games. Whoever signed the contract did not fully understand the extent of the Olympic event program (e.g., men and women, individuals and teams, the various swim and running distances and heats) and did not stipulate the type of hardware that they needed. Instead, EDS was provided a less powerful machine that required additional programming and staffing resources.

Lesa Ukman suggests that you create your own contract and present it to sponsors. This will eliminate the time and expense of hiring a lawyer to go item by item through each new sponsor's contract. Lawyers will advise you that it is better to work from your contract and begin negotiations, rather than rewrite the contract from your negotiating party. Some corporations, like Kodak, always generate their own contracts and send them out before they are even interested in your property in order to lock things up. You must be careful about this action. Look at your own skills and abilities to see whether you can handle the negotiations yourself or need an attorney or agency to represent you.

An attorney is not always recommended for repeat events with relatively few changes and when both parties are satisfied. The general attitude of sport event managers toward attorneys is "we are short on time, and lawyers are long on words."

WHEN TO CONSULT A SPORT MANAGEMENT/MARKETING CONSULTANT

Unless you have specific and extensive expertise in the sport event being negotiated, it may be a wise investment to hire an individual or firm with expertise in this area. For sponsors, this expert can bring more negotiating power to the table and, at least for the first time around, help manage and showcase your sponsorship activities. As mentioned before, companies unfamiliar with the intricacies of sport more often than not find themselves overextended in fulfilling their sport event contracts.

For event organizers, contracting to an outside agency is especially important for an inaugural event, for events lacking an adequate workforce, or for events that will be in multiple cities over an extended period of time. From the beginning, job descriptions must be extremely clear on role responsibilities, reporting, and follow-up. Some firms offer a variety of services, including strategic planning, event management, sponsorship marketing, publicity, hospitality, minority marketing, merchandising rights negotiations, athletes endorsements, sales promotion, sport facility consulting, quantitative sponsorship analysis, and promotional products.

Agency Agreements

Michael Jordan's agent, David Falk, was quoted in the Marquette University *Sports Law Journal*:

> One type of negotiation tactic is to literally walk away. I do not recommend this unless the negotiations are fruitless. Instead, I prefer to set a rigid time frame to keep the pressure on. In one situation, I purposely scheduled my return flight in such a way to imply that time was of the essence.

If you decide that an outside agency is necessary to help manage your event, be sure to select a firm that has experience working on events like yours and understands your needs. See Figure 5-3.

LITIGATION, ARBITRATION, AND ALTERNATIVE DISPUTE SYSTEMS

Whether a contract is written or verbal (and it should always be written), if one party performed a duty that it would not normally provide and could prove that its work benefited the other party, but there has been no compensation for the performance, then its case for litigation is considered strong. In the same vein, if a plaintiff can provide that he or she is the injured party because the defendant did not complete the work specified in the agreement, the plaintiff may be able to file a legitimate complaint against the other party.

With the U.S. court system gridlocked in civil litigation, injured parties in increasing numbers are taking their complaints to a certified arbitrator who is trained to issue a nonbinding judgment. This saves both parties 50 percent or more of the cost of a trial and is much

Figure 5-3

Checklist for Selecting an Outside Agency

_____ Solicit bids from different companies.

_____ Ask for references and speak with previous clients.

_____ Consider the company's historical sport involvement and reputation.

_____ Know what services they offer.

_____ Feel comfortable with the account representative.

more expedient. It is not unusual today for a civil case to take upwards of five years to go to trial, whereas arbitration can find both parties sitting face-to-face in a few months trying to reach a solution.

It is recommended that you include an arbitration clause in your master sport event agreement with all parties. The clause states simply that in the event of a dispute the parties agree to seek arbitration. Make sure to use a trained arbitrator recommended by a reputable group such as the American Arbitration Association. The location of the arbitration will be a negotiable issue.

CLOSING ARGUMENTS

Although verbal agreements confirmed through a handshake between two top-level people can be upheld in a court of law, a problem arises when one of these individuals leaves his place of employment and the terms of the agreement become lost in confusion. For this reason alone, you should insist on a formal written contract. Jennifer Jordan-Lock suggests that you remember the "four corners" rule of contract law: Unless there is a clause in the contract that refers to another document, the totality of the agreement between two parties is represented by the terms contained "within the four corners" of the contract.

William "Woody" Woodruff, a former Xerox employee and now a consultant in event marketing, highly recommends that you "take the time to review the final written contract in detail, as this version does not always reflect previous editions or reflect changes that you verbally thought were agreed upon." Woody adds, "Do not rely on the organizing committee to really understand what it takes from a sponsor's point of view, particularly in the area of service."

Contracts may range from 1 to 500 pages, but the important consideration is not the length but that all parties are clear on their role, responsibilities, rights, and the consequences of any breach in the contract. (See Appendix 1 for sample agreements.)

Negotiations and agreements cannot prevent a catastrophe. That is why Chapter 6 on risk management must be used in tandem with this one.

GAME HIGHLIGHTS

- Make sure your sponsorship agreements include clauses related to exclusivity, territorial rights, option to renew, first right of refusal, termination options, arbitration, insurance provisions, time frames for trademark and logo use, guidelines for trademark approval, and the rights and responsibilities of the sponsor if applicable.
- Provide guidelines in your television agreements on coordination with sponsors, sublicensing privileges, and news access coverage for non-rights-holders.
- Include in your personnel agreements time periods of employment, specific responsibilities, reporting procedures, payments schedules, and provisions for changes. These terms are also applicable to agreements for sport celebrities.
- Ensure that all parties are in full agreement before signing any legal contract.
- Stipulate in contracts the state in which all litigation is to be carried out and include an arbitration clause to avoid the court system.
- Consider hiring an attorney to review first-time or very complex or original contracts. However, developing your own contract is more cost-effective over time.
- Do not rely on the host organizer to serve as your corporate sponsor consultant. If you feel that you are not prepared to negotiate effectively, seek external advice, at least for the first round of negotiations.

6

CHAPTER

Risk Management: Protecting Your Investment

That little white ball won't move until you hit it, and there's nothing you can do after it is gone.

Babe Didrikson Zaharias, multitalented athlete credited with opening the door to the male-dominated domain of sport

How can you reduce the risk of injury to spectators and participants, prevent inventory or personal theft, limit potential financial losses from promotional contests, and protect your event from catastrophic losses due to acts of God?

There are numerous examples of injuries and violence at sport events, including fans storming the field and being crushed to death, fans trying to defy gravity falling from their upper-tier seat, fans pelting snowballs or other objects at players and officials, and fans rioting inside and outside stadiums as a demonstration of their team alliance or victory.

TELL IT TO THE JUDGE

In a comprehensive eight-year study of award and settlement amounts in sports related cases, Gil Fried, M.A., J.D., University of New Haven, reported that the majority of cases involved injuries while swimming, followed by facility-related injuries, with the most common liability at sports events being trips and falls and slip and falls. (See Figures 6-1 and 6-2.) The survey analyzed 281 cases from 1989 through 1996 throughout the United States as reported in the national publication *From the Gym to the Jury*. Of all cases, 22.77 percent involved awards or settlements over $1 million, with the highest jackpot cases reported in California followed by Texas, Pennsylvania, and New York.

Jim Dalrymple, retired executive director of the Washington, D.C., Sports and Entertainment Commission, believes that the increase in number of liability claims at stadiums directly correlates with the leniency of courts in awarding damages against cities and sport venues. Dalrymple states: "When spectators travel to a stadium in the snow and ice, you would think that there is an inherent known risk, but somehow claims for slippage are continually awarded." With this being the case, sport event professionals must be prepared for all challenges.

Figure 6-1

Most Frequent Activity in which Someone Was Injured

Activity	Number of Cases
Swimming	56
Facility	32
Football	21
Administration	21 (i.e., breach of contract, Title IX, etc.)
Baseball	14
Basketball	13
Boating	11
Skating	10
Skiing	10

Figure 6-2

Most Common Incident Which Resulted in an Injury

Incident	Number of Cases
Falls, slips, and trips	60
Accidents	41
Drownings	28
Collisions	26
Battery	21
Breach of contract	19
Diving	18
Discrimination	9
Broken equipment	7
Tackling	7
Medical malpractice	5
Equipment	4
Heart attacks	4
Sliding	3
Stepping	3
Foul balls/pucks	3

TRAINING: THE FIRST PREVENTATIVE MEASURE

Professional education programs such as the Crowd Management Seminar sponsored by the International Association of Assembly Managers (IAAM) and the annual risk management programs offered by the International Special Event Society (ISES) Conference for Professional Development address the most recent developments in this field. University sport management programs also offer courses in facility management, including risk management.

In addition, however, individual sport venues must assess the infrastructure of their facilities to determine how to accommodate present and future fans and implement internal training programs for their staff.

RISK ASSESSMENT

Alexander Berlonghi, author of *The Special Event Risk Management Handbook* (1990), believes the first step in identifying potential risks is to conduct a detailed risk assessment of the event. To do this, event managers may either hire a professional risk management consultant or use the internal expertise of their staff. When you use your own staff to identify potential risks, it is important to involve not only horizontal management positions but also vertical staff. Ticket takers, groundskeepers, security guards, and parking lot attendants, as well as mid- and top-level management, should participate in this process. (See Figure 6-3 for the format to use for this meeting.)

Figure 6-3

Risk Management Assessment Meeting
According to Alexander Berlonghi

1. Assign a knowledgeable person with excellent communication skills to facilitate this meeting. This may be the event director, the director of security, or someone else who has the knowledge and experience to achieve the goals you desire.
2. The facilitator should distribute a meeting notice less than two weeks before the scheduled meeting to alert participants that they should come to the meeting prepared to identify risks in their area and throughout the event.
3. At the beginning of the meeting, the facilitator should briefly describe the seriousness of the agenda and ask for everyone's help in staying focused on identifying real threats that could jeopardize your event.
4. The group may be timid about beginning so the facilitator should suggest one or two risks he or she has identified through research. For example, "The parking areas need more light for the night events in order to help prevent criminal conduct, and the ticket booths need rope and stanchions to establish a lineup area for day-of-events sales. What do you think about that?" This kind of inquiry will promote discussion that helps begin the dialogue and, with continuous facilitation, ultimately helps you identify dozens of real risks that can be easily reduced at little or no cost.
5. This meeting is a mind-mapping exercise. List every potential risk, real and imagined, on a flip chart. This is similar to the SWOT analysis described in Chapter 2. Ask the reporter to explain how the risk was identified and what the potential risk is (e.g., injury, theft, bad public relations). Do not criticize any risk at this point. Instead, dutifully list them all and collect as many as possible before ending this step of the exercise.

continued on next page

Figure 6-3 *continued*

6. Once all risks have been listed, ask each reporter to estimate the total financial cost of his or her risk. With the understanding that this is an exercise, encourage your associates to assign real dollar figures to each potential risk. This helps the entire group recognize that each risk has the real potential of reducing your bottom line revenue from the event. If the risk is one that is covered by insurance, list an estimated dollar increase in your premium due to the identified exposure.
7. Now that you have identified and assigned a cost to the potential risks, encourage the group to act as risk management consultants and make recommendations that will reduce the risks.
8. Before the meeting is adjourned, get agreement from the members of the group that they have, to the best of their ability and with the most recent information available, identified as many risks as possible. Ask them to remain vigilant in reporting other risks that may emerge before, during, or after the event.
9. Assign independent groups from this large group of risk managers to handle the next stage: the actual risk management phase. Ask each small group to design a variety of strategies that will effectively eliminate or reduce the risk at the lowest possible cost to your organization.

Make certain that you document every step of this risk assessment meeting from keeping an accurate attendance roster to creating an action plan of activities you will undertake to reduce the risks. Make certain this document is prepared immediately following the meeting so that you can use it as a measuring stick of your progress in managing the risks.

The risk assessment meeting serves several important and related purposes. First, it is an excellent way for you to empower your line staff and volunteers to take responsibility for identifying and managing risks. Safety is everyone's responsibility, but unless you assign, train, and monitor this activity, it may not become part of each person's job function. Second, you will benefit from the combined expertise of the members of your organization as they share their observations with you in a nonthreatening environment. Finally, you will have taken a significant step toward achieving a standard of care in your industry by convening this informational meeting.

If you should become the defendant in litigation, you will be able to demonstrate in writing that you showed due care in working with your team to identify and correct as many risks as possible to ensure the protection of your valuables and the safety of your guests.

In addition, when organizers take possession of a property for purposes of staging an event, the organizers take possession of the property for a period of exclusive use. At the outset of that period, senior management should walk through the premises with a representative of the owner of the facility. A written or videotaped record of the condition of the premises and any inventory should be taken at this time. Similarly, when possession is transferred back to the facility owner, senior management should be present. This person serves as a repository of information about who bears responsibility for the existence of certain conditions in the event that such conditions give rise to legal claims.

ATHLETE PROTECTION

Since the stabbing of tennis star Monica Seles and the attack on Olympic ice skater Nancy Kerrigan, sport event managers have made security for athletes a key area of concern. Barbara Perry, senior vice president of International Management Group, emphasizes the importance of walking through the sport venue—tracing the route of an athlete from the locker room to the competition or media and hospitality areas—and looking for vulnerable areas. Perry found that older buildings in particular have many nooks and crannies to secure. (See Figure 6-4 for tips concerning athlete protection.)

LOSS PREVENTION

Theft of property or money can be a significant problem in sport event management. These acts range from box office robberies to

Figure 6-4

Athlete Protection Considerations

- Inspect the venue for vulnerable areas.
- Keep security discrete.
- Heighten the awareness of athletes toward the value of security precautions (e.g., credential checks, metal detectors).
- Ensure that credentialing criteria specify reason for and location of access to athlete (i.e., coach allowed in dressing room while family members restricted to hospitality area to meet with athlete).

pickpockets, from pilferage of souvenir merchandise to counterfeit tickets. The 1998 Gay Games in Amsterdam were expected to make money until approximately $2 million came up missing. An investigation of a previous employee is currently being conducted, and to prevent future incidents, an accounting firm is hired to review books every six months. Such checks and balances need to be in place to protect all sport organizations. At the RFK Stadium in Washington, D.C., Jim Dalrymple discovered that kids would sneak under the end zone bleacher seats and steal bags and purses. To prevent this, fences with gates had to be constructed to close off the ends of the bleachers and ushers were placed at each gate.

Each sport event management organization has an implied responsibility to prevent the loss of money and property at the sport event. Three critical considerations must be reviewed prior to commencing operations (see Figure 6-5).

STORAGE

The identification of a secure location not only for counting money but also for selling tickets, storing inventory, and conducting contests and prize-related activities is an important consideration for your loss prevention program. By establishing a secure location for these high-risk tasks, you will automatically reduce the opportunity for a burglary or robbery resulting in a severe loss. To provide a secure location for these tasks, follow the simple guidelines shown in Figure 6-6.

Access to your valuables is an issue that also includes the proper credentialing of your personnel, media, athletes, trainers, coaches, judges, staff, VIPs, and spectators (see Figure 6-7). Also, particular information must be included on the credentials (see Figure 6-8).

Figure 6-5

Loss Prevention Considerations

1. Where will cash, receipts, and valuable inventory be stored?
2. How will access to cash and valuable inventory be provided?
3. Who will supervise your loss prevention program?

Figure 6-6

Securing Your Valuables

1. Select a location with one entrance that is away from the usual spectator traffic.
2. Secure the storage area with a door that has a double bolt lock.
3. When possible, make sure the area is an interior room with additional perimeter walls and a concrete floor.
4. Do not identify this room as a storage or counting room. Identify only box office areas.
5. Find out who has access to this room, including previous occupants who may still retain keys. When possible, change the lock or use additional locking devices as safeguards.
6. When using collection boxes to accept admission or concession tickets, make sure these boxes are secured and that only an appropriate authority has the ability to unlock them.
7. The opening through which the ticket is passed should be the same size as the ticket itself to prevent padding the box with bogus tickets.
8. When possible, chain this box to a secure location in the box office, admission area, or concession operation unit.
9. Involve law enforcement experts in your planning.

ACCESS TO EVENTS

Early in your planning, determine how access will be set up to ensure that only the proper persons enter secure areas. Security guards at each entrance area must be fully briefed on different types of credentials and specific access privileges. Figure 6-9 is a checklist to assist you in developing a secure access plan for your sport event.

According to Terry Cooksey, a 10-year veteran of ticketing operations in Nashville, Tennessee, each ticket must contain at least five basic pieces of information: pertinent event information, seating information, policies unique to the event, applicable legal disclaimers, and the price. Cooksey suggests using a checklist when designing your draft ticket (see Figure 6-10). Remember that if you will be mailing tickets, first send a letter of confirmation asking for any correction in address and/or ticket purchase. High-profile events such as World Cup Soccer use two-day mail service to secure ticket delivery.

Figure 6-7

Credentialing Procedures

1. Review previous credential procedures from past or similar events to determine requirements and areas of improvement.
2. State in writing all credential procedures for each group (e.g., staff, volunteers, athletes, officials, media, participants, VIPs, corporate sponsors).
3. Establish a secure credentialing area with ample space for waiting lines, equipment, security, and other departments. Make certain electricity is available to operate cameras and other equipment and that telephone lines are available for communications.
4. Identify and contract a photography vendor to provide cameras and film for credentialing.
5. Conduct an orientation program for all staff issuing credentials.
6. Consider contingency plans for particular situations such as cameras becoming nonoperational, loss of communications, gridlock among crowds in the credentialing waiting area, theft, and other threats.
7. Keep all credential area signage low key to avoid attention.
8. Provide a separate line or area for athletes, VIPs, and media in recognition of their status.
9. Maintain and protect a computer system that stores credential requests and distribution information. Only persons with proper credentials or authority should have access to this information in a secure place. If necessary, use the services of a security expert to determine any loss of your information through telephonic or even satellite transmission.

Figure 6-8

Critical Credential Information

- Name of credential holder
- Photograph of credential holder
- Code letter(s) for the credential purpose (e.g., press, VIP, official, volunteer, athlete, coach, technical staff, medical staff, administrator)
- Code numbers and symbols detailing event access (e.g., VIP hospitality area, athletes village, media center, competition area, locker rooms, box office, warehouse, all events or specific events)
- Date of expiration or specific usage dates
- Country of origin

Figure 6-9

Tickets, Please!

1. Use a focus group composed of experts in ticketing, security, admissions, concessions, and other tasks in which loss prevention through admissions is an important issue.
2. Ask for the ideas of these experts and then show samples of tickets and credentials used at other successful sport events.
3. Create a draft policy that covers how credentials are granted, where they are issued, how day-of-event changes in credentialing and lost credentials are handled, and how fake and forged credentials are recognized.
4. Integrate your signage program with your credentialing process. It causes confusion, for example, to accept only VIP passes at Gate E when the sign above the admissions personnel reads "General Admissions Only."
5. Establish a process for challenging tickets at the entrance and determining how to resolve these problems. Who has the ultimate authority to grant admission or change the procedure?
6. Remember that passes or credentials should be required for entry to all secure areas such as the box office, the counting room, the warehouse or storage areas, and other areas where valuables may be stored.
7. Does your organization or state or local laws prohibit scalping of tickets or sale of unlicensed, unauthorized merchandise at your sport event? Make sure you have a written policy to handle this possibility. If necessary, create signs to warn individuals who may consider engaging in this activity.
8. Modern sport events often use an advanced ticketing program that has sophisticated printing of the event logo to prevent duplication. Regardless of the technique you use, it is essential that all admissions personnel receive thorough training on how to recognize individualized credentials and tickets.
9. Future credentialing processes may ensure closer scrutiny by including a fingerprint or retina sensor device that matches the recorded computer database image. No two sets of fingerprints or retinas are exactly the same, so this technology may finally end the rash of forgeries that have plagued sport events.

HIRING STAFF

Finding and keeping good, honest employees is a challenge. The good news is that while this burden may be more difficult than it was two decades ago, it is not impossible. Barry Silberman reports that "the key to hiring staff is to continually be on the lookout for quality individuals." He adds, "We typically hire interns who have served us well and have caught on to the business. Rarely do we advertise."

Figure 6-10

Critical Ticket Information
According to Terry Cooksey

Pertinence

- Name of event/opponent
- Location of event
- Day/date/time

Seating

- Section/row/seat
- Gate, portal information
- Facility map

Unique Policies for this Event

- Refunds/exchanges
- Lost tickets
- Prohibited items
- Weather (rain checks)
- Date/time subject to change (televised events)

Applicable Legal Disclaimers

Example: The management reserves the right to substitute performers.

Price

- Base amount
- Amount including applicable taxes
- Amount including applicable taxes and services charges
- Percentage of ticket price going to charity (if applicable)

You should personally select the individuals to supervise your loss prevention program and its individual components, including ticket sellers, concession merchandise supervisors, and other people who collect, transfer, or sell valuable items. And when hiring security, ask about their training. Not all states or jurisdictions require training for private security guards.

For the Super Bowl, the NFL hires a national security firm, Contemporary Services Corporation (CSC), known for its experience in sport events. This firm hires some of the best local security personnel but heavily supplements the staff with people who have no affiliation with the city or local friends who might want to attend. All total, there is an 800-member trained security force in place to ensure a safe and enjoyable event.

Despite all of the mechanical means to guard property, the final responsibility lies with the personnel entrusted with these tasks. The selection and supervision of personnel is the most critical step to master to ensure superior loss prevention practices (see Figure 6-11).

TRANSPORTING THE GOODS

Lisa Delpy Neirotti, a veteran of numerous sport megaevents, states that designing a smooth transportation strategy for goods and valuables is critical. Delays and losses can incur costs that will never be recovered. During the 1996 Summer Olympic Games, for example, merchandise was stolen directly from the unloading docks, causing great loss for a number of licensees.

The preparation, packaging, shipping, receiving, approval, and inventorying of cash and valuables is too often a last-minute consideration by loss prevention personnel when planning sport events.

Figure 6-11

Guardians: Selecting and Supervising Loss Prevention Personnel

1. Use background checks before hiring employees or acquire personnel through firms who use this method to screen their employees
2. Spot-checks ensure the integrity of your loss prevention staff. Spot-checkers are trained individuals whose sole responsibility is to roam—dressed like typical spectators—among ticket sellers, admissions personnel, and concessionary staff to prevent profit skimming from your event through illegal activity. Notify your personnel in writing in advance of the potential presence of spot-checkers at the sport event.
3. Undercover spectators are trained individuals who may display fake credentials in an effort to proceed through admission personnel without care scrutiny. Remember, lost ticket revenue is a tremendous source of lost income for your event. Therefore, the admission process must be checked periodically to guarantee that security has not been breached.
4. Undercover customers may be used to attempt to purchase alcohol products without displaying proper ID or by using an obviously fake ID.
5. Make certain your training program for all personnel includes how to notify the proper authorities when an unusual occurrence is taking place. An authority may be a direct supervisor, a law enforcement agent, a private security official, or anyone who has the responsibility of investigating and preventing a potential loss.

Private companies realize the importance of this aspect of a sport event and have begun to specialize in this kind of logistics. FMI, for example, has orchestrated the delivery, warehousing, distribution, and protection of licensed merchandise for Super Bowls, World Cup Soccer, the 1996 Olympic Games in Atlanta, and the U.S. Open.

Not every sport event requires the services of a private firm or an armored truck to transport cash, but every event does require a confidential plan to ensure the safe accounting of the event's cash and other valuables. Your plan should be developed with the assistance of local law enforcement personnel, your own security director, and line personnel who will participate in the activity. As a further security precaution, the number of participants who craft this plan should be limited only to those who will be directly responsible for its execution. (See Figure 6-12.)

WRAP-UP

The tear-down phase of an event is often not given much attention but is actually as important as the preparation phase from the standpoint of financial and legal consequences. First, from the moment the closing ceremonies end and the crowd disperses, the organizing committee is in possession of a wide variety and a large quantity of equipment from the most technical to the most mundane that must be disposed of. Much of the technical equipment—including computers, pagers, telephones, fax machines, copiers, sophisticated timing devices, cameras, televisions, video recorders, and more—as well as office equipment, must be returned to its proper owner or can be sold or auctioned off after the event to staff, other sports organizations, schools, businesses, surplus stores, or to the public. Whatever remains unsold can be donated to worthy charities to further promote the goodwill of the event in the host community. Each item must be sold "as is" without recourse to the selling entity. The on-site legal council or senior manager must also continue to monitor and attend as necessary to the disassembly of any alterations carried out at the venue by the organizing entity so that it can be transferred back to the care and control of the owners in satisfactory condition.

Figure 6-12

Safe Transport

1. Establish how the cash or valuables will be transported and by whom.
2. Create three routes to transport the protected materials to the final destination. Alter the route for each delivery so that patterns are not established which might be followed.
3. Vary the time the transport is made to further avoid creating a regular pattern that can be monitored by those with bad intentions.
4. Determine whether a uniformed armed guard will be required. Then secure this person through either a private security firm or off-duty police personnel.
5. Plan for backup of personnel if the armed guard does not appear at the appropriate time to transport your materials or if you need to make an early shipment because of a large accumulation of cash.
6. Do not let large amounts of cash accumulate at individual box office locations. Establish a signal for notifying your counting room when pickups must be made to prevent the theft of large amounts of cash.
7. When receiving concession merchandise, make sure a bill of lading accompanies the goods and that you inspect and accept the inventory prior to off-loading the delivery vehicle at your facility. Determine in advance who has the authority to sign for acceptance of this merchandise.
8. Make prior arrangements for secured storage and inventory of merchandise.
9. When transporting goods to individual booths at the sport event, determine who will pull items from inventory and load delivery vehicles, who will accept these goods for transport, and who will sign for acceptance at the final destination. Receipts should match in order to prevent loss.

SAFETY FIRST

Most successful sport event professionals admit that safety is a paramount concern. Steve Schanwald, vice president of Marketing and Broadcasting for the Chicago Bulls, says:

> Some of our players have always received escorts to and from their cars and the locker room. We also have security people positioned intermittently throughout the court area. There is nothing more important to us than the safety of our players and fans. It doesn't make sense to bury your head in the sand and not take precautions.

The night before Nancy Kerrigan was attacked at the ice rink, her agent Jerry Solomon feared for her safety because the only transportation provided by the organizing committee to a midnight practice in the middle of Detroit was a hotel shuttle van with no security.

Safety generally involves three areas: fire, medical, and crowd control. Official procedures and protocols are most likely to be encountered in those three. High school coach Tom Hilton states, "Crowd control is essential. We always hire a uniformed off-duty police officer and make certain the police car is highly visible in the parking lot. This acts as a deterrent."

Security must be tight at all levels or it creates a domino effect. If tickets are not checked for appropriate seating, a rush of people could enter a section close to the field and players, overburdening the security personnel in that area. It is also important to understand that safety is a global issue to which every department concerned with planning and operating the sport event should be committed. (See Figure 6-13.)

Figure 6-13

Safety as a Global Concern

1. At the first planning meeting, include the word *safety* as a benchmark for producing a successful sport event. Without overall attention to safety, no event can possibly succeed.
2. Remind your event team that everyone is a safety consultant and that you want the input of all personnel in devising a successful safety plan.
3. Establish a safety committee to formulate final plans and set a time frame for its development.
4. Locate a first aid station on your sport event site. In the case of larger events, locate as many stations as medical and law enforcement officials recommend.
5. Determine through consultation with medical personnel, or from reviewing other sport events of similar size, attendance, and scope, the number of medical personnel that your event requires. To ensure complete coverage, remember to staff these positions from the time personnel arrive for the event to the time the venue is shut down.
6. Utilize the services of the fire marshal to inspect the venue, to confirm the capacity allowed for the event, and to help you determine proper signs for crowd control.
7. When using special effects such as pyrotechnics, check with the fire department about requirements for special permits and/or personnel.
8. Check with the fire department to determine requirements for concessions, decorations, and special areas that may require separate inspection.

Risk management preparation is crucial to any event and relies heavily on the ability of event managers to communicate the venue's emergency medical system (EMS) to staff, spectators, and participants. The following scenario illustrates the elements involved in an EMS and how—through oral, visual, and physical means—the emergency system is communicated and implemented.

Scenario: Emergency Medical System

The Super Bowl is in progress and a middle-aged man clutches his heart and falls over. His wife remembers reading a notice in the program (visual) and hearing an announcement over the loudspeaker (verbal) giving directions on what to do in an emergency. The wife immediately asked a neighbor to call an usher, security guard, or the medical team. An usher was easily identified by an orange vest (visual). He immediately notified the central communication center (CCC) by portable radio and gave an assessment of the situation before beginning CPR. The CCC then contacted the EMT on location and the doctor and nurse on duty to prepare for advanced medical care and transportation. The CCC also alerted other ushers and security to maintain crowd control. After the usher's initial contact to the CCC, all communication was carried out by the CCC to keep radio lines clear. After the victim was safely cared for and taken away, all individuals completed written reports. Supervisors read this documentation to evaluate the effectiveness of the system, after which the reports were stored in case of litigation.

Note: Prior to this event, the facility manager conducted EMS in-service training for all employees. Each employee was also certified in CPR and given a copy of the policy handbook.

ANTICIPATING PROBLEMS

For large-scale events, plans should be coordinated between the organizing committee and the local law enforcement. For the 1994 World Cup Soccer events held in Washington, D.C., 214 individually numbered patrol post locations were designated in and around RFK

Stadium, and individual officers were assigned to each post from three and one-half hours prior to every match until approximately two hours after the end of the match or whenever the crowd dispersed, whichever was sooner. In addition, each post was associated with a designated responsibility such as access control, vendor patrol, crime patrol, and missing persons. The organizing committee had a list of all officers and their reported posts and duties.

Contingency plans for an abnormal increase in arrests, processing of detainees, and possible defectors should also be arranged. This includes formulating an emergency court plan mandating emergency weekend court assignments capable of being activated with a single telephone call from a representative of the judicial task force that issued the plan. This task force should be a collaborative effort of representatives from the law enforcement and justice communities, as well as the local organizing committee.

As part of the "Marks" protection strategy, a blanket court order should also be secured before the event is underway, allowing enforcement personnel to seize counterfeit merchandise, to escort unlicensed vendors and concessionaires off the premises, and to issue "cease and desist" letters or notices in the event of ambush marketing or other unfair competition situations.

Furthermore, local organizing committees should be very familiar with constitutional rights and local ordinances such as free speech, ticket scalping, and minority business contracting policies. Although the First Amendment generally limits the government's ability to regulate speech on public property (street, sidewalks, public parks, and many public sports arenas), the courts have interpreted the First Amendment to permit the government to place some restrictions regarding time, place, and manner of speech in public forums. Therefore, for the 1984 Olympics in Los Angeles and for the nine World Cup venues in the United States in 1994, the organizers designated two special areas in and around the venues for the exercise of free speech.

The public-address script should be reviewed as well to ensure that it is factually accurate, contains adequate forewarning of the conditions of entry (for example, when video cameras, sticks or poles, noisemakers, coolers, glass containers, or other items are prohibited from being brought into the premises), and directs spectators to exits or other emergency personnel. Be sure the script is free from any discriminatory language.

An amateur video made by the local organizing committee can successfully memorialize not only the general festivity and atmosphere of the event, but weather conditions, decorative elements, commercial activity, seating vantage points, signage, and other circumstances which could ultimately become relevant in a legal dispute.

Accurate and consistent incident-reporting procedures can serve to protect the organizers from unnecessary liability and are a useful means of disseminating information to headquarters and management staff, so as to ensure consistent operations and response to emergencies.

INCIDENT REPORTING

When and how to report an incident are two important pieces of information to share with all event volunteers and employees. Figure 6-14 provides examples of "incidents" requiring reporting and investigation. Language used in reports can often have repercussions that a person not experienced or trained in the insurance or legal fields may fail to recognize. Incidents should be relayed without conclusory language. Nothing in the incident report or notice letter to the insurance company should suggest fault, causation, negligent or reckless conduct, or other legal conclusions. For example, terms such as *fault, negligent, careless,* and *cause* should be avoided. The facts should be related without speculation from the writer as to what particular act or oversight led to what consequences.

World Cup USA 1994, Inc., at the suggestion of one of their on-site legal counselors, printed their incident report forms on quarter sheets of ordinary 8½- by 11-inch paper. These pages were then glued in pads of 50, which fit comfortably in the uniform pockets of all management staff. In this way, every person authorized to collect information on reportable incidents had reporting forms on hand in case an incident occurred in his or her presence.

The incident report included spaces for the following information: date; venue; severity (critical, significant, or minor); incident type (automobile, concessions/food, concessions/novelty, facilities, fan incident, medical/injury, merchandise infringement, property dam-

Figure 6-14

Incidents Requiring Reporting and Investigation

1. Staff or volunteer suffers physical injury or illness related to event-related duties
2. Personal injury or property damage to third party caused by event-related activity or personnel
3. Physical damage to, loss of, or theft of event organizers' property, or property leased, borrowed, rented, or contracted to organizers
4. Auto property damage and/or physical injury caused in an accident involving an event-related vehicle
5. Threats to security, spectator violence, personnel problems, facility or equipment malfunction, ticket scalping, spectators' ticketing complaints, marketing or merchandise infringement, unauthorized concessionaires, trespassing, or other difficulties while event organizers have possession of and responsibility for the licensed premises
6. Breach of contract by event organizers or other parties
7. Complaints concerning organizers or other parties
8. Broadcasting of media problems

age, property theft, security/accreditation, ticketing, or other); time of incident; location of incident; description; and resolution/action. The report asked, "What was the staff member doing at the time of injury?" If there was a physical injury, the report asked for the injured person's description of the injury and attitude of the victim and for comments in addition to the aid given. If a vehicle was involved, the report asked for a description of the damages and an estimate of the value. If the incident was insurable, the report asked the venue incident coordinator to submit a claim to the insurance company.

SECURING ADEQUATE INSURANCE

The best laid plans often are circumvented because of circumstances beyond your immediate control. This is why maintaining adequate levels of insurance is critical. This issue is of such importance that members of the International Special Events Society (ISES) are required to have adequate levels of comprehensive liability insurance in order to maintain their membership.

Indeed, most venues require that the promoter, sponsor, or organizer of the event maintain a minimum level of insurance. Insurance coverage that is typically required is shown in Figure 6-15. The premiums for these types of insurance are based on the level of risk. Obviously, a tennis event is at greater risk of cancellation because of player injury or weather than a rugby match is. With a reduction in gate receipts, the burden of proof is on the policyholder to quantify the loss and justify the anticipated attendance. For this type of insurance, it is best to agree upon values, based on average historical records, prior to the start of the events.

Cancellation Policies

Cancellation insurance requires that the criteria for canceling an event be specified in advance. A hot-air balloon race or air show may be canceled because of low clouds and high winds, while other events may be canceled if the humidity level is too dangerous or if players fail to arrive because of travel difficulties. Cancellation insurance also should cover loss of merchandise sales, with the merchandise vendor's costs and expenses typically guaranteed for loss of profit.

Prize Indemnity

The conditions for prize indemnity must also be stipulated in advance. These include the type of technology that is allowed in the contest or the prior experience of the contestant. A successful contestant of the half-court million-dollar shot offered by the Chicago Bulls was ultimately disqualified by the insurance company, as he had played a semester of college basketball. Although the insurance company did not pay the prize money, the contestant ended up receiving the money from local sponsors and the Bulls organization. Premiums are based on the number of attempts available to win the prize and the probability of success. Contests for large prizes (e.g., hole-in-one, half-court shot) are frequently required to be videotaped for proof. A lawsuit over possible fraud occurred between a race car driver and an insurance carrier. The race car driver won three races and alleges that, according to the contest rules, the driver is due a cash bonus. However, the insurance company inspected the vehicle and discovered that it was an enhanced version of the technology initially approved by the insurance company; therefore, the underwriter alleges that the coverage is null and void.

Figure 6-15

Types of Insurance Coverage

1. **Comprehensive General Liability**
   A package policy that includes fire, theft, and injury also typically includes several exclusions such as pyrotechnics, aerial or participant activities, and other high-risk activities.
2. **Cancellation or Contingency**
   Provides coverage for the cancellation of the event. A comprehensive cancellation or contingency policy will provide adequate coverage for nonappearance of celebrity performers and rain, lightning, or other acts of God.
3. **Prize Indemnity**
   Indemnifies the sponsors against loss of income due to prize fraud or contest awards. Often used for hole-in-one golf tournaments.
4. **Workmen's Compensation**
   Required by most states to provide reimbursement of medical expenses for workers injured on the job.
5. **Automobile Liability**
   Provides compensation to those who are injured by automobiles used for the event covered under the insurance policy.
6. **Property Insurance**
   Insures sets, props, and other material items.
7. **Participant Accident Coverage**
   Provides coverage for the accidental death or dismemberment of an event participant.
8. **Inland Marine Insurance**
   Provides coverage for goods in transit or goods that do not have a fixed location.
9. **Board of Directors Liability**
   Protects volunteer board members from personal liability.

Selecting the Appropriate Insurance and Insurance Company

When purchasing insurance, the best advice is to select an agent who is knowledgeable about your business and can thus suggest the most appropriate coverage. Most event management firms purchase an annual policy covering all business activities. In the case of high-risk events such as skiing, however, it is advisable to purchase a separate policy in order to keep premiums to a minimum. For one-time events, however, the first point of contact should be the associated sports governing body. As part of the sanctioning fee, most sport organizations provide comprehensive general liability coverage.

LeConte Moore, senior vice president of Marsh & McLennan, one of the world's largest sport and entertainment insurance brokerage firms, says that it is essential for the sport event professional to seek expert, experienced advice when determining the type, amount, and length of coverage required to manage the risk of financial loss. Moore, a 20-year sport and entertainment industry veteran, states that "the broker's technical expertise and experience, examples and references of past events, and access to a large group of specialized underwriters should provide the purchaser with enough information to make an informed and confident decision."

Moore describes the professional insurance broker's function as "providing the transactional capabilities to link clients with appropriate insurance companies that can adequately underwrite the risks presented. Typically, the broker receives a fee or commission from the insurance company based upon a percentage of the premium paid." You can also go direct to insurance companies without using a broker.

Fewer than 10 insurance firms, by Moore's estimation, have the knowledge and experience to accept the coverage for a major sport event—a great contrast with other forms of insurance where the purchaser may have dozens of options. Therefore, the relationship between the broker, client, and insurance company in sport event management is critical. Paramount in this relationship is the level of understanding between the client and the broker. The broker must listen carefully to the needs of the client to best evaluate the risks involved in the sport event and then properly communicate these needs to the insurance company to provide appropriate coverage.

K&K and Bollinger Fowler are two insurance companies that specialize in sports-related insurance. Other companies specialize even further. For instance, SCA Promotions specializes in prize indemnification, including kick-off return promotions, halftime promotions, or rebate promotions based on a particular sport or season.

By matching your needs with a company that specializes in sports-related or promotion-related insurance, you are more likely to find a specialist that understands your specific risks and can better assist you in buying the appropriate type and amount of insurance for your team or event. These insurance specialists can also guide you on how best to minimize risk and reduce claims and provide a breadth of information through their brochures, application forms, underwriting guidelines, risk management information, sample releases, and other business materials.

A good reputation is another important criterion. According to Jim Pearson, a lawyer with Pearson, Milligan & Horowitz in Denver and an authority on adventure sport insurance, it is important to "talk with other entities that have similar operations to yours, as they may have already found the ideal insurance program for you or may know which insurance programs to avoid."

Todd Overton, an account manager with SCA Promotions, advises people to look for companies that have been in business for at least three years and to get a list of contact names and phone numbers for claims the company has paid out. "Anybody can issue a contract, but you want to make sure that they can pay out," said Overton.

State insurance commissions, which regulate insurance company activities, can also provide valuable information about the legal status of a company in their state, as well as the number and type of complaints or operational problems reported in the past. That information also helps you evaluate how a particular insurance company handles its claims and treats its customers. You should also research the insurance company's industry rating, which is available from Standard & Poor's, Moody, and A.M. Best.

Yet another concern in selecting your provider should be the size of the agency that is selling the policy. "Insurance agents with purchasing power are often better able to negotiate special requests or waivers from insurance companies than an agent with only a few clients," said Elaine Curl, president of Sports Transportation Management and The Convention Store in Edgewater, Maryland.

According to Curl, a reputable insurance broker with experience in writing policies relating to sports should be able to discuss important coverage issues such as deductible limits, whether lawyers' fees and litigation costs will reduce the amount of coverage, what happens if more than one person is injured or if you have more than one loss in one year, policy limits, and applicable state and federal laws. Curl said her insurance agent has even been helpful in reviewing and responding to requests for proposals.

Finally, as with any business decision, price is important. But be careful when quoted premiums are substantially lower than others you have received. Small agencies trying to break into the business frequently offer lower rates but are unable to satisfy commitments when claims come in, and they often end up going out of business.

When selecting an insurance provider, take the time to research and interview several insurance providers. Make sure that you feel confident and comfortable with the provider you choose, for when things go wrong, and they invariably do, the insurance company you've selected can either make or break you. Figure 6-16 provides a list of questions to ask before purchasing insurance.

Figure 6-16

Twelve Questions to Ask Before Buying Insurance
(Adapted from a list provided by Jim Pearson)

1. How long has the company been in this type of business, or how long has an agent handled this type of client?
2. What is the procedure for handling claims? Who does it, and how long does it typically take? What is the claims reporting period? What is the company's philosophy about settling claims? Who selects the attorneys handling the defense of a lawsuit, you or the insurance company?
3. Exactly what is covered under the type of policy you are considering for purchase, and conversely, what is not covered?
4. Who is covered under your policy or policies—for example, spectators, participants, employees, volunteers?
5. What kind of risk management program does the company or agent offer?
6. How are premiums calculated (for example, are they based on the number of participants or upon gross receipts), and can they be paid in installments?
7. Is the agent's commission structure the same for each company the agent represents?
8. Is the policy a "claims made" or an "occurrence" type?
9. What are the policy limits, and how are the limits determined and applied to different claims?
10. How many clients of your type has the agency or company handled, and what are the names of some references?
11. Does the agency or company offer any discounts or incentives for certifications, enhanced safety features, good safety record, and so on?
12. Can the agent identify risks and exposures associated with your event?

THE FINAL SCORE

For one-time events, however, the first point of contact should be the associated sports governing body. As part of the sanctioning fee, most sport organizations provide comprehensive general liability coverage.

The most important final tally is not the score recorded on the athletic field. The tally that will be recorded in a great number of record books will be that of your professional management of the risk, loss, and safety. A good record here is one truly to be proud of and is the most important championship of all. In the words of Gil Fried, always remember the "ects" of risk management:

Reflect on why you engage in risk management.

Deflect by passing liability onto someone else through insurance, releases and waivers, hold-harmless and indemnity clauses in contracts, and by being named as an additional insured on other insurance policies.

Detect all your risks.

Inspect to make sure risks are minimized.

Correct any problems that are identified.

Reinspect to make sure the work ordered was complete.

Reflect on what did and did not work to improve future events.

One area where risk is increased and opportunity expanded concerns the celebrity in your sport event. As you will see in Chapter 7, the right celebrity can be an excellent addition to your sport event.

GAME HIGHLIGHTS

- Risk management, loss prevention, and safety are effective management tools to use in producing profitable and successful sport events.
- Use a focus group composed of event staff to help you identify a wide range of potential threats and plan for their efficient management.

- Provide effective oral, visual, and physical communications so that employees, spectators, and participants will know what to do in an emergency. Use one central control center for EMS so miscommunication will not occur and radio lines are left open. Write a report after each incident for litigation and evaluation purposes.
- Select an insurance broker knowledgeable in the sport event field who can advise you wisely about the amount and type of coverage you need.
- Involve external groups such as athletes and spectators in the safety review process to ensure universal acceptance and usage.

Effectively Recruiting and Leveraging a Sport Celebrity

On the day of the race, a lot of people want you to sign something just before you get in the car so that they can say they got your last autograph.

A. J. Foyt, race car driver

PLANNING A CELEBRITY SKI WEEKEND, golf tournament, an awards banquet, or your company's annual sales meeting?

If so, the thought of inviting one or more celebrity athletes is sure to be on your mind. The reasons for the high interest and demand for sport celebrities include their ability to (1) draw people to an event and sell tickets; (2) gain media exposure for an event or organization; (3) motivate and entertain corporate employees, organizational members, and guests; and (4) sell more product. Despite these benefits, event planners need to consider a number of items before soliciting a sport celebrity.

First, you must determine if a celebrity athlete is right for your event. This is often based on the event's purpose and audience profile. If the purpose of your event is to raise money, you need to decide if a sport celebrity will positively enhance your goals and objectives. For example, will more participants register and more pledges be collected for a multiple sclerosis walkathon if a sport celebrity starts the race? As far as the audience profile, would a sport celebrity be the best speaker to invite for an international computer science conference? If in fact a sport celebrity is deemed appropriate for your event, the next question to ask is "What type of athlete, referee, coach, or mascot should I invite?"

Here again the demographics of an event play an important role. Jim Palmer, a retired baseball player, may be great for a corporate senior sales meeting but not so good for a youth event. Obviously, an active or just recently retired player will have more appeal for a younger audience. It is also important that the athlete have the ability to relate to the audience. Can the sport celebrity apply lessons learned on the field to the boardroom or to daily issues applicable to both men and women, sport fans and nonsport fans in the audience?

Marketing a sport event, sport tour, or any other sport-related special event or product through the use of a celebrity athlete is not always a slam-dunk. Advance research and planning needs to be done to maximize an athlete's appearance power.

FINDING THE RIGHT MATCH

Fortunately, there is assistance in identifying an appropriate celebrity for your event. Marketing Evaluations/TVQ, a research company in Manhasset, New York, ranks 375 active and retired sport personalities in terms of their familiarity and appeal to the general public as well as to specific markets (e.g., 40- to 55-year-old males on the West Coast). The cost for this service ranges from $950 for a profile on one athlete to $13,500 for profiles on all athletes studied.

If this research is beyond your budget, informally survey your audience by requesting information on the sports in which they personally participate or regularly follow. You can also research the television ratings of different sports. Ratings offer a breakdown of viewership by demographics. Another resource is participation statistics calculated by the Sporting Goods Manufactures Association (SGMA) and the National Sporting Goods Association (NSGA), some of which are provided in the *Sports Market Place Directory*. Lastly, speakers are often identified solely on the intuition of the event organizer's personal knowledge of the athletes and the audience. Remember, it is also possible to use a nonathlete celebrity to enhance a sport event. Jack Nicholson attending Los Angeles Lakers' Games or Garth Brooks playing ball at spring training are two good examples.

Regardless of the identification process, the next step in the selection process should be a reference check. An investigation should be made as to whether the athlete is reliable, capable of making a good presentation (without using "locker room" language), and can relate to your audience. Speaker bureaus such as Burns Sports Celebrity Service, Inc., the nation's oldest source for sports celebrities since 1970, and the Washington Speakers Bureau can assist with this research, as well as the logistics of booking the sport celebrity appearance. Burns Sports Celebrity Service, Inc. maintains a 3,500-name database in their Chicago office and with a keystroke can call up the name, location, agent, and general fee for any sports celebrity, from megastar Michael Jordan to a lesser-known Olympic wrestling champion. After 25 years, David Burns, the founder of this service, knows which athletes, coaches, referees, and team mascots are likely to make a client happy and which ones will leave them gasping for air.

Ideally, you would personally meet and witness the athlete in a setting similar to your event. If this opportunity is not available, be sure to request a videotape of the athlete presenting. No matter what, always request references. When checking references, be sure to identify the nature of the event in which the athlete was involved, whether or not the athlete interacted with the audience, how well he or she related to the audience, the athlete's reliability, any special requests that the athlete may have made, and the appearance fee—if the reference will provide it.

CONTACTING AND PERSUADING THE SPORT CELEBRITY

Once you have narrowed your selection, you need to contact the appropriate person, whether it is a family member, an athlete's personal friend, the athlete's agent or team, a speakers bureau, or the athlete directly. This initial call allows you to check on the athlete's interest, availability, and fees, and to identify any other criteria that may be important to the sport celebrity. Be sure to check the athlete's practice and game schedules before calling to make sure there are no conflicts with the date of your event.

The next step is to write a brief letter to the athlete stating your request and mail it in care of the athlete's contact person. Within the letter, provide the details of the event, including the purpose, beneficiary, date, time, location, schedule of activities (e.g., cocktail reception, dinner, speech, autograph signing), and a response date. Also list in descending order of importance the benefits the athlete will enjoy from participating in the event, such as an appearance fee or honorarium, media exposure, a donation to the athlete's charity, an opportunity to meet corporate executives that may be interested in signing endorsement deals, or an opportunity to sell books, CDs, or other merchandise related to the athlete. Always include a suggested response date to remind the athlete or his or her representative that your publicity is being developed and requires confirmation to proceed.

Unless you are involving multiple celebrities in your event, contact only one athlete at a time. Do not send out simultaneous letters to a dozen athletes hoping that one will respond. The world of celebrity athletes is a small one; publicists and athletes get extremely upset when they learn that you have sent multiple invitations.

Most athletes admit that their chief concern is compensation but that they realize public appearances are part of building their resume. They also want to know about the credibility of the organization putting on the event and the demographics of the people attending. Some athletes will only participate in events targeted to youth, while others focus entirely on the corporate market.

Getting the right person to pitch the celebrity is essential. Bob Geoghan, founder and president of Sports America, Inc. in Rockville, Maryland, remembers when a famous sportscaster turned down his invitation to speak at a NFL "Player of the Year Dinner" only to accept a few weeks later after the sportscaster's boss presented the same invitation. Other useful inside sources are the family members, trainers, coach, or agent of an athlete. A request can also be made directly through the public relations or community relations office of the athlete's team, as most players are required to make a certain number of community appearances per year. Obviously, the personal approach is usually more successful.

Another suggestion on how to attract a sport celebrity to your event is to offer the athlete an award. Unfortunately, this can often turn into an expensive proposition when the athlete starts requesting that their agent, family members, and friends also be invited to partake in the celebration. Now, instead of paying first-class air, accommodations, and meals for one or two people, you are paying for three or more.

Once a sport celebrity expresses interest, a contract or letter of agreement is drafted and signed by all parties. The agreement should specify the length of appearance, number of breaks (if appropriate), cancellation or no-show penalties, and type and class of transportation, accommodations, food, and beverages. The type of attire should also be discussed for two reasons. First, you want the athlete to dress for the occasion. Second, the athlete may wear sponsored clothing that conflicts with one or more of your event sponsors. At the same time, travel plans and any other special requests should be arranged. In addition, specific materials about the organization and audience should be mailed to the athlete (or appropriate contact) so that the celebrity's speech, which is usually canned, can be tailored to the group. The benefit of working through a speaker's bureau is that all these details are taken care of, as well as most of the worrying about whether the athlete will show up.

WHAT DOES IT COST?

The cost of booking sport celebrities for charitable events is considerably less than for corporate events. Depending on the event, cause, and the person making the request, athletes will often attend charitable events for free. This is where research plays an important role. Find out whether any athletes are currently serving on the national board of the charity or have been linked historically to the cause. It is always easier to attract a celebrity who has a personal interest in the cause, as is the case with quarterback Boomer Esiason and cystic fibrosis, a disease that has afflicted his son. Also check with your major corporate sponsors. Many companies retain sport celebrities on their payroll. You could cut the costs of appearance fees if these celebrities are asked, as part of their corporate contract, to make the appearance.

For charitable events that occur on a regular basis and for which the same athletes are frequently asked to participate, such as the Washington Redskins' weekly luncheon benefiting Children's Charities, it is advisable to offer a small honorarium ($150 to $300). This token of appreciation not only makes the athletes feel more special but makes them feel more accountable to the event. Typically, the more money a sport celebrity is paid, the less likely they will cancel; however, emergencies do happen!

For those events with a budget to pay for a sport celebrity, the best recommendation is to identify a local sport celebrity who will not require first-class airfare or accommodations. Local athletes are often more effective as well because of their recognition level. According to Bernie Swain, partner of the Washington Speakers Bureau, "The fee for sport celebrities ranges between $5,000 and $50,000." For instance, Tony Dorsett commands a fee of $7,500, Bob Costas gets $35,000, and John Madden asks $50,000. (Note: Madden is extremely selective with his engagements and may speak a total of three times per year.) The cost of a sport celebrity may also depend on whether the athlete is asked to deliver a keynote speech, to attend autograph and/or photograph sessions, or to simply attend the event to meet and greet guests. If your event charges admission, some athletes may negotiate a deal for a percent of the gate. This is especially helpful for event organizers short on cash. Other athletes may request that a donation be made to his or her charitable foundation or another nonprofit organization.

In addition to their appearance fees and associated travel expenses, some of the more notable sport celebrities include contract clauses requiring local limousine transportation, additional security, special dietary requests, and even the stipulation that a PGA golf course be within 40 miles of the event location.

MAXIMIZING THE CELEBRITY'S APPEARANCE

One of the best ways to capitalize on an athlete's appearance is for the athlete to have something on which to sign autographs, such as posters, playing cards, or event programs. Such items can often be provided complimentary by one of the athlete's sponsors (e.g., Nike or Wilson) if requested in advance.

If an athlete is being used to help promote an event, be sure to request a biography and picture of the athlete to include in a press release, as well as posters or other marketing materials that an agent, team, and/or a sponsor can provide to distribute in the local area to increase public awareness of the athlete's appearance. You may also request that the athlete travel to your city prior to the event in order to schedule media interviews and/or a press conference. Whenever possible, recruit the celebrity athlete to be your promotional partner.

If the athlete is expected to make a presentation and he or she is not experienced at public speaking, it is advised to provide a draft speech or talking points and to designate time to rehearse the presentation. If the athlete frequently speaks, be sure to work with him or her to personalize the athlete's standard presentation so that it will better relate to your specific audience. If applicable, a demonstration by the celebrity athlete may also enhance a presentation.

Finally, small details can often make the greatest difference. Arrange for someone to pick up the athlete at a scheduled time so that you are certain the athlete will arrive to the event on time or make his or her flight on time. Make arrangements for the appropriate amount of security and a photographer to be at the event, as well as for delivery of the memorabilia to be signed and waterproof marking pens. In establishing the schedule, prepare a window of time for each activity that is longer than actually needed so that if the sport celebrity pauses to greet fans or is late, you will still end on time. By adding minutes to the published schedule, you can compensate for delays beyond your control. It is also wise to assign a specific staff member to host and handle any unique requests that may arise during the appearance. A backup plan should also be ready just in case the athlete becomes ill or is not able to appear for another reason. One such plan is to build a relationship with an agent representing various athletes so if your first choice is a no-show another athlete is on standby. The checklist in Figure 7-1 provides step-by-step instructions for organizing an effective sport celebrity appearance.

Figure 7-1

Steps to Producing a Successful Sport Celebrity Appearance

Before the Appearance

- Review all correspondence and contracts to be certain you are in full compliance.
- Set time lines for scheduling air travel, ground transportation, hotel reservations, and other amenities.
- Ascertain whether the sport celebrity has any special needs during travel such as airplane seating preference, food and beverage likes and dislikes, and entertainment or other amusement activities in which they may wish to engage, including sport events.
- Confirm in writing all travel arrangements.
- Check with the celebrity or his or her representative about any specific security arrangements that must be made locally.
- Send a written logistical plan to each venue where the sport celebrity will appear, describing the setup with the help of graphic visuals.
- Confirm that each venue has received plans, understands requirements, and can comply fully.
- Send the final itinerary listing all scheduled activities and ask the sport celebrity to approve, comment, or change with his or her initials. This letter of agreement is essentially your contract and should begin with "This letter is to confirm that…."
- Schedule and confirm in writing all travel arrangements.
- Assign a person to be available on a 24-hour basis to handle the sport celebrity's last-minute needs upon arrival.
- Notify the hotel that you will be using a pseudonym for the celebrity to avoid pranks or intrusive calls to the celebrity's room.
- Ask the hotel to provide special amenities such as a fruit basket, welcoming gifts, and so forth for the sport celebrity.
- Simulate the travel and walking path of the celebrity to the event venue so that your event plan contains the actual time it takes for the celebrity to get to his or her destination. This will avoid miscalculations and delays later.

Day of Arrival

- Call the airline to confirm the flight.
- Call the hotel to confirm room availability and welcoming gifts.
- Call the transportation company to confirm the limousine or shuttle pickup at the airport or for local engagements at the celebrity's home.
- Arrive at the airport one hour prior to flight arrival.
- Stage the limousine or shuttle for prompt pickup.

continued on next page

Figure 7-1 *continued*

- Greet the sport celebrity and escort to transportation.
- Retrieve luggage and deliver to the hotel.
- Prior to the sport celebrity's leaving the limousine, retrieve the room key and escort him or her directly to the suite, or have the limousine driver call ahead to make sure the sport celebrity's room key is available upon arrival.
- Hand the sport celebrity an itinerary that describes all previously approved and scheduled activities. Ask the celebrity to review and query it.
- Reconfirm the time for pickup and/or transfer to the first engagement.
- Notify hotel security that a sport celebrity is in the hotel and ask for assistance in providing coverage for transfer from room to transportation or lobby.

During Events

- Arrive one hour prior to the sport celebrity appearance to reconfirm all logistics.
- Confirm that the arrival area is secure and free of casual bystanders.
- Confirm that all personnel are standing by for arrival. Personnel may include host, police, security, and other staff.
- Select an escape route if the arrival area fails because of breach of security. Ideally, this will be a nearby room where the sport celebrity can be secured until crowd management is handled.
- Escort the sport celebrity to the appearance area.
- Make sure the crowd lineup is proceeding according to plan and that all personnel are at their posts.
- Keep your eye on the clock and begin checking the departure route for clearance 15 minutes prior to the end of the appearance.
- Do not announce in advance the departure of the sport celebrity. Make the movement as quiet and inconspicuous as possible.

Appearance Physical Requirements

- Use a stage with a height of 24 to 48 inches (48 inches deters guests from sitting on the stage).
- Use rope and stanchion to clearly mark areas where autograph seekers and guests are to queue up to meet the sport celebrity.
- Use a table (8 feet long, skirted on the front and two sides) for autographs.
- Use pre-autographed photos and have the celebrity add initials at the event.
- Make certain the area is well lighted with sufficient candlepower for videotaping if required.
- Provide bottled water or other refreshments for the sport celebrity in this area.

continued on next page

Figure 7-1 *continued*

Appearance Personnel Requirements

- Make certain private security and police have established communication and are working together.
- Place one guard on each end of the stage and beside access ramps or stairs.
- Place one guard near the front and back of the sport celebrity.
- Place a public relations staff member immediately beside the sport celebrity to serve as buffer for unruly fans or guests.
- Assign one person as a gofer to restock autographed photos, bring refreshments, or perform other essential tasks.

IDEAS FOR SPORT CELEBRITY APPEARANCES

The possibilities are limitless for your sport celebrity appearance. Figure 7-2 offers some creative possibilities to illustrate this point.

The growth of the business of booking celebrity athletes continues to escalate as more and more companies realize that sports figures as speakers have the ability to motivate employees and entertain clients. In addition, they have the capacity to raise the recognition level and appeal of the products they promote. If well researched and properly courted, a sport celebrity can be an event planner's most valuable resource.

In the next chapter, you will discover how to integrate a variety of marketing techniques to maximize the visibility and profitability of your sport event.

Figure 7-2

It's Showtime!

- Schedule a bush league star baseball player to provide batting lessons for your corporate sales team.
- Engage a state championship runner to carry the flag into your celebrations and have him or her hand the flag to a national running star.
- Turn your shopping mall into a Little League baseball tryout area using a Nerf baseball to avoid damages, and invite a former major leaguer to sign autographs.

continued on next page

Figure 7-2 *continued*

- Invite a local golf pro to provide putting tips or work with a golf club manufacturer to bring in a PGA pro to sign autographs and answer questions.
- Introduce the speaker with video clips from his or her best games.
- Take your guests to a major league hockey game, and as a surprise, arrange for one of the players to drop by the reception after the game to greet and meet your guests.
- Hold your banquet on the 50-yard line of Texas Stadium in Irving, Texas (home of the Dallas Cowboys), and invite one of the assistant coaches to scrimmage with your team.
- Schedule a clay target-shooting tournament at a resort, and hire a professional trick shooter to mix with your regulars and keep them on their toes.
- Arrange for an early morning jog for your group and engage a presidential lookalike complete with five or six secret service types to join you.
- Invite the local team mascot to welcome your audience to the city and have the mascot lead your guests to the next activity, such as an exhibit hall where he/she will pose for photos.
- The sky is the limit! While en route to the big sales meeting on board your 747 aircraft, invite an Olympic gold medalist to speak to jet-setting business leaders about never giving up and going for the gold!

GAME HIGHLIGHTS

- A sport celebrity includes athletes, coaches, team owners, officials, mascots, and members of the sport media.
- Always determine the purpose of the sport celebrity appearance before signing a contract.
- Do your homework and find out the sport celebrity's schedule, personal or sponsor affiliations, and previous appearances and their success.
- Use market analysis (e.g., Q ratings) to determine the most suitable celebrity for your event and audience.
- Be sure to add time in the event appearance schedule for delays and other problems that could occur with an uncooperative celebrity.

Event Marketing

> So many sports organizations have built their entire budgets around television, that if we ever withdrew the money, the whole structure would collapse.
>
> *Roone Arledge, former ABC sports director*

What are the two types of event marketing and how can both be accomplished successfully?

Traditionally, event marketing refers to the actual marketing of an event by event organizers. For sport events, this type of event marketing involves marketing to: (1) athletes to secure their participation in the event, (2) the media to cover the event, (3) the general public to attend the event and/or follow the event via print and electronic media, (4) corporations to sponsor and support the event, (5) government officials to provide public support, and (6) private vendors to provide efficient and reasonable services.

The contemporary use of event marketing, however, refers to a new strategy companies and communities are implementing to reach consumers beyond traditional, cluttered advertising mediums. With companies competing in a world characterized by even greater competition, market saturation, and change, it is no longer possible to effectively communicate with the consumer in traditional ways.

Companies are looking for ways to differentiate their brands through emotional positioning and to create innovative communication devices. Through events, companies try to develop an active relationship between the brand and their consumers.

Information on both of these types of event marketing will be covered within this chapter that will be helpful to event organizers and event sponsors looking to maximize opportunities.

PART I: TRADITIONAL EVENT MARKETING

Obviously, each of the six target audiences mentioned above requires a unique marketing approach. For example, event organizers may need to pitch athletes' parents, coaches, or agents to secure the athlete's participation. For the media, press releases, special invitations, and gifts are standard. Depending on the type of event and size of budget, direct mail, advertising, and now the Internet are effective marketing vehicles to reach the general public. Corporations expect to receive a concise sponsorship proposal clearly outlining the event's target market and benefits to the company. Government officials look for studies detailing the event's positive economic and social impact on the community and how the event will benefit their personal agenda. Finally, vendors are interested in working for events professionally run, with well-written requests for proposals, and events offering long-term or new business opportunities. Since marketing to corporations, government officials, and vendors are covered in Chapters 9, 12, and 3, respectively, the focus of this section will be on promoting the sport event to participants, spectators, and the media.

Attracting Participants and Spectators

The 2000 Susan G. Komen Breast Cancer Foundation Race for the Cure in Washington, D.C., set a new record for participation in a 5K foot race. Over 69,000 runners registered for the event. How did this event grow from 7,000 in 1990 to this new record? "With lots of hard work, excellent volunteers, sponsors, and a good cause," states Vanessa Collier, director of public relations. Registrations were received by mail (4,000); online (9,700); at one-stop registration sites such as Fresh Fields or Hechts stores, where participants could register and pick up their T-shirt and goody bag in advance (26,900); team packets (20,000); late registration at the 97.1 Soft Rock Health Expo (6,500); and another 2,800 through other means. A director of teams, in addition to the director of registration, was hired primarily to visit companies and encourage them to form a team to participate in the race. This maneuver turned out to be extremely successful. In addition, the event recruited a media partner, the local NBC affiliate that ran a number of public service announcements (PSAs); placed advertisements in newspapers, in magazines, and on radio stations; and distributed entry forms through various local companies. All total, the event raised more than $3 million to be designated for breast cancer research, education, screening, and treatment. According to Jim Vandak, race director for the Army 10-Miler, the most common way to market a road race is through running publications, race brochures, and the Internet.

For event organizers and marketers, Internet sites such as ActiveUSA, Acteva, Do It Sports, and SignMeUpSports all provide event registration technology and marketing opportunities. These sites will assist you in developing an individualized event Web site outlining all the necessary information regarding the event, along with the possibility of registering online. For each online registration, a 2 to 8 percent transaction fee is charged either directly to the registrant or to the event organizer. When you sign up your event with one or more of these companies, your event will be listed in their calendar of events by date, location, and type of sport. ActiveUSA, for example, offers more than 75,000 events nationwide in more than 50 sports, from running and triathlons to skiing and fishing.

Marketing to Athletes

With over 36 million youth participating in sport each year, the opportunity to capture this market is huge. Considering that coaches make the majority of decisions regarding tournament selection and team travel, we will consider this group as primary gatekeepers. Parents, however, are also an important audience, as they make the ultimate decision concerning whether or not their child will travel and if so, how many (if any) family members will accompany the athlete. On average, 3.2 spectators attended for each participant in The Lone Star Junior Volleyball Classic for girls 10 to 18 years old held in Austin and Dallas, Texas. It is important to note, however, that boys events typically do not involve the same travel commitment from parents and family as girls events.

The Lone Star Junior Volleyball Classic attracts over 520 teams to Austin and Dallas. When coaches were asked why they chose the Lone Star over other tournaments, their response was good competition, unique venues (held in convention centers), and a fun location, and because the tournament was well organized, attracts many college coaches, and was shown on tape-delayed television. One of the marketing strategies of the Virginian Soccer Tournament, which attracts over 650 teams, is scheduling four games plus finals, whereas most tournaments offer only three games and finals.

For professional events, Lee Coorigan, tournament director of the State Farm Senior Golf Tournament, understands that in order to attract high-quality athletes to his tournament, the airport and hotel must be close to the course, the purse needs to be high, and family activities must be planned. As an example, Coorigan throws a private fireworks party just for the golfers and their families.

Selling Out the Stands

To sell out a sport competition or special event, be it the Olympic Games or a fund-raiser dinner, ticket sales require both a creative and scientific approach. To begin, the price of the ticket must be determined. To do this, the type and purpose of the event, total expenses, sponsorship revenue, the location, anticipated demand, and local competition must all be considered. If you are hosting the only golf pro-am within a 300-mile radius at an exclusive golf course in a relatively affluent community, your entry fee should fall toward the upper end of the fee spectrum. On the other hand, if you are trying to gain exposure and increase public interest in your sport, a lower price may be charged (e.g., WNBA or MLS).

Once the ticket price is determined, target markets must be identified. Target markets may include individuals residing in a specific zip code; school, church, or civic groups located within a geographical area; previous supporters/customers; subscribers to related sport publications (e.g., *Golf Magazine*); or members of related sport organizations or clubs.

Specific names and contact information of individuals within a target market can be attained through existing proprietary databases or by purchasing or bartering mailing lists. Many groups provide mailing lists in exchange for a discounted group ticket price or for a ticket commission (i.e., for every ticket sold to someone on the mailing list, $1 goes to the associated group or organization). Some groups even work out a deal where their newsletter is printed on the back of the promotional brochure mailed to the list, saving the group postage fees. Publications may lend their mailing list if offered a free program advertisement, a booth, or other form of recognition at the event. Event sponsors are another possible source for lists, particularly car dealers. Exclusive country club or sport organization membership lists may also be attained through the board of directors, staff, or acquaintances of both who are members.

While identifying the target markets and building a database, decisions as to the type of ticket sales campaign implemented (e.g., telemarketing, Internet, direct mail, personal sales, print/TV/radio advertisements, promotions) should be based on the amount of the marketing budget, the size of the target audience, and the time frame. Mass media may be more practical for a large, diverse audience, while telemarketing is preferable for a more select group.

Direct-mail pieces range from a simple postcard to an elaborate four-color glossy ticket brochure. Postcards are especially useful to remind people that the event is approaching or to highlight a special offer. If an event is held close to a holiday (i.e., Christmas or Mother's or Father's Day), a postcard can be used to encourage purchasing tickets as gifts.

Placing ticket brochures on cars in designated parking lots is another inexpensive approach to targeting an audience. At The George Washington University, cars parked in the staff/faculty lots receive ticket brochures offering discounted season tickets to staff and faculty.

Packaging tickets with extra amenities such as parking, concessions, or merchandise has proved most successful in reaching the family market. Such discounted promotions can be cost-shared and marketed in cooperation with existing team or event sponsors or concessionaires. As an example, for a limited selection of games, the Colorado Avalanche offered four tickets, four mini Pizza Hut pizzas, and four Cokes for $99. Pizza Hut and Coca-Cola each participated in the promotion.

To sell end-zone or other less desirable seats, consider creating a concept such as the Citrus Bowl did when they established the "Zonies." Anyone who purchases a ticket in the end-zone section is coined a "Zonie" and is entitled to a variety of added-value benefits such as a special T-shirt, hat, and party. "This concept not only sells seats but creates a fan loyalty beyond the athletic event" states Joe Lathrop, president of OCG, Inc. in Orlando, Florida, an organizational development company that focuses on customer service.

Contingency and theme promotions are two additional techniques to encourage ticket sales. Contingency promotions include those that require the attendee or the players to do something before the attendee receives a benefit. Theme nights attract people to the event who might not be the consummate fan and help make their experience more enjoyable so that they may return in the future. Refer to Figure 8-1 for examples.

The cost of most of these promotions should be absorbed by existing sponsors and not by the event organization. Two additional ways corporate sponsors can assist in the marketing of an event are to contribute, or sell to you at a discount, some of their prepurchased advertising spots or purchase additional spots for you at a volume discount. In addition, have corporate sponsors identify all they can bring to the table besides cash. Airlines, for example, frequently have the right to sell merchandise in airports. This provides an opportunity for prepromotion of the event and an additional revenue source.

Unfortunately, no two events or audiences are the same, thus it often takes a trial-and-error approach to determine the best marketing mix for your specific event. For example, postcards and telemarketing were primarily used to sell tickets to the first Champions Tennis Tour in Washington, D.C. After careful analysis, however, it was determined that ticket brochures providing all relevant information and newspaper advertisements were the most cost-effective techniques and were therefore emphasized in the tournament's second-year marketing plan.

Coding the different marketing pieces is also essential to determine which mailing lists, advertisements, or promotions generated the largest response. Mailing lists with a high response should be scheduled for a second mailing (if time permits), while those with a low response may be eliminated.

Figure 8-1

Promotional Ideas

Theme Promotions

- Bald night (This was a popular promotion at The George Washington University during the tenure of coach Mike Jarvis, who was bald. Not only did all the bald men get into the game for free, there was a contest at half-time to find the closest resemblance to Coach Jarvis.)
- International week (The New York Mets, in conjunction with the New York City Transit Authority, dedicated certain games to Hispanic, Irish, Jewish, Asian, African-American, and Italian fans).
- Lawyers Appreciation Night (The Tampa Bay Devil Rays charged attorneys double and billed by the third of an inning.)
- Conversion Day (Tampa Bay fans were rewarded for getting rid of New York Yankee caps.)
- Birth night (A minor league baseball team invited expectant mothers to a game, led breathing exercises between innings, voted on potential names, and offered a year's supply of diapers to the woman who delivered first.)

Contingency Promotions

- Offer a discounted ticket to a future game with every ticket purchased.
- Offer a coupon with each game ticket for a free Coke at the next game they attend.
- Distribute coupons for free food or drink if the team scores a certain number of points.
- Feature season-long themes such as collecting a different baseball card at every game and then entering the fans with the most cards collected into a drawing for free tickets to the World Series.
- Offer a final ticket free to customers who purchase tickets for the first three days of a tournament.

Another fast-growing option for selling tickets is through the Internet. A number of teams currently offer fans a spectator's view from the different sections and seats (e.g., Houston Astros site at http://www.astros.com). For those customers uncomfortable with the security of electronic transactions, the Internet sites can also provide valuable ticket information such as price, availability, and purchase alternatives.

Contests and Giveaways The purpose of most sport-related contests and giveaways is to generate interest in a sports team, event, or organization in order to increase ticket sales or membership. No matter how creative or exciting a contest or giveaway may be, if your target audience doesn't know or care about it, it will not succeed. Likewise, if it costs more to implement than it brings in, the contest may not be deemed successful.

To ensure a successful contest or giveaway, sport marketers must first know their audience (who they are and what they like), create or borrow an idea that appeals to this audience (there are few copyrights in sports marketing), and then work with corporate and media sponsors to sufficiently promote the contest or giveaway. If the prize is of a significant value, marketers should buy insurance for protection.

Although borrowing marketing ideas is acceptable in sports, you must understand your market and know that a successful promotion in one sport or community may not have the same response elsewhere. Research and trial and error are part of the process.

Using the Right Marketing The success rate of any contest or giveaway increases dramatically as the marketing behind it increases. That marketing includes public address and video scoreboard announcements at events leading up to the promotion, as well as during the event at which the contest or giveaway takes place; advertising in newspapers, on radio and television, and on the Internet; and point-of-sale displays at sponsor locations. According to Grady Raskin, corporate sales account executive at the Southwest Sports Group, the purpose is to increase consumer awareness and lead people to say, "How can I get involved?"

The advertisements should be a call to action and drive people to the local retailer-sponsor or Web site to sign up for the contest or giveaway and then actually come to the event involved. Working with sponsors to create and promote contests and giveaways has proved to be the most successful model. It not only distributes costs but also offers companies the opportunity to leverage their sponsorship and, if done correctly, provides a winning situation for all involved.

Effective Sports-Sponsor Partnerships Following are some examples of this type of partnership. The Texas Rangers teamed with Chick-Fil-A to offer the Friday Night Pop-Up contest. Individuals registered at Chick-Fil-A stores, and the selected winner tried to catch three pop-ups in the outfield before a Rangers game. If he or she caught all three, then everyone in the ballpark won a free drink at Chick-Fil-A and the contestant won free food.

Christian Carlson, assistant general manager of Sales and Marketing with the Salem Avalanche minor league baseball team, worked out a deal with Harley-Davidson to donate a motorcycle and then sold the contest idea to title sponsor Coors (later Pepsi), who then promoted the contest through posters and other material in grocery stores, bars, and restaurants. As with Chick-Fil-A, people registered at each of the sponsor outlets, and the distribution truck drivers collected the registrations from the various sites.

Eighteen contestants were selected to attend the game where the Harley would be won. At a pregame picnic, each contestant was given a key, and local radio celebrities escorted contestants to the field between innings to see whether their key started the motorcycle. The radio station was a media partner and provided in-kind advertisements for the contest. For most promotions, a media outlet can be secured through a barter agreement.

The key to success for most contests and giveaways is how much the individual sponsors support the promotion with large point-of-sale displays, media tie-ins, and a prize valuable enough to keep everyone excited. Timing is also essential. In the case of the Harley-Davidson contest, the optimal time for the bike to be won was determined to be in the fourth or fifth inning.

"Before that inning, the sponsors do not receive enough recognition, but after the inning the excitement dies down," Carlson said. To keep the winner truly random yet ensure that the contest does not drag on, each contestant selects a numbered key out of a hat, with the number corresponding to the fourth or fifth inning previously identified as the winner.

Selecting participants of the correct age for a contest is another important factor. An adult is much more entertaining trying to spin around a baseball bat in a bat race than a young child with a low point of gravity. A child, however, may be a better choice for a dress-up dribble-and-shoot contest.

Connecting the promotion to team performance is another way to generate interest in the sponsor as well as the team. Domino's Pizza received a tremendous amount of media attention when they offered a dollar off a pizza in Washington, D.C., for each touchdown the Redskins scored. In the 1999–2000 season, the Redskins' offense cost Domino's more than $2 million. Similarly, Bank One launched a promotion in conjunction with the Dallas Cowboys' offense. For every point the team scores, interest rates on certificates of deposit increase by a hundredth of a percentage point.

For contest prizes that are not donated and have a high dollar value (such as cars or cash), insurance should be taken out. Since premium costs are based on the statistical possibility that someone will actually win the contest, the structure of the contest can reduce the premium. For example, most contests are constructed so that an unlimited number of entries are received. However, if only a few of these entries will be selected as finalists to win the grand prize, and of those finalists, the winner must pick the final score of a game, kick a 50-yard field goal, or achieve some other difficult task, the possibility for a true winner decreases, and often no one wins.

Creating Successful Giveaways The success of giveaways, like contests, depends on the publicity around the promotion and how the actual item given away will be used in the future. Giveaways with the team schedule printed on the items or the name and date of the event being promoted (magnetic schedules, sport cups, lunch sacks) are best.

Giveaways that are then used in another promotion are also successful. For example, at one game you hand out posters, and at the next game you have a pre- or postgame autograph signing party and ask that the fan bring the poster to be signed. Or distribute T-shirts at one game and offer half-price tickets to another game for fans wearing the shirts. The Washington Capitals handed out screen savers to game attendees, which tied in well with the launch of their revamped Web site. Collector items such as Beanie Babies, Barbies, and Hot Wheels have also been used as successful giveaways. Such items not only draw attendees but also increase media attention.

Giveaway promotions should be prominently noted on all game schedules and promoted over Web sites, public address systems, video scoreboards, and voice mail. Although sponsors pay for most giveaway items, you need to consider the staff time spent implementing the giveaway as well as marketing costs. If the giveaway does not provide an additional benefit to the team or event, you should consider not including it in the marketing mix. Also, be careful what kind of item you give out; some giveaways have been thrown onto the field and have disrupted the game.

Contests and promotions are important tools in marketing sport teams, events, and organizations. As the competition to attract and keep sports fans increases and fans continue to look for extra value, the quality and creativity of promotions must also increase. (Figure 8-2 includes additional ideas for promotion.)

Figure 8-2

Additional Promotional Ideas

- Organize a sport training program in conjunction with a local hospital or sports medicine clinic prior to a public event (e.g., a road race) to train and motivate participants.
- Sell or give away T-shirts, posters, lapel pins, and stickers before the event. The more people who wear these items before the event, the more publicity the event receives.
- Organize a communitywide contest to design the logo and mascot for your event.
- Create a theme song or jingle that is connected to the event and can be repeated on local radio stations. Put the name of a star athlete in the jingle.
- Invite school children to come to the event in their school uniform or school colors.
- Create stories about the event, sponsors, athletes, and spectators and share with the press. The New York City Marathon provides each journalist with a press kit filled with statistics and facts from dimensions of the "longest urinal" to the "pounds of pasta" served at the pre-event pasta party. You must give the press something to write about.
- Ask local movie theaters to show a short clip of some of your athletes in action or highlights of one of your previous events.
- Solicit endorsements from celebrities as well as sponsors. This not only attracts interest from the public but also encourages press coverage. A current example is Michael Jordan endorsing bowling or Gina Davis trying out for the 2000 U.S. Olympic Archery Team. Encourage sponsors to hang event banners or post information about your event at their place of business.
- Display information and hold exhibits at malls or public areas. For example, to promote a freestyle ski competition in a nearby mountain resort, athletes perform stunts on a trampoline in the city center.

continued on next page

Figure 8-2 *continued*

- Create a holiday theme. For St. Patrick's Day, the SkateNation ice rink outside of Washington, D.C., partnered with a local radio station and advertised that the person wearing the most green would win a "lucky pot of gold." Additionally, they dyed the entire sheet of ice green. The promotion was very successful, and the rink sold out in 2 hours.
- Piggyback with high-profile events to gain mass exposure. This is what the National Handicap Sport Association did when they partnered with the NBA and held exhibition matches during halftimes.
- Distribute promotional material at similar-type events. For example, when promoting a fun-run hand out fliers or place fliers on car windshields at or near other road races.
- Develop a Web site, include the URL on all marketing collateral, link to similar events and other Web sites that attract a similar demographic as your audience.
- Add information about your event to your voice mail message and encourage sponsors to do the same.
- List your event in the Digital Cities area of AOL or the Microsoft City Scapes.
- Children and animals always generate lots of media and fan excitement so periodically schedule autograph and photo sessions and even a pregame pet show in the parking lot.
- Direct mail is also very effective in marketing to a targeted audience. The United States Postal Service is currently working with various sport entities to help maximize direct-mail opportunities through the delivery of creative mail pieces such as sending CD-ROMs, Frisbees, pop-up stadiums and postcard schedule magnets.

Marketing via the Internet

The key to successful Internet marketing is a marketable registered URL, extensive and updated content, a site that is easy to use, pages that download quickly, cutting-edge technology, incentives, games, purchasing ability, and customizable content. Interestingly, advertising is not considered negative if it enhances the visitor's experience through contests and promotions.

The decision of what will be communicated and how it will be expressed through words, pictures, animation, audio, or video is essential to Web development. The content must be compelling enough to keep Web users coming back to the site. The Web site's URL needs to be incorporated into all online and offline marketing including voice mail, press releases, banners, video scoreboards, and advertisements. It is also important to keep the site to less than four levels deep. This prevents users from becoming lost in the site. In addition, the icons or bars on the Web pages need to create clear navigational paths. On each subpage of the site, always provide a way for the user to return to the home page.

Relationships are also key to successful Web sites. Most of the well-known Web sites (e.g., ESPN, CBS SportsLine, CNN/SI) have prospered because of the media exposure received through their respective television partners. Developing relationships with sports marketing agencies and leagues is also important. International Management Group (IMG) was an early investor in CBS SportsLine, offering access to valuable athletes such as Tiger Woods. As far as leagues, Mark Hardie of the Forrester Group predicts that "the Web will shift control of the sports experience from broadcast networks to professional leagues." Rather than depend on one or two mass-media outlets, organizations like the NBA, NFL, MLB, NASCAR, and IOC will reach fans through a constellation of Internet-based and offline outlets. Some fans will utilize these outlets separately or simultaneously.

For athletes, teams, and organizations, the decision of whether to explore Web development independently or to work with an established Web site often comes down to customization or distribution. Athletes that sign on with AthletesDirect.com will receive tremendous exposure but may not have as much flexibility as if designing their own Web site. Similarly, a team or organization that joins Myteam.com may receive financial guarantees but may have some rights limited.

Another point to consider is the time and risk involved in developing your own Web site. Event organizers will need to devote valuable resources toward Web development that may not provide dividends for some time. For example, Michael Payne, marketing director for the IOC, issued a friendly reminder to the Salt Lake City Olympic Organizing Committee that their Web site needs to break even, as there is no budget for this venture. Sydney spent over $30 million and did not break even.

The issue of Internet rights is yet another heated topic among athletes, teams, leagues, and organizations. Since its inception, the NBA was the only league that incorporated all of its team sites under the NBA.com site. Recently, the NHL and MLB have taken steps in this direction. In March, The George Washington University hosted a MBA Case Competition concerning "The Future Internet Strategy of the IOC" that posed questions related to Internet rights of broadcasters and other Olympic Family members. The consensus of most all research is that the league or association at the highest organizational level must take control of rights and sell digital and analog rights individually.

By controlling rights, direct and deeper relationships can be made with fans and sponsors, and additional revenue can be generated. Currently, the most popular revenue models for sports Web sites are advertising, commerce, subscriptions, and ticket sales. Licensing digital rights and digital content are two additional revenue sources expected to grow in the near future. Just look at the 11-year $6 billion CBS/NCAA television/Internet deal. By 2004, Web revenues are projected to contribute 15 percent of league revenues, with overall advertising on sports-related sites reaching close to $2.5 billion and e-commerce related to sports estimated to rise to $5 billion.

To compete in today's high-technology business world, sport event managers need to understand the value of the Internet and be able to utilize it to its full potential. Refer to "Selecting a Web Partner" in Chapter 3.

Turning Negatives into Positives

With some quick thinking and luck, some of the most disappointing or potentially damaging incidents can become a promoter's dream. Dewey Blanton, former director of public relations for ProServ, recalls a tennis event from which Andre Agassi pulled out because of an injury:

> For three months Andre's name was promoted as the headliner for the event, but a few days before, he canceled, disappointing a number of fans. In an effort to rectify the situation, we convinced Andre to speak to the press and explain the injury in his own words. The media attention received through this personal announcement gave a huge boost to the tournament in terms of public awareness. The interview was covered by every major television and radio station, as well as all the print media in the area.

Another example of how a negative can turn to a positive is described by Christian Carlson, assistant general manager of Sales and Marketing for the Salem Avalanche minor league baseball team:

> We originally scheduled a séance to end the first half of the 1997 season to exorcise the evil demons that were hanging like a black cloud over the team. It was an effort to make fun of how bad we had been, not making the playoffs since 1988, including not having a .500 half in that time. We had booked a magician/performer to hold the ceremony, billing him as a local medium in contact with the spirit world.
>
> The response was not at all what we expected. The Christian radio stations in town came after us with a vengeance. They started running an editorial every half hour telling people to call and tell us how upset they were for taking something like a séance so lightly and threatening to bring evil spirits down on the Roanoke Valley. They were going to boycott the team and deluged us with phone calls.
>
> Our response was to cancel the ceremony, instead holding a good luck ceremony with a different performer (the first one backed out when the heat came down). We made the announcement on the Friday before the ceremony was to take place, holding a press conference at the stadium in the morning that was broadcast live on all the Christian radio stations. In exchange, the Christian stations promised to fill the stadium on a separate Christian Family Night two weeks later, also on a Saturday. It was a logo ball giveaway night, so we expected a good crowd, especially on a Saturday. We were not prepared for what happened.
>
> They did fill the stadium, setting a stadium attendance record with 8,379 fans that night. The radio stations asked everyone to wear white, and it was a sea of white in the stands that night, especially considering our stadium only seats 6,300. The concession stands were slammed and couldn't keep up with the demand. We ran out of french fries in the first inning and were cleaned out of almost everything else by the end of the night. The crowd was into the game, cheering loudly at all the right times and getting the players real excited. To

thank everyone for their patience and support, we told them they could bring back their ticket stub from that night's game and exchange it for a ticket of equal or lesser value at any remaining home game that season. The PR value of the free tickets was worth any revenue lost, plus we had a guaranteed renewal for our logo ball sponsor after the tremendous exposure they received that night.

Overall, it was the best night at the stadium, with the crowd happy, the sponsor happy, the players excited, and a negative was turned into a positive with a little spin.

Working with the Media

When contemplating how to improve media relations, consider the three factors of *time, timing,* and *times to remember*. *Time* refers to the amount of time spent working on developing relationships. *Timing* pertains not only to the best time to communicate with media but the actual timing of activities during an event that will assist the media in completing their work. And finally, *times to remember* involves any stunt or activity that will catch the attention of the media before, during, and after the event.

Without question, there is no substitute for taking the time to get to know journalists and broadcasters on a personal level. Personal relationships are key to getting telephone calls accepted and to reaching a more receptive listener. It is therefore imperative that time be set aside to contact targeted media not just the day or two before the event but on a continuous basis year-round. Basically, the media needs to be convinced or "worn down" over a period of time. All verbal communication should be followed up with written documentation via fax, e-mail, or express or regular postal delivery at the specific time requested by each media entity. The story also needs to be laid out so that the editors or reporters see it as beneficial to their audience.

Personal relationships aside, the type and level of event, as well as the content and twist of promotional materials, will influence the media's interest in a story. From a survey of over 20 sport editors across the United States, Figure 8-3 lists the top 10 reasons for selecting stories.

Unless your property is the Super Bowl or Olympic Games, one of the most difficult challenges for a publicist is obtaining pre-event edi-

FIGURE 8-3

Top 10 Reasons for Story Selection

1. **Newsworthiness**—Is this an important event in which readers should be informed?
2. **Oddity**—Is there something unusual about the event that would make interesting reading?
3. **Prominence**—Will high-profile celebrities attend or participate in the event, and what are the financial stakes?
4. **Urgency**—Is the story something that readers need to know immediately?
5. **Timeliness**—Is this an "in" event or current "trend" of interest to readers?
6. **Relevance**—Is there someone participating in this event from the local area or is a local business supporting the event?
7. **Conflict or tension**—Is there some scandal or heated rivalry that would spark the readers interest?
8. **Impact**—Will this event personally effect readers or the community at large?
9. **Competition**—Is it a slow news day? If yes, profiles and features are more likely to be run.
10. **Instinct of editors**—Based on experience and knowledge of the readership, is this story appropriate for the newspaper?)

torial coverage. A fairly successful tactic is to sign on a local television or radio station, or a newspaper to be a sponsor or promotional partner. Even then, however, the media needs something "provocative" or "unique" about which to report (the oddity factor). For the Nuveen Tour of Champions, Steve Griffith worked with a local television station to promote the "Tweener" contest. A "tweener" is when a tennis player returns a lob shot in between their legs. The contest challenged viewers to try and duplicate a "tweener" shot during breaks in the tournament. Each day of the tournament a different person was selected to try the "tweener" from those who entered the contest. This contest not only achieved great event exposure one month out but created tremendous media interest during the tournament as well.

Another way to attract media attention is to add local celebrity flavor. When the NBA All-Star Game was held in New York, cast members from 11 of the running shows performed in a halftime show called "Basketball on Broadway."

Providing the media with a video news release is also a powerful way to gain media coverage. Television exposure of the Sydney Olympic torch relay jumped when the organizers provided media with a video news release picturing the torch being carried underwater by a scuba diver through the Great Barrier Reef. This also certainly helped boost Australian tourism.

Once you attract the media and they come to the event, there is no substitute for servicing them to the highest degree. They should be provided both technical and personal support. Technical support includes the availability of telephones, computer hookups, copiers, and even closed-circuit television. Refer to Figure 8-4. Personal support includes easy access to food and beverages, restroom facilities, and hotel accommodations. This may require serving or having food service available for breakfast, lunch, dinner, and late-night meals, depending on the schedule of events. Special bus shuttles to and from the media hotel to the event facility may also be required.

Figure 8-4

Steps to Setting Up a Media Center
Created by Jennifer Jordan-Lock

1. Determine the size of media center needed based on the number of media who will attend the event and will need a place to work.
2. Identify a location at the sport venue. The site must be convenient to media seating, press conference room (if separate from the media center), and mixed zone (if applicable). Also, if there will be photo processing in your media center, the location needs to be convenient to water and drainage.
3. Create a layout for the center with media staff offices; work area with tables, chairs, power and phone distribution; lounge for hospitality; results distribution area; help desk; administrative areas; and storage. If the media center will also house press conference area, create a layout for dais, seating, and camera platform.
4. Use the layout to create an equipment list for tables, chairs, platforms, storage units, banners and other look elements, temporary walls, and any items that need to be custom made.
5. Determine technology needs: phones, faxes, computers, copiers, televisions with live feed of the competition, microphones, sound systems, and power distribution.
6. During move-in, make sure that equipment is placed according to layouts.

continued on next page

Figure 8-4 *continued*

7. Test all technology once it's installed to make certain it is working properly.
8. If your event has multiple venues, you may need to create a primary media center and one or more subcenters. If this is the case, the primary center may not be located at a sport venue, but will still need to be conveniently located to facilitate transportation to the competitions. The steps to set up a subcenter are the same as above, but on a smaller scale.

Furthermore, the pressroom should be open long before the event commences and should not close until all reporters have had sufficient time to file their stories. This means making certain arrangements for lights and air-conditioning or heating systems to remain on in the building once the event is over. This also requires keeping certain gates open near media parking or shuttle pickup so journalists do not have to walk halfway around the building to exit.

Before the pressroom opens, all equipment should be checked to ensure it is in working order. This is especially true if a press conference is scheduled. Timely materials should also be ready, as the media expects to receive current facts, quotes, and statistics pertinent to the day's competition and activities. The more information that you can provide, the better.

Helping journalists get to their destinations in a timely manner is also important. Although the solution may seem somewhat elementary, Sue Carpenter, who previously worked for World Cup Soccer and Olympic Soccer, received great acclaim for placing duct tape along the different travel routes that the media took during these international events. For the Olympic preliminary soccer matches in Birmingham, Alabama, different-color duct tape outlined the path from the press box to the photographer's area, to the mixed-zone, and to the field of play. This not only reduced the number of questions asked but increased the comfort level of the media, especially for foreign journalists. Figure 8-5 suggests ways of getting the most out of the media.

PART II: CORPORATE EVENT MARKETING

According to Ton Bil, director of De Produktieven Effective Marketing and Publicity, there are five P's of event marketing: partic-

Figure 8-5

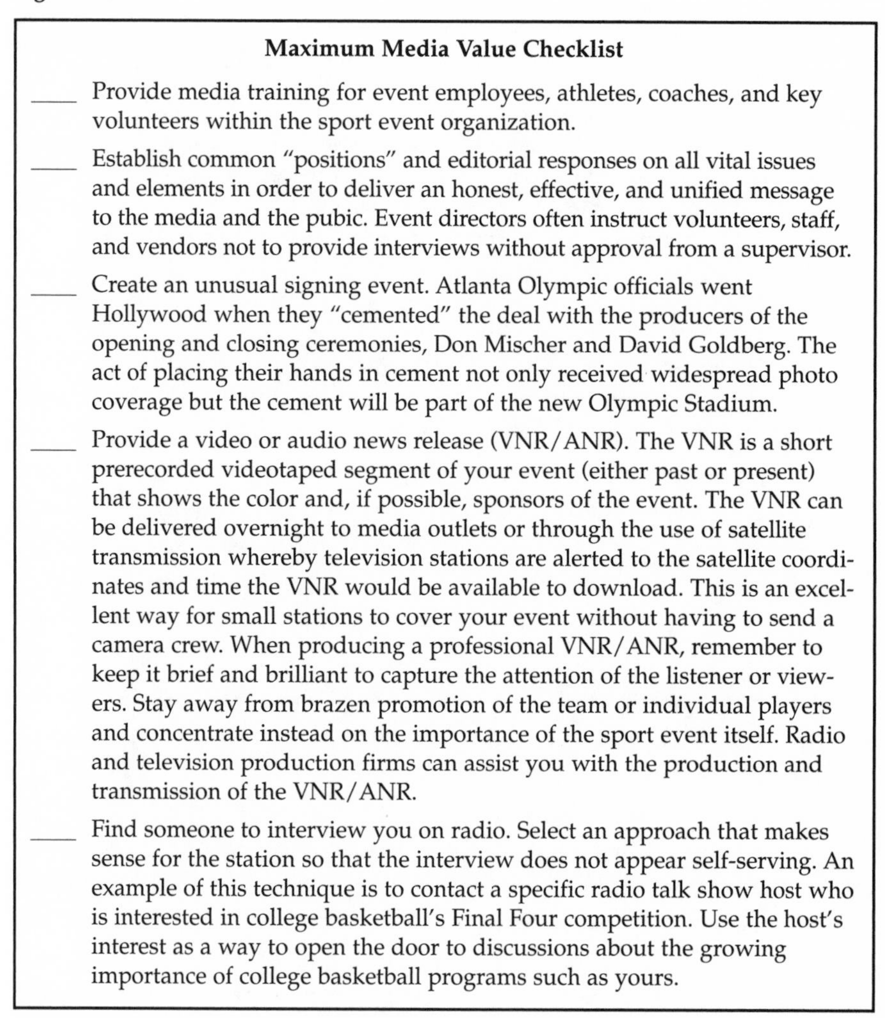

Maximum Media Value Checklist

____ Provide media training for event employees, athletes, coaches, and key volunteers within the sport event organization.

____ Establish common "positions" and editorial responses on all vital issues and elements in order to deliver an honest, effective, and unified message to the media and the pubic. Event directors often instruct volunteers, staff, and vendors not to provide interviews without approval from a supervisor.

____ Create an unusual signing event. Atlanta Olympic officials went Hollywood when they "cemented" the deal with the producers of the opening and closing ceremonies, Don Mischer and David Goldberg. The act of placing their hands in cement not only received widespread photo coverage but the cement will be part of the new Olympic Stadium.

____ Provide a video or audio news release (VNR/ANR). The VNR is a short prerecorded videotaped segment of your event (either past or present) that shows the color and, if possible, sponsors of the event. The VNR can be delivered overnight to media outlets or through the use of satellite transmission whereby television stations are alerted to the satellite coordinates and time the VNR would be available to download. This is an excellent way for small stations to cover your event without having to send a camera crew. When producing a professional VNR/ANR, remember to keep it brief and brilliant to capture the attention of the listener or viewers. Stay away from brazen promotion of the team or individual players and concentrate instead on the importance of the sport event itself. Radio and television production firms can assist you with the production and transmission of the VNR/ANR.

____ Find someone to interview you on radio. Select an approach that makes sense for the station so that the interview does not appear self-serving. An example of this technique is to contact a specific radio talk show host who is interested in college basketball's Final Four competition. Use the host's interest as a way to open the door to discussions about the growing importance of college basketball programs such as yours.

ipation, product and brand experience, promotion, probing, and prospecting.

1. Participation refers to having your consumers attend the event and actually interact with the company during the event, whether visually, verbally, or tactually.
2. Product and brand experience involves distributing samples or having the consumer physically try on/try out your product on-site at the event.

3. Promotion includes generating media exposure by creating stories within the event and further increasing corporate awareness via event-related coupons and sweepstakes.
4. Probing entails conducting research before, during, and after the event to make sure you are effectively reaching and penetrating your target audience.
5. Prospecting implies that companies should approach event marketing as a long-term commitment to effectively see returns on investment.

Basically, for this type of event marketing to work, a company must be willing to incorporate all marketing resources into the event from sales, advertising, public relations, and promotions. Therefore, event marketing is an integrated marketing approach (see Figure 8-6). Sport event marketing has proved to be one of the most effective event marketing platforms because of the opportunity to reach a specific target audience in an enjoyable and healthy environment. At sport events, there is ample opportunity to interact with consumers on-site before, during, and after the sport event, as well as off-site through direct mail, advertising, and promotions.

Budgeting

A corporation that enters a sport event sponsorship should not think of the rights fees as the end of its commitment or view this event as a one-time involvement. Companies should adequately support their sponsorship agreement by budgeting at least one to three times as much as their initial sponsorship fee for promotions, advertising, and hospitality and another 3 to 5 percent for market research. Olympic sponsors, for example, spend $40 to $60 million on rights fees, as well as an addition $60 million on television advertising around Olympic programming, along with additional millions on hospitality and promotions. Companies also need to allow equity to build over time. Research shows that it takes from 10 to 50 images to make one impression on a consumer. Figure 8-7 provides ways to maximize sponsorship value.

Getting Your Event Televised

Because of the growing number of broadcast mediums, there is a great demand for sport programming. Television stations, however,

Figure 8-6

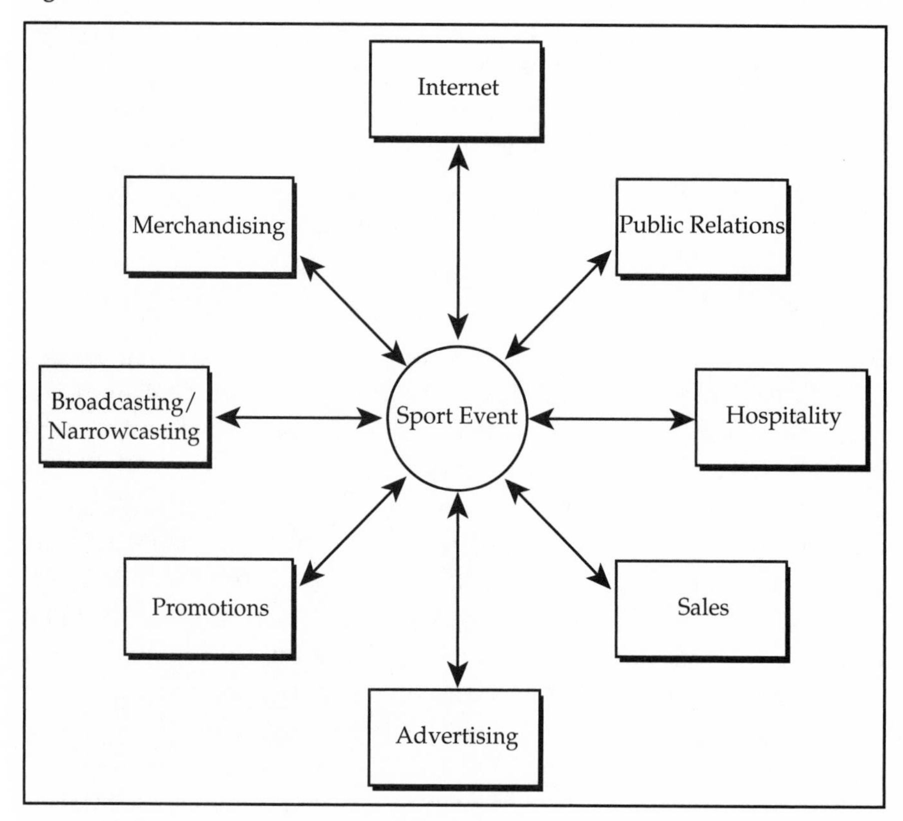

are driven by advertising dollars, and cable stations are driven by both advertising and subscription fees. Your event must therefore meet certain criteria in order to interest a network or cable station in televising your sport events.

If you are fortunate enough to have what the industry calls "a hot property," then you may reasonably expect that a television station will pay all production costs as well as a rights fee for your sport event. Rights fees for hot properties such as professional sports and collegiate basketball and football are typically negotiated by the leagues, conferences, or teams to allow one network exclusive rights to broadcast their sport events. Millions of dollars are paid for the exclusive rights to the Olympic Games, and to major league baseball, football, hockey, and basketball.

If your sport event is considered good but not hot programming, the station will sometimes enter into a barter agreement with you,

Figure 8-7

How to Increase Sponsorship Value

- If you purchased the rights to be a title sponsor, turn around and try to sell a tie-in to someone with whom you are conducting business. A perfect example is Home Depot's leveraging of its 1996 Olympic sponsorship by allowing its vendors (for a price) to use the Olympic rings on product packaging sold only in Home Depot stores, not on products carried in other stores.
- Incorporate the event name and logo in existing advertising.
- Sponsor an entertainment stage or pin-trading center where spectators and participants gather before, during, or after an event.
- Create a theme for your sport event sponsorship. To promote the "Popwatch," Swatch freely distributed popcorn, lollipops, and Popsicles during an event the Swiss watch manufacturer sponsored.
- List the competition results in your entrance office window.
- Offer a special prize to the first person to pass by a branch office or corporate headquarters (assuming the sponsor has an office located along the course).
- Produce a limited number of specially designed beer and soft drink cans or posters that make interesting collectibles.
- Provide a shuttle bus to and from your place of business to the sport event. Local media will frequently promote this service, which generates free publicity for your company.
- Telecommunication sponsors could make it possible through public or cellular phones for athletes to reach out to friends and relatives immediately after their event.
- Sponsors that fly blimps or hot-air balloons with their name and logo attractively displayed should offer rides to the press, photographers, television reporters and crews, and guests before, during, or after the event.

which means that you provide the program free to the broadcaster (produce the show) and split the commercial inventory (advertising spots) with the station. In this case, you hope to recoup your production costs through the sale of advertisements or increased sponsorship fees.

Another option, usually the least appealing and most expensive, is to purchase airtime directly from the station. This option makes you responsible for producing the entire sport event program and for selling all the advertising spots.

Depending on your programming status, radio stations will offer you similar arrangements. Figure 8-8 describes ways of increasing

Figure 8-8

Increasing Your Chances for Media Success

- Make sure talent or celebrities are involved. Celebrities attract people to watch.
- Network and get to know the station director, general manager, or someone who will get you in the door. People listen to people they know and trust.
- Be organized and respect the decision maker's time.
- Offer a quality sport event attractive to advertisers.

your chances for success in getting the media to broadcast your sport event.

GAME HIGHLIGHTS

- Whether you are a sport event marketer or working for a company incorporating event marketing, the steps in planning your marketing strategy are to consider the type of sport event, research the sport and event, determine the target audience, identify the various type of marketing opportunities, devise a budget, delegate responsibilities, plan for evaluation, and implement the plan. Commitment and creativity from everyone involved are key ingredients to success.
- To maximize a sponsorship, companies need to spend one to three times the amount of rights fees in leveraging the sponsorship.
- The first step in attracting an audience is to determine the price threshold and appropriate target markets. A marketing campaign should then be developed and individualized toward the different audiences and within the designated budget.
- If you want to get your event on television, understand the value you bring to either a cable or network station and make a proposal.

P A R T

PRACTICAL METHODS FOR ACHEIVING SUCCESS

If you have confidence, you have patience.
Confidence, that is everything.

Ilie Nastase, tennis player

FINANCING SPORTS EVENTS

The more money you have, the faster you go.

A.J. Watson, car designer, on the importance of money in auto racing

THERE ARE NUMEROUS OPPORTUNITIES to host and produce sport events, but the questions remain: How will the event be financed and be profitable? Where do you find starting capital? What is required to achieve profitability for your sport event?

Maybe you are a volunteer who has agreed to chair a local fund-raiser road race and just realized that it typically costs at least $8,000 to $15,000 to produce a 10K race. Or, perhaps you are an entrepreneur who has a unique sport event idea but no capital to support it. The challenge for cash, support, and profitability are universal across the event industry.

FINDING CAPITAL

A sound business plan is one way to find investors who will provide you with start-up capital for your sport event (see

Figure 9-1). If you are an employee or member of a sport commission seeking funding to bid for an event, this plan may take the form of a grant proposal submitted to a government entity (e.g., Office of Economic Development or the State Tourism Department). For most events, however, corporate sponsorship is the primary source of financing.

Why do corporations sponsor sports events and how can you build successful partnerships? As Lisa Delpy Neirotti describes in her sponsorship seminars, "Sport events offer corporations endless opportunities to introduce, showcase, differentiate, and move product; reward sales staff; entertain current and/or potential clients; increase media and public exposure; enhance or change an image; improve employee morale; reach new market segments and distribution channels; and lock out competitors." The medium of sport is not

Figure 9-1

Elements of a Successful Sport Event Business Plan

- List the key persons responsible for planning and managing the sport event and their relative experience.
- Find people who will vouch for their experience (include written testimonials).
- Briefly describe the sport event including date(s), time(s), location(s), history, and purpose.
- Identify what you have to sell and all of your rights (e.g., merchandise, TV, and signage). Determine the rights that you wish to keep and those that are available for sale.
- Determine how to protect the rights that you have for sale so that competitors or non-rights-holders have no opportunity for ambush marketing.
- Briefly describe the demographics of the participants and spectators and the estimated economic impact they will generate.
- Describe your marketing, sales, advertising, public relations, hospitality, and promotions plans.
- Explain how you will amortize this capital investment and repay the loan.
- Describe your risk management procedures, including cancellation insurance, to further assure your investors that their investment is well protected.
- Name your accountant or chief financial officer, and describe the type of record keeping you will provide and when you will distribute periodic statements of income and expenses.

only valuable to corporations because of its universal appeal, but it delivers a captured and defined target audience in an environment encompassing their lifestyles. In brief, a consumer is motivated to attend the sporting event, and a corporation is motivated to sell a product or service to these consumers.

Securing a sponsor may very well be the single most important factor in determining the success of your sport event. Sponsorship dollars bring revenue that buys better facilities, additional staff, and a greater experience for participants. Considering the importance of sponsorship, learning and applying a successful strategy is extremely critical. Mike Dyer, vice president of New Development for the NBA, recommends listening as much as speaking when recruiting sponsors. Find out what the sponsor needs or wants. Be sure to include measurable components and then validate through research and follow-up reports. Sponsorships are relationship-driven, so service at the high level but within reason—a sponsorship should not cost you money! The following suggestions have been gathered by Lisa Delpy Neirotti from a variety of experts in the sport event marketing field and serve as an excellent footprint.

Step One: Know Your Event

The first step in securing a sponsor is determining if sponsorship is even beneficial for your event. Richard Nealis, race director for the Marine Corps Marathon, has just recently entered the sponsorship arena. Mr. Nealis stated that "for most of its existence, the Marine Corps Marathon has been known as the 'People's Marathon.' We conducted the Marathon without sponsors, prize money, or much media coverage. Our goal was simple—to promote athletics and the Marine Corps ideology. In the last few years, however, we have been open to a limited amount of sponsorship to help offset our increasing costs for police coverage and street closures. We wanted to keep the cost to the participants as low as possible, and corporate sponsorship is helping us achieve that. Our entry fee is $35, while most other marathons range from $55 to $75."

Assuming that sponsorship is a good thing for your event, you must then decide what your event has to offer to a corporation. What benefits can you bring to the table to make your event look attractive? Refer to Figure 9-2 for an example of potential benefits for a title sponsor. Be sure that you can deliver on all proposed benefits. For example,

Figure 9-2

An Example of Benefits for a Title Sponsor

Title Rights: Corporate Name and/or logo to be incorporated in event name

Media Coverage: (Separate out only if you have TV coverage; otherwise, include with pre-/post-event exposure) For example, in negotiation with ESPN to cover the event or ESPN will air event for 1 hour live on Saturday; invitations will be mailed to all local radio and TV stations with a personal follow-up to encourage coverage of the event.

Pre-/Post-Event Exposure

Name and/or logo included in:

- Press releases mailed before and after the event to ...
- Registration packets or direct mail brochures mailed to ...
- Promotional fliers/posters distributed at all local sport retail outlets, other road races, and so forth
- Tickets
- Web site with reciprocal link to the sponsor's Web site
- Bill stuffers with phone or electric bills or bank statement
- Point of sale (POS)
- Street banners
- Pre-event functions (pro-am, press conference)
- Thank-you letters mailed to ...

On-site Exposure

- Signage (Two 10-foot x 10-foot, banners to be provided by sponsor)
- Half-page advertisement in program (1)
- Public address announcements (3 per match)
- Video scoreboard advertisement
- Name and/or logo included on:
  - Athlete bib
  - Volunteer and staff uniforms
  - Official merchandise
- Single-event sponsor (special recognition around one specific event; e.g., 100-meter dash)

Merchandise Opportunities

- Booth space for product display, promotion, or sale products/services
- Sampling and/or coupon distribution
- Interactive kiosk or activity
- Official location for registration pickup
- Exclusive product concession rights

continued on next page

Figure 9-2 *continued*

Entertainment Opportunities

- 10 event tickets
- 7 VIP parking passes
- One 10-foot x 20-foot private tent (catering not included)
- 10 invitations to VIP post-event reception

Additional Benefits

- Market research opportunity
- First right of refusal option
- Event evaluation report
- Access to event mailing list
- Exclusive concessionaire rights (depending on venue)
- Access to event athletes for one promotion or advertisement
- Opportunities for cross-promotions and cause-related marketing

do not offer street banners if your community has a law prohibiting them. Most sport events also offer different levels of sponsorship, as outlined in Figure 9-3. The higher the level of sponsorship, the more benefits should be received.

In addition to the physical benefits listed, you must know the size, demographics, and psychographics of your audience so that a correct match can be made between the event and corporate sponsor. To calculate the size, consider the number of people who will actually attend the event, as well as the number of people who will watch the event on television (if applicable). It may also be of interest to sponsors to see how many people participate in the sport, especially if it is on the rise. Demographics include age, sex, income, educational level, and marital status, while psychographics include attitudes, opinions, and lifestyles. Such statistics can be found by either conducting research on-site at your event or a similar event or by contacting the national governing body of the sport or a related trade publication or organization or purchasing the data from sports-related research companies. The *Sports Summit Sports Business Directory* and the *Franklin Quest Sports Market Place Directory* provide contact information for all these sources. Some statistical facts can also be found in the *Sports Market Place Directory*.

Figure 9-3

Generic Levels of Sponsorship

Title Sponsor (e.g., The Kemper Golf Open)

Presenting Sponsor (e.g., The Fiesta Bowl presented by Tostidos)

Supporting or Associate Sponsors (Companies that sponsor but at a lower level than the first two categories)

Official Suppliers (Companies that provide value-in-kind, or VIK, services or goods)

Individual Donors

- Sponsorship titles are not consistent throughout the industry.
- Each level of sponsorship should offer different amounts of benefits based on the value of the sponsorship.
- There should be only one sponsor per product category, but many categories can be divided into various components (e.g., the beverage category could be separated into water, carbonated drinks, isotonic drinks, fruit drinks, coffee/tea, malted beverage, and distilled beverages).

Another aspect of knowing your event is knowing how much it is worth. Unfortunately, there is no magic formula on pricing sponsorships. Begin by evaluating the value of each of the benefits identified, including the amount of media in terms of number of newspaper column inches and television ratings (if applicable). Also try to calculate the number of impressions your event receives. This is especially important to advertising types who are familiar dealing with cost per thousand impressions (CPM). Finally, look at what the market will bear...what are other similar events in your area receiving for sponsorships?

According to Lisa Ukman of the International Events Group, "One of the primary factors in the determination of sponsorship fees is the cost of media in your market. The same property in Cleveland is not worth nearly as much as the same in Los Angeles. Then you look at the competitive marketplace." Is your sport event the only such event within 200 miles, or are there five others? Is your event a first-time event or is it established? What is the cost to sponsor other properties similar to yours? Is there more value for one product category over another? For example, if the event entitles the sponsor to on-site sales rights of soft drinks or candy, then it may be worth more to sponsors in those categories than to a bank. However, when you ask corporate management for $50,000, their first consideration will be, what else can we do with this money? How much other media time can we buy? How many people will we be reaching? How many trade deals could we cut?

Although tangible benefits are important, do not completely discount the intangibles of your event. As pressure increases on companies to be socially responsible, your event worth also increases with the number of intangible and cause-related images. Ukman explains that "where sponsorship can beat out measured media is its ability to increase a company's share of heart, its qualitative as opposed to quantitative impact." Cause-related marketing involves a commitment to your event above and beyond sponsorship dollars. Visa, an Olympic sponsor, donates a percent of all U.S. customer purchases during the period of the Olympic Games to the U.S. Olympic team. General Motors, a WNBA sponsor, donates $1 toward the Breast Cancer Foundation for every WNBA ticket purchased.

Step Two: Prospecting Corporate Sponsors: Primary and Secondary Research

Although the thought of research may frighten some people, it is the most important factor, other than luck, in recruiting corporate sponsors. There are two basic types of research: primary and secondary. Primary research ranges from personal observations to original surveys and interviews. Secondary research involves reading local and national newspapers and trade publications and using industry resource books.

Examples of primary research include walking or driving through the commercial district where the event will take place, noting the types of businesses there, and questioning participants and attendees at the event about what products they use or intend to buy within the next six months or on what items they most frequently spend their discretionary income. For instance, a survey conducted by Lisa Delpy Neirotti at the Lone Star Junior National Volleyball Tournament in Austin, Texas, revealed that 100 percent of the participants spent discretionary money on clothes and primarily shopped at the Gap. Guess who then received a sponsorship proposal?

Attending Rotary Club and Chamber of Commerce meetings or presentations by corporate CEOs and executives are also examples of primary research. Through these activities, you can learn more about your business community and personally meet people who may have an interest in your event.

Another example of primary research is attending events similar to yours and taking notes on the type of corporate sponsors as well as the benefits those sponsors receive. Then you can take those notes and either specifically design a proposal to those companies or go shopping. Shopping literally involves walking through the aisles of a supermarket or store and recording the different brands and products surrounding those of the sponsors on your list. If the sponsor provides a service, go to the yellow pages and research their competitors. This leads us to the discussion on secondary research.

Secondary research sources include the yellow pages, your local newspaper, The *Wall Street Journal*, the *IEG Sponsorship Report*, *Advertising Age*, and the *Sports Business Daily and Journal*. Reading such publications keeps you current with both business and social trends. The local newspaper is helpful in identifying businesses that are moving to or expanding in your area. The *Wall Street Journal* and *Advertising Age* provide information on corporate strategies and future marketing campaigns. And the more industry-specific publications such as the *IEG Sponsorship Report* and the *Sports Business Daily and Journal* offer examples of sponsorship deals that have been signed or are in negotiation. It is here that you may learn of a company's interest in a particular sport or demographic that fits your event. Other important resources are the *Fact Book*, *IEG Directory*, and the Internet. The *Fact Book* provides a comprehensive listing of companies that sponsor sports, as well as a detailed description of those companies, including a company profile, current sport marketing activities, and names of decision makers and outside agencies. The *IEG Directory* provides information (number of spectators, budget, and sponsors) on more than 4,000 events produced in the United States from art festivals to sports events. The Internet also provides access to corporate information through annual reports or other documentation posted on a company's Web site. The wording used to describe their company can also be incorporated in the body of your sponsorship proposal.

Often the method of identifying and recruiting sponsors depends on the type and size of your event. Figure 9-4 offers more specific

Figure 9-4

Suggestions for Recruiting Sponsors

- If your event involves or honors Olympic or professional athletes, find out the companies those athletes have endorsement contracts with. Your event offers those companies an opportunity to leverage their athlete's endorsement deal and further solidify the relationship between the athlete and the company.
- If your event benefits a nonprofit organization, survey the organization's board to see whether members would personally forward your sponsorship proposal to decision makers in their respective businesses or introduce you to other influential business leaders. For university sport teams, successful alumni can serve in this capacity.
- If your event is small, research the sponsors of larger events or attractions in your community, as those companies may view your event as a way of enhancing their existing investments. Derek Murphy, former director of Sports Marketing for American Express, said that "American Express may consider sponsoring small or grassroot events in Austin, Texas, because they would enhance or piggyback on their sponsorship of the Dallas Cowboys, who train in Austin."
- Ask committed sponsors to provide endorsements and evidence supporting the value of the sponsorship. Existing sponsors could also be offered an incentive of a 10 percent refund on their sponsorship fee or increased benefits if they bring another corporation to the table. This works well with companies such as McDonald's or Pizza Hut, who have strong ties to companies such as Coca-Cola and Pepsi, respectively, or a grocery chain that works with a number of consumer products.
- Offer your media sponsor a category that you are unlikely to sell and allow it to bring in a cosponsor (one of its advertisers).
- Approach businesses that your organization or your existing sponsors support such as legal, accounting, and telecommunication services; printers; and other vendors. This includes companies that have expressed an interest in conducting business with your organization. Existing sponsors may also be able to provide a list of vendors or companies that have courted their business.
- Guarantee or enhance sales volume. For example, the sponsorship agreement between the American Canoe Association (ACA) and Subaru included a sales promotion that offers a three-year service contract ($500 value) to any of the 25,000 ACA members who buy a Subaru plus a $150 rebate per car to the ACA. In less than a year, the ACA became the largest Subaru dealership in the United States, accounting for the sale of over 200 new Subarus.
- Offer a discount for an early sponsorship commitment.

suggestions for identifying and recruiting sponsors that involve both primary and secondary research.

Step Three: Making the Contact: Writing a Proposal

Once you have narrowed down the field of prospects, the next step is to make contact with or identify the correct person at each company. Some corporations have an entire department dedicated to sport marketing (e.g., Anheuser-Busch, Coca-Cola), while others assign one employee to scrutinize incoming proposals and forward the best to appropriate departments. The *Fact Book* provides contact information for each company. Although difficult, try to set up a telephone or in-person meeting to introduce yourself and to discuss your event and the needs of the company. If this is not possible, be sure to do your homework. Confirm the correct spelling of the name and mailing address of the appropriate contact person, and find a personal reference or link that you can use to tie the company and event together. Include this information in the first sentence of your cover letter (e.g., "I recently met Mr. Connection who suggested I contact you." Or, "I recently read that your company wants to increase your market share of 10- to 14-year-olds, and this is the target audience for the XYZ event"). Refer to Figure 9-5 for a sample cover letter.

If you do make a call and the person contacted is not interested, ask if there is another person or division within the company to contact or send a proposal to. For events that involve a large amount of media exposure, the company's advertising agency may be appropriate to contact. For charitable events, see if the company has a non-profit foundation with money to support the event. Still other areas to research are human resources, public relations, brand promotion, special events, and ethnic marketing.

The written proposal that should accompany the cover letter need not be an expensive four-color production, but it should be professionally executed. Refer to Figure 9-6 for a sample layout. Be sure to ask whether the company has any sponsorship guidelines. M&M Mars, for example, will provide this information to you upon request.

While every event marketer has his or her own personal preference or ideas on how to develop a proposal, Marty Grabijas, director of sales and market development for SnowSports Industries America, offers nine qualities of a successful proposal:

Figure 9-5 *Sample Cover Letter*

[Date]

Mr. John Doe

New Product Development

Eastman Kodak

Four Concourse Pkwy, Suite 300

Atlanta, GA 30328

Dear John:

Eastman Kodak means quality images. The sports of canoeing, kayaking, and rafting mean having fun while getting wet.

Capturing the fun experienced on river trips has always been a problem for both serious paddlesport enthusiasts and occasional commercial raft customers. Eastman Kodak has solved that problem with its line of waterproof FunSaver cameras and the American Canoe Association is the vehicle to deliver that message.

Founded in 1880, the American Canoe Association has grown into the nation's largest paddlesport organization. Steeped in tradition, we are quick to respond to the rapid evolution of our sport and represent all aspects of paddling. In addition to certifying whitewater instructors across the United States, we sanction over 700 events per year, govern the United States Wildwater Team, and aggressively promote river conservation and stewardship. We also represent corporate sponsors such as Subaru of America.

The enclosed program will provide Eastman Kodak with great exposure throughout the paddlesport community. Its real strength, however, is its ability to ***motivate sales to over 4.2 million adventure seekers***.

Thank you for reviewing the enclosed information, John. I will take the liberty of contacting you within the next few weeks. In the meantime, I can be contacted at XXX-XXXX.

Sincerely,

Marty Grabijas

Director of Sales &

Market Development

Enclosures

Figure 9-6

Sponsorship Proposal Blueprint
Lisa Delpy Neirotti

1. Overview paragraph to describe proposed event, managing organization, and those who will benefit.
2. Event facts and history:
   - Title
   - Date
   - Location
   - Participants (names of athletes and/or artists)
   - Attendance—previous and expected
   - Media coverage—previous and expected (include examples in appendix)
   - Benefiting charity or cause (name benefactors and level of charitable contribution)
3. Demographics of participants and spectators
4. Benefits available to sponsor (refer to Figure 9-2)
5. Sponsorship fee

1. *Satisfies prospects wants and needs*—You may think that your proposal is a work of literary genius, but look at it from the perspective sponsor's viewpoint—it is just another piece of junk mail.
2. *Differentiates your event from other marketing opportunities*—The truth is that your proposal is among many others that land on an already overtaxed marketing manager. You must therefore efficiently show that manager how your opportunity is different and how the event will deliver (a performance guarantee in the proposal adds to your accountability). Whenever possible, use examples of how your event has increased sales for other sponsors and how it can affect the bottom-line.
3. *Details the benefits, rather than the features, of your event*—When buying a new car, you may not care that it has a six-cylinder, dual overhead cam engine with four valves per cylinder. All you care about is that it is *fast*. Use this mentality when writing your proposal and explain, in very concise terms, the benefits that the event offers.

4. *Pushes the prospects "hot-buttons"*—While corporations ultimately sponsor events to impact their bottom line, their inherent corporate culture may place a high value on providing educational or volunteer opportunities for their employees, maintaining a high community profile through community support and economic development, or aligning themselves with environmental efforts. Hot-buttons can be identified by reading annual reports as well as sales and marketing material and by listening to presentations made by the CEO or reading articles written by a corporate executive.
5. *Identifies cross-promotions*—Above and beyond the face value of your event, opportunities should exist for your potential sponsor to cross-market with other event sponsors. This business-to-business facet of the sponsorship deal provides added value.
6. *States precisely what you are selling, the specific cost of entry, and the expected return on investment*—This may include a large, up-scale targeted market, categorical exclusivity, signage, hospitality, product sampling, and the ability to leverage sales. You need to provide enough information for the proposal to be appropriately evaluated and to sell the event internally to the company.
7. *Calls for action and closes*—You must be the aggressor and take the lead on all follow-up unless directed otherwise by the prospect. You must also strongly state why your opportunity will be successful for them. If the prospect lives in another city, arrange to meet whenever traveling in that area or at a mutually attended conference/trade show.
8. *Is a strong business document that could be three pages or less*—Consider your proposal to be viewed as junk mail. Therefore, it is vital to provide managers information in a well-organized, concise format. Do not make them search for the key points of benefits, cost of entry, and why your opportunity is their best choice. Have someone else proofread your material. For many companies, key points are knowing the difference between, for instance, *two*, *too*, and *to*. *In addition*, names should be spelled correctly. Also, check for obvious oversights; make sure, for instance, that a proposal meant for Subaru doesn't list Ford Motor Company as the potential sponsor of the event.

9. *Includes support material*—Support materials includes fact sheets, news clippings from previous years, market research, testimonials, and specific items targeted to the prospect. This material should further strengthen your proposal and can be included as an appendix or in a folder attached to the proposal.

Timing is also crucial when you are writing and mailing out proposals. Find out the budget cycle of companies, and know when budget decisions are made. Eighteen months is an ideal lead time. If you are approaching a company within six months, consider offering the company a discounted fee for the current year, with the stipulation that they sign a long-term agreement at full price. For companies that are cash poor, consider a barter or value-in-kind arrangement in which goods or services (e.g., drinks, T-shirts, equipment, marketing) are provided in exchange for sponsorship benefits.

Aside from mailing out proposals, the Internet can also be useful in disseminating information about your event and associated sponsorship opportunities. Such announcements can be sent to target audience Usenet newsgroups, incorporated into related Web sites, and delivered over appropriate mailing lists and bulletin boards. For example, an announcement about the 1995 St. Patrick's Day United States versus Ireland rugby match was sent to managers of various rugby Internet sites. The announcement included information about the various levels of sponsorship opportunities. As a result, the marketing manager of Murphy's Irish Stout got in touch with the event director, and a title sponsorship deal was negotiated.

Step Four: Follow Up with the Company

Rarely will a sponsor call you, so be sure to mark on your calendar when you are to follow up with the company. Typically, 10 to 14 days after mailing the proposal is a good time. Frequently, you will not reach a live person, so leave a brief voice mail introducing yourself and the event and asking if they received the proposal and if they have had a chance to review it. If you do not hear back, wait another week and follow up with another call or fax. You might also try sending an article that mentions or would be of interest to your contact with a note that says "Thought you might be interested in this and looking forward to discussing the XYZ proposal."

When you do finally make contact, ask for an opportunity to meet and make a presentation in person. Be sure that you bring ideas that expand beyond the sponsorship proposal, and present them in a multimedia format. If all goes well, a verbal agreement will be reached with the next step being a formal contract. Refer to Figure 9-7 for clauses to include in a contract, as well as Chapter 5.

One negotiating point is the length of the contract. A long-term multiyear agreement reduces the annual labor of courting and re-signing the sponsor, allows a sponsor to build equity in an event, and provides both parties the opportunity to budget more precisely. For start-up events, however, Ukman discourages long-term agreements with locked-in fees. She says that the main problem to avoid here is getting stuck if the event takes off. As a new property, you also want to find sponsors who are interested in promoting the event for you. Sometimes it is better to go with a sponsor such as Coca-Cola, who will promote the event on truck backs and through co-op ads, than someone who gives you more cash but no promotional commitment. Sponsorship priorities may change as the event grows.

On the other hand, if after two months you receive no feedback, it may be time to close the door. But don't lock it. Believe it or not, that contact is not dead yet! A database of all of your contacts from throughout the years provides an excellent target for press releases that highlight your successes. Previous contacts should be informed every few months of new corporate partners, successful marketing ventures, and upcoming events. This "build it and they will come" approach is low-maintenance and relatively low-cost. It also builds your credibility in the eyes of potential corporate partners by showing them that your event or company is a viable marketing tool that they can use to increase sales. Your message should be, "It worked for this other company and it can work for you."

Whenever possible, also extend an invitation to potential corporate sponsors to attend your event or another event that your organization produces. That is a great way for the corporation to sample your event and witness firsthand the excitement and opportunities available.

To be successful in sport event sponsorship, Ukman advises you to first find a media and a supermarket sponsor; then you have the guaranteed reach and trade commitment that make selling cash

Figure 9-7

Sponsorship Agreement Checklist

The Parties
Who are the legal parties responsible for executing the agreement and how will they be referred to throughout the agreement?

Category Description and Exclusivity
What specific product or service category is being purchased? Is it exclusive? Will sponsor have approval over other sponsors or suppliers?

Performance Responsibilities
What specific tasks is each party to perform? Ambush marketing protection, signage, promoting/marketing the event, hospitality, competition schedule.

Date, Time
What is the date and time of the sport event(s) activities during which the parties are liable for performance of their duties as specified in the agreement?

Location(s)
Where will the sport event take place and what is the official name and address of this venue? Are there territorial restrictions to the sponsorship?

Financial
What are the financial responsibilities of each party?

Terms of Payment
When is payment due, what happens if payment is late, and is there a benefit for early payment?

Risk Management
Who is responsible for insurance, bonds, permits, and other risk management procedures? Who is to be named as additional insured? When must certificates of insurance be received? What types of insurance are required and in what amounts? Who indemnifies whom?

Trademark/Logo License
Under what circumstances and during what time period can a sponsor use the event trademark logo?

Expiration Date
When does the sponsorship offer expire if it is not accepted?

Execution
Who are the official signers?

Date of Execution
When was the document jointly executed?

sponsorships much easier. Unfortunately, the first two anchor sponsors are always the most difficult to secure. As Jeff Ruday says, "Securing and keeping sport event sponsors is a true challenge.

Corporate objectives change all the time, and no company absolutely needs to spend money on sport events."

Basically, your search for corporate partners is limited only by your imagination. Yes, personal contacts are extremely valuable, but most of us eventually run out of friends. And, although cold calling is frustrating and time-consuming, according *IEG Sponsorship Report*, this approach accounts for a surprising 77 percent of all sponsorship dollars. Like any form of cold-call selling, plan on 100 calls netting 10 appointments, with one of those 10 appointments turning into a new corporate partner.

Securing corporate partners means selling yourself and your event. It means separating yourself from the 20, 30, or 40 proposals and contacts that marketing managers may see every day. A good exercise in formulating your proposal is to look at the reams of junk mail you receive each week. What catches your eye? What motivates you to open an envelope? What button needs to be pushed to make you *want* to write in, call with your credit card, or order through e-mail? These same principles can be applied to your proposal.

Step Five: Servicing Sponsors

Finally, the most important consideration to remember is that the easiest way to recruit a sponsor is to re-sign an existing one. That requires that you service your sponsors and treat them like your most precious asset. Wine and dine and involve them in continuing decisions related to your event. The more they feel as if they have a stake in your event and the more benefits they receive, the more likely they will continue to support your event.

Just having a company's name associated with the sport event is not enough. To maximize the sponsorship, it needs to be leveraged to include sales, advertising, promotions, merchandising, hospitality, and public relations. Your job is to assist the sponsor in getting the most out of your event and to help them quantify that success.

Before a corporate sponsor can move fully ahead on its marketing plan, it must receive guidelines and direction from the event organizer. If the organizing committee continually changes its plans and builds roadblocks, credibility will be lost and the potential for the corporate sponsor's future involvement will be minimal.

One extra touch that Melissa Minker, marketing manager for USA Track and Field, provides sponsors is a marketing newsletter that highlights each of the organization's sponsors and their sponsorship activities. This not only provides more visibility for the companies, but it also opens the door to cross-promotional opportunities among sponsors and improves communication. An example of a cross-promotion is when Bank of America and Visa teamed up to offer a special Olympic Visa credit card. Each time the Olympic credit card holder used his or her card, the holder was eligible to participate in a variety of Olympic promotions, including a free trip to the Games. Other benefits Minker offers sponsors are to invite them onto the track and to introduce them to the athletes or arrange for a signed number bib or picture to be given to sponsors.

Event organizers should also work with the sponsor and the local jurisdiction to prevent ambush marketing. Ambush marketing occurs when companies engage in activities that make them appear like a sponsor when in fact they paid no rights fees. The best defense is often a good offense. Identify all areas that could be used for ambush marketing and secure these areas. For example, make arrangements with outdoor advertising companies or airport/metro authorities to give first right to purchase advertising to event sponsors. Also make sure the public knows who the "official" sponsors are through an aggressive public relations plan, and encourage action against companies that try to take advantage of the event.

A warning should also be made about keeping sponsors informed yet at a distance, particularly in terms of budgets and production. On more than one occasion, major sport event sponsors have taken complete control of events, removing the entire promotional and event organization or replacing the original promoter for a less expensive one. In one instance, a large bottler "stole" an event from a major charity—just another example of the competitive nature of the sport event business.

CONTRACTING OUTSIDE AGENCIES

As an event organizer, you can chose to sell sponsorships in-house or hire an outside sports marketing company. The pros for outsourcing this responsibility are that the sport marketing agency provides the expertise, corporate contacts, and workforce. In some cases, the agency will pay your organization a guaranteed dollar amount, and anything they sell over that amount will be their profit. Most agreements, however, work on a commission basis in that the company keeps 15 to 25 percent of the amount of the sponsorship sold. Care should be taken, however, to make sure that the sports marketing agency is not so busy with larger clients or has a conflict of interest that causes your event to receive inadequate attention.

The greatest disadvantage of outsourcing sponsorship sales is loss of control. Excellent communication and a detailed contract are required between the marketing company and the event organization to make sure both understand their roles and responsibilities. For example, if an event employee identifies and secures a company that wants to work directly with the event and not through the marketing agency, how can this be handled in a manner that is agreeable to all parties? Melissa Minker also suggests that the marketing agency provide a biweekly activity report outlining the companies being approached and the status report of sponsorship sales.

NONSPONSORSHIP FUNDING SOURCES: FOUNDATIONS AND FINANCIAL INSTITUTIONS

One of the easiest sources of funding to identify but extremely competitive to receive are foundation grants. A foundation is a charitable trust or other tax-exempt, tax-deductible organization whose purpose is to distribute financial grants. The Foundation Center in Washington, D.C., and similar organizations maintain extensive databases of foundation tax forms. Through computer searches, a targeted list of potential sponsoring agencies based on key words (e.g., athletics, education) can be identified. Pam Gerig, executive director of the Palm Beach County Sports Commission, has been extremely successful in soliciting grant money for grassroot sport programs in her community. Many of these were funded through the tobacco settlement money.

Before approaching a foundation, make a telephone inquire about the accuracy of the printed information that you have reviewed and whether any of it has changed. You do not want to mistakenly prepare your grant proposal only to discover the deadline has been moved ahead two months. Simple mistakes of this kind can be avoided by making one telephone call. While calling, also ask if the foundation has any formal guidelines or examples to follow.

An alternative source of financing is through banks. Typically, however, such loans or lines of credit are as part of a sponsorship agreement. Bank of America, for example, is a sponsor of the 2002 Olympic Games and has arranged for a line of credit for the organizing committee based on expected revenue. Depending on your leverage, you may be able to negotiate an interest-free loan to support the organization while sponsorship funds are being solicited. Without a direct relationship to a sport event sponsorship, banks are usually a poor choice for start-up capital because of the risk involved. Unless your sport event has a long and successful history of financial stability, you will be asked to provide large amounts of collateral (frequently equal to the loan amount) and pay a prime interest rate.

Recently, some government entities and venture capitalists have been providing loans to sport commissions to bid on and host sport events. (See Chapter 12.) If you do enter into a loan agreement with either a bank or another investor, be sure to ask what type of loan it is. For example, you could ask for a nonrecourse loan or nonreimbursable loan where you are responsible for paying back the loan only if the event makes a profit. If no profit is made, then the loan becomes forgivable. This kind of financing is usually made through government entities, and the arrangements are negotiated in terms of public security and emergency personnel. If the event makes money, the city where the event takes place will usually expect to be paid for these services. If the event does not make money, the city will write it off as an overhead expense.

CONTROLLING COSTS

Another way to make money is not to spend it, and this is especially true in sports events. There are numerous ways to minimize your financial exposure through clever negotiations. First of all, each event employee and volunteer must be a salesperson and find ways to reduce costs through in-kind services and products. For instance, why pay for trash cans if you can borrow or barter for them? The same applies to refreshments, decorations, equipment, advertising, transportation, and almost every other logistical aspect of an event. (Refer to Figure 9-8.)

Figure 9-8

Barter Examples for Sport Events

Product/Service	Supplier
• Waste management	Recycling company
• Satellite parking shuttle bus	Shopping mall/department store
• T-shirts	Clothing/sport manufacturer
• Power generators	Air/heating company
• Cones	Department of Transportation
• Portable toilets	Construction company
• Chairs and tables	Religious institutions/schools
• Public-address system	Radio station
• Transportation vehicles	Car dealership
• Gasoline for vehicles	Oil/energy company
• Printing	Printer
• Food and beverage	Grocery store/restaurant

FINAL WORDS OF ADVICE

Event sponsorship takes many forms; however, the basic process is essentially the same. Ron Thomas, CEO of the Tennessee Walking Horse National Celebration, has brought $5.2 million to his event. Mr. Thomas states that "sponsorship principles are the same if you are after $1,000 in sponsorship from a small-town drugstore or if you are after $1 million from a major firm in their corporate board-room....Certainly, however, the higher up the flagpole, the harder the wind blows, so you better be prepared."

Ultimately, the effectiveness of all these ideas is most dependent on the appropriate demographic match between an event's target market and the company solicited; the direct and indirect benefits available to the sponsor; and the manner in which the proposal is presented. The written proposal should not only provide information about the scope and nature of the event but also include spectator or participant demographics and the associated benefits. Such details, collected through primary and secondary research, are necessary for a company to make an informed decision and to sell the proposal internally.

As businesses become more fiscally conscious, one of the most important concepts to remember is that companies sponsor sport events to impact their bottom line—their profit margin. Through sponsorship, companies are able to align themselves with a lifestyle, or demographic group, that best suits their image. Sponsors of events are able to establish a dialogue with consumers, rather than just speaking at them as in traditional advertising. When approaching potential sponsors, also remember that you will be competing with many other forms of advertising and you will have to establish why your proposal deserves consideration.

GAME HIGHLIGHTS

- Building a corporate sponsor base is a time-consuming process that relies on your entrepreneurial sense for tracking future trends, your ability to conduct meaningful research and obtain the right information, and your ability to network and to present your proposal in the most meaningful way to a potential sponsor.
- Focus on the benefits to the sponsor, not the needs of your organization.
- Service the sponsor and involve them in as many activities as possible.
- Conduct a post-event summary for each sponsor quantifying their exposure and return on investment. In the outset, make sure goals are measurable.
- Research foundation grants and confirm specifications before writing or submitting the grant proposal.
- Saving money will ultimately make you money, so look for ways to reduce costs.

10
CHAPTER

LICENSING AGREEMENTS AND MERCHANDISING

Be everywhere, do everything, and never fail to astonish the customer.

Macy's motto

HOW DO YOU MAXIMIZE INCOME and exposure through merchandising, and when and how do you implement the licensing program?

Licensing is an arrangement whereby rights to use a trademark, trade name, or copyrighted design on a product or service are granted from the licensor (property rightsholder) to a licensee (company interested in manufacturing and selling licensed merchandise). The three P's of licensing are profit, promotion, and protection.

Depending on the popularity and uniqueness of your event and the process in which the licensing program is organized and marketed, licensed merchandise can be a lucrative revenue source for your event. Within the first two hours of announcing the three mascots for the 2002 Salt

Lake Olympic Games, $75,000 worth of merchandise was sold. The 1996 Atlanta Olympic Games generated a record $50 million in licensing revenue, and Sydney achieved similar results. In 1999, the U.S. Tennis Open attendees spent close to $7 million on merchandise, while Wimbledon rings up close to $100 million in retail sales each year; almost as much as the Super Bowl.

To protect your merchandise rights, however, all names, logos, slogans, or graphics associated with your event must be copyrighted or trademarked. Names and pictures of venues should also be registered. Applications for a copyright are made through the Library of Congress and for a trademark through the U.S. Patent and Trademark Office. Although some events elect to change their logo annually to increase merchandise sales, the costs associated with such change must also be considered, such as new event signage, artwork, and fees associated with copyrights and trademarks.

Licensed merchandise range from traditional souvenirs, such as T-shirts, hats, key chains, and mugs, to more unique products, including furniture, jewelry, and linens. According to anthropologist Valene Smith, T-shirts tend to be the most popular item because not only are they functional, they allow the wearers to associate themselves with an event, statement, or design that proclaims their values or shows their allegiance.

Relatively inexpensive items such as posters and lapel pins can be sold at a premium price if the design is considered fine art or a collectible. Annual events often create limited-edition posters frequently designed by a famous local artist. These posters can be framed and will serve not only as a decorative item but as a conversation piece.

THE LICENSING PROCESS

One of the first decisions an event producer needs to make concerning licensed merchandise is whether to manage the licensing program in-house, to grant/sell these rights to a corporate sponsor, or to hire an external organization to coordinate the effort. Whoever ends up with the job will be responsible for the following:

- Development of the license application, design handbook, and marketing plan

- Distribution and collection of license applications
- Review and selection of licensees
- Collection of minimum guarantees or bank guarantees
- Development and dissemination of approval process guidelines
- Review of all products and promotions for quality and appropriateness
- Accounting for all sales and royalties
- Protection against counterfeit merchandise

The number of licensees depends on the exclusivity of the license category. This decision is usually influenced by the philosophy of the management and market size, as previously discussed in Chapter 5. Applications are scrutinized in terms of the company's product, reputation and knowledge of the retail business, financial status, and distribution channels.

Based on the experience of one licensee who is involved in many different sport events, the key ingredient in a licensing program is to hire knowledgeable people. If you are going to handle licensing in-house, this means that you need to pay to attract the best talent. If you decide to contract out this part of the event, be sure to hire a company experienced in sport event licensing. It is also vital to listen to the advice offered by your licensees, as they are in the business of selling product year-round. Mattel, Inc., for example, steered the Salt Lake City Olympic Organizing Committee away from a moose as the mascot toward a bear because the moose had too may sharp angles. Based on the toy company's experience, rounded curves are more attractive to consumers.

VENDING LOCATIONS, DESIGN, AND OPERATIONS

Location is critical when selling merchandise at sport events. Whenever possible, try to position your merchandise stand or kiosk in the path of the spectators. Look at crowd flow as an indicator of where to position permanent or temporary selling areas. Whenever possible, set up your displays so that the arriving public will see active buyers purchasing merchandise. Consumers tend to follow crowds. Also keep in mind the need to restock your inventory and the proximity of the location to the inventory. After all, you can't sell what is not on the shelf.

Design your kiosks or stands with raised displays that can be easily seen over the heads of standing crowds. Research shows that lighted signs and three-dimensional displays are more effective in attracting consumers. Colors also play an important role in attracting customer response. Red and white attracts customers at close range, while black and yellow is more visible from a distance. The kiosk should be designed to stop traffic en route to rest rooms, concession stands, or exits.

Many venues allow a menu of merchandise items to be placed in each seat, particularly in the club or reserved level and in the luxury boxes or suites. From this menu, spectators can place an order with the roaming vendor and pay for it with a credit card. The items are then delivered to the customer's seat, eliminating the need to stand in line.

When ordering inventory and stocking kiosks, remember that large T-shirts are the most popular size, so be sure to have plenty on-site. In addition, larger, bulkier items tend to be purchased toward the end of the event. Also note that the busiest times for merchandise sales are during the arrival as well as departure. Make sure you have peak staffing during these critical times.

For larger events, companies such as FMI and SES can also be hired to select the line of merchandise and orchestrate the delivery, warehousing, distribution, and protection of licensed merchandise. In addition, a separate concessionaire company may be hired to set up, staff, and stock selling areas. According to licensees, the major problem with this is that the organizing committee tends to charge the concessionaire a royalty fee in addition to the licensee royalty that makes the cost of the product sold to spectators too high. A $12.99 Olympic Barbie sold in Toys R Us was turned into a $35 souvenir at the venue.

MARKETING LICENSED MERCHANDISE AND GUARANTEES

Before licensees make any guarantees, they should inquire about the marketing effort of the organizing committee to promote the event and its merchandise. In the case of the 1996 Atlanta Summer Olympic Games, a number of promises were made in terms of marketing the mascot "Izzy" to the world through a television cartoon show and other activities, none of which transpired. In fact, Izzy was hardly visible before, during, or after the Games. This misrepresentation allowed some licensees to renegotiate their final guarantees with the organizing committee, since merchandise sales did not go as well as expected.

Event organizers should approach local merchants to sell and display event merchandise in store windows. Sponsors should also be asked to assist in marketing licensed products. JCPenney, for example, a sponsor of the United States Olympic Committee, created an Olympic merchandise section within each store.

For licensees, it is also important to look at possible threats such as a player lockout or boycott that could influence merchandise sales. Such clauses may be included in the licensing contract. The NBA player's lockout, for example, hurt many of the NBA and WNBA licensees.

Another decision that licensees need to make regarding marketing is which marks will be more appealing. For the Olympic Games, will the Game marks (e.g., the Salt Lake Olympic logo) sell more or will the marks of the national team (e.g., the United States Olympic Team)? For some products it is possible to combine both marks, whereas the packaging incorporates the Games marks and the actual product has the team logo.

Douglas Frechtling, associate professor of tourism studies at The George Washington University, suggests that every product be test-marketed carefully to determine consumer likes and dislikes, to set appropriate pricing, to fine-tune sales techniques, and to develop ideas for further product development.

TRAINING YOUR SALES TEAM

When Joe Jeff Goldblatt was retained by the Sells Floto concession company (a division of Ringling Bros. and Barnum & Bailey Circus) to train the concession sales personnel who travel with the circus, the first thing he did was assess the skill and language level of the group and determined that they were primarily profit-driven. He asked the group, "When someone orders popcorn or cotton candy, how do you respond?" He asked them to demonstrate a typical example of selling these products in the stands and watched as one of the salespeople raised his index finger and another galloped up 30 steps to fill this single order. "Tonight when someone signals that they want to buy, I want you to stop, shout 'How many?,' and wait for them to respond." The salespeople looked at him quizzically, but he now had their full attention. "The customer will most likely hold up two or more fingers. Whatever the number he displays, you are to shout it at the top of your lungs and then go into the stands to fill the order," Goldblatt continued. He then demonstrated this procedure several times, using members of the audience as buyers. "The goal is multiple sales with less time and effort per sale. Each time I catch you doing this tonight and it results in a sale, I will reward you with an extra dollar. I'll be watching." In less than 30 minutes, he had taught them a simple skill that would increase the sales that evening by an amazing 43 percent.

SELLING MERCHANDISE AT SMALLER EVENTS

For many events, there will not be a great demand for licensed merchandise beyond the athletes participating in the event and their family and friends. In this case, it would be more appropriate to either handle the process in-house or to sell the rights to an event sponsor, usually the sportswear category sponsor, such as Nike, Adidas, Fila, or Reebok. The benefit of controlling the merchandise sales is obviously more profit, but the advantage of selling the rights is a guaranteed revenue stream and fewer headaches.

The steps to handling merchandising in-house are to design the logo; decide on the type, quality, and quantity of merchandise; order the merchandise from a local merchant; and set up selling areas in the registration area during team check-in, near the front entrance of the event, and near the playing area during the event. Be sure to have enough cash boxes with a minimum of $50 in small denominations in each. Designate one or two responsible people to collect the money, and schedule volunteers or staff to work the booth according to peak times. Don't forget to post signs directing people to the merchandise area.

A number of events also organize a trade show or health exposition that concurs with the sport event. This is another revenue generator, as booths are sold for $100 to $5,000, depending on the length of the event and amount of traffic generated to the show. Most major road races incorporate trade shows that draw a variety of exhibitors, from fitness-related companies to financial institutions and insurance companies all seeking the business of the target audience. The next chapter presents additional ideas that are involved in organizing sport events.

GAME HIGHLIGHTS

- Determine if a licensing program is appropriate for your event and if it should be outsourced or handled internally.
- Incorporate sales training in your strategy.
- Always seek multiple sales.
- Test-market the product to determine the projected level of sales.
- Select the location to sell the product based on traffic flow, visibility, and ability to restock quickly.
- Listen to the advice of your licensees.

11
CHAPTER

The Ins and Outs of Sport Events

I find baseball fascinating. It strikes me as a Native American ballet—a totally different dance form. Nearly every move in baseball—the windup, the pitch, the motion of the infielders—is different from other games. Next to a triple play, baseball's double play is the most exciting and graceful thing in sports.

Alistair Cooke, journalist and broadcaster

WHAT SPECIAL TOOLS and skills do you need and how do you apply them to produce successful sport events?

"The success of any event is in the details as well as the flexibility to react to inevitable problems," exclaims Emilio Pozzi, managing director of events for the United States Soccer Federation. It also depends on the event manager's experience and confidence in what he or she is doing. In Chapter 3 general logistical requirements were described for all sport events. In this chapter, additional sport-specific considerations are provided to offer a deeper understanding of the requirements needed to organize a successful sport event. Keep in mind that many of the logistics presented apply to other sports with similar needs (i.e., timing, registrations, and first aid).

CYCLING

The most common cycling event is the long-distance road race, with the most popular being the Tour de France. Crossing great distances creates logistical challenges far greater than those of a sport event performed in a stationary venue do. When asked what the most difficult logistical aspect of cycling races, Jim Birrell, vice president of Operations for the Goodwill Games, quickly answered, "The two-way communication system. Walkie-talkies or cellular phones are fine until your cyclists and management team is on two sides of a mountain. To combat such geographical elements, a fixed-wing airplane carrying three repeaters is hired to fly above the event, allowing signals to be transmitted over the mountain." Another technical device used to help position both the television helicopter and the fixed-wing plane is the global positioning satellite (GPS). Since planes can normally only fly four hours and the event lasts six, at some time the plane must land and refuel. Once back in the air, pilots can immediately locate the cyclist by calling up GPS geographical coordinates. Birrell says, "Without a GPS, it takes pilots a long time to relocate the cyclists, wasting both time and money. Remember, from 2,000 feet in the air, it isn't easy finding a pack of cyclists in a forest.

Another logistical challenge of the cycling tours is that they cross numerous police jurisdictions, each with its own political bureaucracy. Birrell says that the best way to handle this is to "begin at the state level, followed by the county, then the city. This is especially important when traveling on state highways."

Cycling and running events share similar logistical considerations such as numbers, rest areas, and timing systems.

RUNNING RACES

More than 12,000 road races take place each year, and each one requires an organization to make it successful and profitable. A number of logistical considerations will help you to produce a successful and profitable race.

Considerations for Races

1. *Race application and permits*—To become a sanctioned event, organizers need to complete an application form available from the local association of the national sport governing body, which in the case of road races is USA Track and Field (USATF). The cost of sanctioning depends on the number of racers, ranging from $30 to $5,000. The benefits of sanctioning an event include comprehensive general liability insurance, the opportunity for USATF course certification (necessary if performances are to count toward records and for national and international team qualifications), listing in association newsletters and on Web sites, and the right to use the USATF name and marks on event collateral. At this time, proper paperwork should be submitted for what is usually called a "proposal for a parade permit," or permission to use the streets or parks on which your race will take place. This should be performed at least six months prior to the race date.
2. *Budget*—Obviously, the budget of a road race varies with the number of entrants, the length of the race, and the diversity of the course. "But," said Jim Vandak of 10K/Sport Productions in Arlington, Virginia, "there will always be some fixed costs if you have 500 people or 5,000." Both Vandak and Susan Kalish, head of the American Running Association in Bethesda, Maryland, said the most expensive element is the purchase of the T-shirts. The cost of contracting someone to organize the finish line is next. A typical 10K race costs between $8,000 to $15,000 to produce. In some cities, however, fees are charged for police support that can run $10,000 to $18,000 for 30 to 40 police. In addition, if the new chip system is used for timing races, this could increase costs another $2 to $10 per racer, especially if racers do not return their chips to the race organizer.

   According to Vandak, "In general, sponsorship revenue determines the profitability of smaller races. Take the time to develop your event sponsorship and sponsor relationships. A well-organized race that offers sponsors good value will produce a successful race and a successful bottom line." Kalish further explains that for this type of sport event, "your best bet for sponsors today are not the big companies but the small local businesses that are interested in promoting their name." Mom-and-pop businesses are great for prizes, while banks and insurance companies are by far the most prevalent race supporters looking to capture the upscale runners market.

3. *Promotions*—To receive "more bang for your buck," develop a Web site, place advertisements in newsletters and magazines in the local community, distribute brochures at other road races, and make sure your race is listed in running publication calendars and on event-related Internet sites. The race should be promoted to a targeted audience with ample time for runners to train.
4. *Race equipment*—To set up the race, you need equipment including measuring devices, numbers, pins, time sheets, surveyor's chalk to line the course, stopwatches, finish-line clock, flags, banners, scaffolding, ladders, tools, computer and printer, result board, awards, megaphone or public-address system, water, ice, cups, and some form of shade (trees, awnings, umbrellas). National magazines, such as *Running Times* and *Runner's World*, set up promotions in which they supply race organizers with numbers, pins, and "goody bags" in exchange for the distribution of discount subscription order forms to participants by the event organizer.
5. *Course monitors*—You must have volunteers or staff serving as monitors on the course to direct runners, watch for cars, and manage water stations. These individuals should wear bright colors and be briefed extensively about the course and responsibilities (e.g., have water in cups lined up on tables ready to distribute to runners and assign people to resupply the cups). Monitors should also be stationed where a crowd is expected to form in order to restrain the crowd from surging forward and interfering with the runners. A police escort is suggested for the first-place runner. Use the media to notify the public about roads that will be closed to avoid traffic problems.
6. *Medical attention and transport*—Every race must have a medical unit available. Although racers complete a wavier freeing race directors from prosecution for injuries, event organizers still have an unspoken responsibility to equip the race to handle run-

ning injuries and emergencies. Many races actually assign a race medical director to be responsible for assisting in the choice of the day, start time, evaluation of the course for potential hazards, and selection of the location for refreshments, shade, and medical stations.

7. *Course measurement*—The worst way to measure a course is by using an automobile odometer. Many race associations will not accept race proposals that have measured the course this way. The best way to measure a course is with a Jones counter that is attached to the front wheel of a bicycle. This system is authorized by USATF to certify courses. Race organizers can also select to use an existing certified course.
8. *Brochure/entry form*—Brochures and forms should provide to the runner the following important information about the race:
   - Race name
   - Sponsors
   - Time and date
   - Location
   - Cost
   - Awards
   - T-shirt information
   - Entry form
   - Mailing address
   - Liability waiver
   - Brief history
   - Course map and distance
9. *Registration*—An average race currently costs between $5 and $30 to enter. Fun-run courses are usually measured by odometers and rarely offer any awards or T-shirts. The registration fees for these events are therefore at the low end, and races are usually organized for the social aspect of racing. Many clubs organize fun-runs to solicit new members. The larger the expected race, the more you should charge for the entrance fee.

   Decide whether to allow race-day registration or preregistration only. Runners registering on the race day are often charged an additional $5 to $10. Those who register prior to the race usually receive a break on the fee and have the luxury of picking up their "race packet" a day or two before the race.

Sponsors of fund-raising events, such as the National Multiple Sclerosis Society, require entrants to collect pledges for eligibility, usually a minimum of $25.

10. *Race packet*—The race packet contains a course map, the entrant's race number, safety pins for the entrant's number, sponsor information and/or giveaways or coupons, and other information such as medical services, the awards ceremony, and so forth.
11. *Split times*—Larger races have mile-marker signs 10 feet high so that the runners can see the mile they are approaching. Other races simply mark the mile on the road with paint. Either way, the runner knows he or she is approaching a mile marker when you hear a volunteer, ideally dressed in common volunteer attire or a specific color, yelling out split times.
12. *Finish line*—Make the finish line noticeable by using flags, balloons, sponsor banners, race name banners, and cones. You must decide whether you want all finishers to cross into the same finish line chute or whether to separate the male finishers from the female finishers.

    Recording runners' times is another aspect of the finish line. At smaller races, two people complete this procedure. The caller, using a stopwatch, calls the time of each person as he or she crosses the line, while the second person records the time. We suggest that you create a time sheet with preprinted numbers and times so the recorder has to only circle the times as they are being called. Most large races, however, have automated this procedure. A small handheld device about the size of a large calculator can be purchased or rented. You push a button on it each time a runner crosses the finish line, and the time is recorded and later printed out on a small sheet of paper. Even more sophisticated is the chip system in which runners wear a chip on their shoe, and as they cross rubberized mats (antennas embedded), the system captures runner data. Whatever the system, however, always have a backup.

    The next responsibility is placing the finishers. At small races, an index card with the place written on it is given to each finisher. After the runners have caught their breath, they walk to a table and complete the card with pertinent information. The cards are then combined with the information received by the timers in order to match places and names with the corresponding times. Another option is to purchase the numbers that come with a tear-off tab. Organizers apply the runner's information on this tab as each runner crosses the finish line. The tab is then torn off and placed in order of finish. This obviously expedites the greatly anticipated posting of results. With the chip, results are computerized, greatly reducing the required workforce and alleviating human error.

13. *Cleanup*—One of the least favorite yet inescapable aspects of a sporting event is cleanup. This is becoming even more important with the emphasis on environmentally friendly events. Jim Vandak shares a valuable lesson on how to deal with the arduous task:

> With over 11,000 runners completing the Army Ten Miler, lots of trash is produced. My first year working on the event, we ordered two big Dumpsters, thinking that this would be sufficient. It turned out that the Dumpsters were not so big, especially when we started filling them with trash and cardboard boxes. Also, our event site was spread out, so we were hauling trash in and on top of any vehicles we could find, making legions of road trips to the Dumpster. The next year, I spent $250 on disposable trash containers and $600 for a rear-load, compactor truck to drive around and pick up trash. It was the best $850 I ever spent. Plus, I imprinted event and sponsor logos on the trash containers and packaged them as collateral advertising in sponsorship packages.

Changing Demographics

Road races are no longer just for the young and fit. The age of those involved with road racing is increasing, with 30 percent or more of the entrants over 40 years old. Races are also more popular among females and families. In 1999, 38 percent of finishers were females, compared to 20 percent in 1985, and many races are also now including a children's event.

Organizing a road race, even one that expects only 200 runners, demands strict preparation and delegation of resources. Manage these tasks by breaking them down into committees. Even for smaller races, this relieves some of the burden placed on the race director, who is busy overseeing the entire race. The Road Runner Club of America publishes a very comprehensive handbook for club and race administrators that covers every event detail and even outlines budget items for a major road race.

GOLF TOURNAMENTS AND OUTINGS

Golf events include corporate outings, celebrity and pro-am tournaments, fund-raising tournaments, and professional tournaments. The *corporate outing* is probably the most prevalent type of golf event and can range from a small group of corporate executives getting together on a specific day to play golf to a major corporate tournament involving suppliers, clients, employees, and corporate executives. The success of corporate golf outings relates to the amount of business that is conducted on the course. Where else can you spend four to six hours in conversation with someone over things in common and, of course, business opportunities?

Celebrity and pro-am tournaments match celebrities and professional athletes, respectively, with participants who have paid $500 to $5,000 to play in the tournament. Celebrity tournaments are typically designed around a popular celebrity who can bring in equally celebrated friends to attract sponsors who want to share in the limelight and glitz. Pro-ams are typically scheduled early in the week of professional tournaments. Both types of golf outings usually benefit a charity.

Fund-raising tournaments tend to take the name of the major sponsor or are presented by a corporation, such as the Junior Achievement Golf Classic sponsored by 3M. This type of golf outing is designed to be supported by members and friends of the organization or cause hosting the event.

Professional tournaments are the most exciting spectator golf tournament. This consists of the top professional golfers in the world who qualify to play for a predetermined money purse. Although there are different levels of tournaments that offer many prizes, the most popular are the PGA (Professional Golf Association), the Senior PGA, and the LPGA (Ladies Professional Golf Association). These tournaments are sponsored by corporations and play in preannounced cities throughout the country.

Organizing Golf Tournaments

Before planning any golf tournament, you need to identify the level of players who will be participating. Other data vital in the early stages are the number of people expected to play and the reason for the golf event (e.g., fund-raising, sales staff incentive, relationship building, corporate anniversary), along with the intensity of the event—competitive, friendly, or educational. The level of players and tournament purpose will affect your decision about what type of tournament to have, as well as the course to use. If you are looking to impress guests, an exclusive country club would be appropriate, but if you are more interested in making money, a public course or private course out of town may be your best choice. Remember, however, the more exclusive the course, the higher the tournament fees. If your players are mixed-level, select a course that is challenging but not too difficult.

Player information also helps determine the format of the tournament. The "shotgun start" is an excellent way to get everyone in the tournament energized. In the past, the golf pro would fire a shotgun—hence the name—to start the play. The teams arrive simultaneously, have refreshments, start their cart engines and drive to a preassigned individual tee, and tee off simultaneously at an agreed upon time.

For a team event, a "scramble format" (aka captain's choice) enables the different levels of players to participate regardless of ability. Every person in the group tees off, and then the ball closest to the hole is selected and played by the entire group until the hole is finished. The scramble is also the fastest tournament play. If you have more competitive participants, consider a "best ball" format in which each person plays his or her own ball, but only the lowest team score is recorded per hole. This lets those individuals keep track of their own scores, if desired, as if playing straight medal play.

Typically, the registration fee of a golf tournament is based on the price of the greens fees and cart. These could be as low as $45 or as high as $250 a head. On top of this you need to consider food and beverage costs. Most tournaments provide a light breakfast or lunch before play, beverages and snacks during the tournament, and an awards lunch or dinner following the tournament.

As far as revenues, the two main sources are registration fees and sponsorships. The cost of a foursome generally costs more than four single players, as there is a premium added for the right to group four specific players. Sponsorships include title, presenting, as well as hole and contest sponsors (e.g., hole-in-one, closest to the hole, longest drive). Silent auctions are also often organized in conjunction with golf tournaments and serve as an excellent fund-raiser. Auction items are displayed and bids are placed while participants are waiting to tee off and/or upon their return to the clubhouse. The winners are then announced at the closing award lunch or dinner. Silent auctions can raise thousands of dollars, depending on the number and type of auction items. The NFL Players Association raises close to $6,000 through a silent auction offering 35 items for only one hour before the "Unsung Heroes" awards banquet.

Auction items are not as difficult to obtain as you may think; all it takes is a letter of request. The letter should clearly state the type of item requested, the purpose of the request, when the item needs to be received, and where it should be mailed or delivered. To increase silent auction revenues, promote the auction before the event by sending out a list of the auction items with tickets or other marketing material, arrange the flow of the event so that participants must pass through the action and so that the items and accompanying bid sheets are visible and easily reachable, include a minimum bid for each item, and finally, allow time for the bidding to increase. Serving alcohol also seems to inflate bids!

For golf event planners, the golf professional at your selected course serves as a good point of reference. Most courses have a full-time outings coordinator on staff marketing special event packages and assisting with tournaments. There are also a number of companies such as Advantage Golf that consult with groups interested in hosting a golf tournament and Golf Group International that will organize the tournament for you. The benefit of outsourcing is that companies that specialize in producing golf tournaments have the experience to make the event a success and can often get a volume discount on signs, insured contests, gifts, T-shirts, and awards that are passed on to the client. A basic tournament management fee ranges from $3,000 to $5,000. The first question any consultant should ask is "What are the goals and objectives of the tournament?"

Planning should begin at least six months prior to the golf event to be sure you get the date, times, and service you require. Following are some of the details involved in organizing a golf tournament:

- Marketing the tournament
- Designing and ordering signage and gifts
- Setting up scorecards
- Arranging the pairings based on average scores or handicaps
- Assigning tee times
- Making sure people get to their tees on time
- Posting winners at the end of the tournament
- Orchestrating hole contests and obtaining prizes
- Arranging transportation
- Preparing the award ceremonies or banquet
- Coordinating a silent auction in conjunction with the tournament to raise additional funds

Most golf tournaments are planned through a tournament committee. The golf tournament organization chart shown in Figure 11-1 is also adaptable to other sport events.

All facilities used by the athletic competitors should be assigned to one person to ensure compliance with competition standards as well as to provide security and safety for the athletes. Supervision of auxiliary facilities such as hospitality tents or merchandise and concession kiosks should be assigned to appropriate committee representatives.

The checklist in Figure 11-2 will help stimulate your thinking about the abundant possibilities available to you and your team to organize a successful golf event. Despite your best-laid plans, however, you have no control over what Mother Nature has in store. Figure 11-3 offers ideas for what to do during inclement weather.

Finally, when planning golf tournaments don't forget the importance of involving women golfers. The National Golf Foundation reports that women account for 19 percent of all golfers and 36 per-

Figure 11-1 *Golf Tournament Organization Chart*

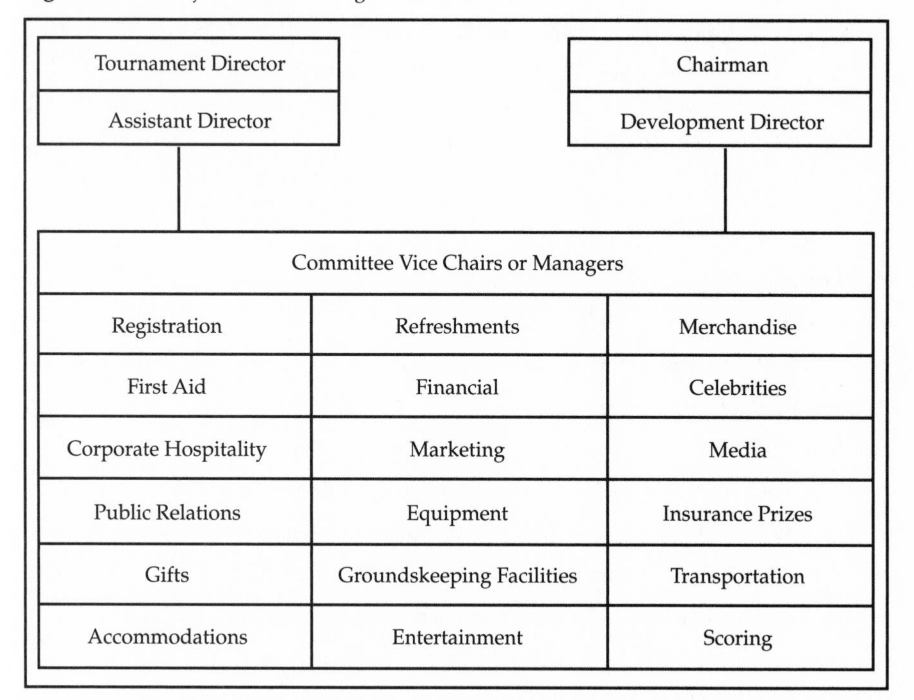

cent of all beginning golfers. There are currently over 5 million women golfers in the United States. Part of this planning is to include gifts and prizes appropriate for women.

3-ON-3 = 7 TIMES THE FUN

One of the most popular basketball events today is the 3-on-3 tournament (see Figure 11-4). As described by Tom Swanson of the Championship Group, a sports marketing firm based in Atlanta, Georgia, "3-on-3 basketball is a weekend street fair, a block party, an event born in the neighborhood, a family event, a media event, a charitable fund-raiser, and a unique promotional opportunity." Companies not only sponsor one-day tournaments but a series across the United States and Europe. Hoop-It-Up, the official national 3-on-3 basketball tour of the NBA, is held in 44 cities across the United States as well as in Europe and culminates in two 1-hour televised Hoop-It-Up events. The largest of these tournaments is held in Dallas,

Figure 11-2

Tournament "Hole-in-One" Ideas

- Select a golf chairperson who is interested in and knowledgeable about the game.
- Include with the invitation or registration form a golf participant survey that requests the participant's average score or handicap, rental equipment needs (shoe size if applicable), and the number of spouses of partners playing.
- Determine the number of attendees not participating in the tournament. This will help you plan alternative programs such as instructional clinics, putting tournaments, and tourist or shopping excursions.
- Remind players to clearly mark and identify all equipment and shoes before arriving at the course.
- Design and order personalized merchandise early.
- Decide what number of prizes will be needed (e.g., twosomes or foursomes), and the categories of winners (e.g., lowest score, highest score).
- Avoid changes in handicap and last-minute changes in pairings.
- Meet with the golf operations coordinator to finalize all scheduling, group requirements, and special needs, including celebrity players. Provide a list of the pairings and rental needs at least one day before the tournament.
- Ask about tipping and gratuity policies at the course.
- Assign check-in people to greet players as they arrive to drop off their golf bags. Greeters should ask the players' names, inform them of the hole number at which they will start and tag their bags with this number, and place the bags on the corresponding cart. A receipt showing this hole number is a helpful reminder to golfers.
- Assign a parking attendant to direct all tournament traffic.
- Assign an individual or several individuals to pick up VIPs on tournament day to ensure schedule is maintained properly.
- Publicize the availability of lockers, locker room facilities, and showers.
- Use beverage cart sponsors to provide refreshments to players on the greens.
- Hole sponsors can offer prizes for the best score at each hole.
- Sponsors can offer special prizes for contests such as closest to the hole, longest drive, accurate drive, and so forth.
- The "hole-in-one contest" is a great idea to generate excitement and lots of free advance publicity. Try to get someone to donate a vacation trip or even a new automobile as the prize for this contest. To build excitement, park the automobile near the hole.

Figure 11-3

Making Sunshine on Rainy Days

- In case of inclement weather, be prepared to offer your golfers a suitable substitute that will at least provide entertainment until the weather clears.
- Ask the course golf pro to be prepared to offer a demonstration trick shot clinic or a special educational session. A surer bet is to bring to the event your own golf pro, who can be ready to provide assistance on the course or in the clubhouse.
- Provide waterproof clothing, golf umbrellas, and golf club covering for your guests who might like to continue playing in the rain.
- Ask audiovisual personnel to set up a television and video machine so that you can show instructional video tapes or championship footage while golfers wait for the weather to improve.
- Research and secure cancellation insurance in your contracts. You also might consider a rain date.

and in 2000, it attracted 6,800 participants. The tour is run by Streetball Partners International, a grassroots event company that also organizes the NHL Break-out tour (5-on-5 hockey), MLB Yard Ball (4-on-4 plastic bat and ball), Toyota Golf Skills Challenge, and Let It Fly (4-on-4 flag football).

ALTERNATIVE OR ACTION SPORTS

What once was referred to as extreme sports, now dubbed alternative or action sports, is one of the fastest growing yet least-tested area of sport event management and marketing. The first lesson shared by those who have ventured into this new field is to listen and respect the athletes. Once an extreme athlete herself, Bonnie Crail, partner of Disson Furst and Partners and On Board Entertainment, strongly suggests involving the most influential athletes in your planning. "The paradigms that work in other sports don't work in alternative sports. Disciplines are so fluid and what is considered cool or uncool or too commercial or exploitative of athletes can dramatically affect the reputation of the event and sponsors." Jim Downs, director of Sports & Competition for the XGames and now general manager for the Great Outdoor Games, concurs with Crail that the learning curve for event mangers working in action sports is extremely high and it is impera-

Figure 11-4

3-on-3 Basketball Tournament Checklist

____ Site selection
____ Permits
____ Advertise through leagues in the area
____ Registration
____ Sponsors
____ Volunteers
____ Game officials
____ Insurance
____ Medical, first aid
____ Equipment (e.g., backboards, balls, scoreboards, whistles)
____ Awards
____ Booths for vendors
____ Food and beverage concessions
____ Sound equipment, staging

tive to work closely with the athletes. "These athletes do not accept orders or negative responses easily. Providing explanations regarding requests and decisions have more favorable results." It is not the same as in older sports where sports federations more influential. Event organizers must go to the athletes first, or they will be seen as suffering from arrogance.

Aside from the unique human dynamics involved, action sports require additional safety precautions and logistical challenges. For the X Games' street luge competition, 5,000 to 6,000 bails of hay must be strategically placed to protect athletes as well as spectators. Half pipes and other venues need to be constructed and thoroughly investigated for raised screws, splinters, and other loose ends. Be forewarned: Don't ever try to hire a construction company with no experience—the athletes will laugh you out of town. And don't forget, snow for the snowboard jump needs to remain frozen in 100-degree weather and the FAA needs to clear airspace for sky surfing. These are but a few of the unique challenges facing action sports event managers. In the words of Crail, "To be successful in this area of sport, you need to reinvent the wheel. The audience demands innovation and will not settle for the same show week after week." A snowboarding event today looks dramatically different than last year, so if you try to copy what you saw last year, it would be a waste of time and money. The best place to seek advice and to stay abreast of hot athletes and new trends in action sports are the specialty magazines. Successful producers of action sports also try to blend music and entertainment into the events.

ULTRA SPORT EVENTS

For organizers of long-distance events such as AIDS Ride 2000, a four-day, 330-mile bike ride to benefit those with AIDS or HIV, there are additional logistical requirements to consider. Because of an event's cause and the increase in modern medicine, organizers must be prepared to deal with a variety of medical conditions. For example, heart transplant recipients, liver transplants recipients, double amputees, HIV-positive participants, and people with AIDS who swallow protease inhibitors along with their Gatorade at pit stops may participate in your event.

For both the strong and weak, rest stops need to be set up every 15 to 20 miles where participants can replenish themselves with nutrition bars and orange slices, smear on sunblock, and seek out medicine and massages. Ice baths and water sprays are also popular.

Staffing of the medical tent for the AIDS ride consisted of a corps of volunteers: 5 physicians, a physician's assistant, 2 nurse practitioners, 45 registered nurses, 6 physical therapists, and a smattering of paramedics. This corps turned vans into rolling medicine cabinets.

Plans for those far behind also need to be made. Typically, participants still on the road at 7 p.m. are asked to ride the rest of the way in a support vehicle. It's known as "sagging," and for many events, there is honor in it!

MULTICITY SPORT EVENTS

For sport events that travel to various cities across the United States such as Toyota Golf Skills Challenge, Hoop-It-Up 3-on-3 Basketball, and the Adidas Golden Spike Indoor Track and Field Tour, a number of special logistical considerations must be arranged. To transport the equipment and signage, trucks need to be purchased or leased and drivers hired. Hiring a moving company is not always reliable or economical warns Melissa Minker, marketing manager for USA Track and Field. Plus, by hiring your own truck and driver you have on-site storage and one more event hand to help off-load and set up the equipment and signage. Care should be taken when producing event signage so that durable yet light material is used. Dismantling and packing heavy signs is extremely labor-intensive. If the events are split between the East and West Coasts, it is wise to have two trucks and drivers. Drivers are typically paid a flat fee (half paid in advance and half paid upon completion of the tour) and provided a gas card. To help promote and staff the events in each market, it is a good idea to hire a local company if your organization does not already have an office or affiliate in the area.

Now that you know what to expect in terms of hosting sport events, it is time to learn about sports tourism, why this field is growing, and how you can participate. Chapter 12 will also discuss how to secure the right to organize events through a bidding process and the need to measure and research techniques to measure the success of the events you host.

GAME HIGHLIGHTS

- The technical rules and regulations for producing specific sport events are fairly standard and can be obtained through national sport governing bodies or affiliated sport federations. Action sports are the exception to the rule.
- Test communication systems and make alternative arrangements in areas with no cell sites.
- Develop rain contingencies.
- Plan events through committees; don't try to do it all yourself.
- Action sports require you to reinvent the wheel and to continually involve the athlete.

12

CHAPTER

SPORTS TOURISM: AN ECONOMIC CATALYST FOR CITIES

> ...for what image would be conjured if the noun "marathon" were used without the adjective "Boston" in front of it. Would the "Kentucky Derby" or the "Indianapolis 500" mean as much if a mental picture of those places were not summoned each time we hear the event's name?
>
> *Tim Schneider, Publisher,* SportsTravel *magazine*

WHY ARE CITIES INVESTING IN SPORTS EVENTS, and how can they maximize and measure the return on investment?

Throughout the United States, the development of municipal, regional, and even state sport commissions has been accelerating at an Olympian pace. In 1994, there were 75 sport commissions, and in 2000, there were 228 sport commissions registered as members of the National Association of Sports Commissions (NASC). The economic impact that sport events can create has spurred many cities into the sports tourism arena.

Based on the research of Lisa Delpy Neirotti, a pioneer and expert in the field of sports tourism, the notion of people traveling to participate and watch sport dates back to the ancient Olympic Games and the practice of stimulating tourism through sport has existed for over a century. Just recently, however, sport and tourism professionals alike are realizing the significant potential of sport tourism and are aggressively pursuing this market niche.

Sport tourism is a three-dimensional concept involving travel away from home to play sport, watch sport, or to visit a sport attraction (e.g., hall of fame, stadium) and includes both competitive (i.e., tournaments, championships) and noncompetitive activities (i.e., recreational hiking, biking). For this chapter, the focus will be on competitive sport tourism.

Numerous reasons explain the increased interest in sport tourism. Elected officials and their constituents realize that sports events can generate media exposure, stimulate business and infrastructure development, generate direct economic income, and improve the quality of life in the community.

According to estimates made by University of Georgia economists, a total of $5.1 billion was pumped into Georgia's economy from the 1996 Olympic Games. The State of Utah reports that the 2002 Winter Games in Salt Lake City will provide significant economic benefits to Utah, including $2.8 billion in economic output, 23,000 job years of employment, and $970 million in income to Utah workers and business owners. State and local governments will generate an estimated $236 million in sales, income, property, and fuel taxes, as well as service charges and other revenue sources. According to Brenda Pitts, a professor of sports management at Florida State University, "The 1998 Gay Games attracted over 800,000 people and generated a little over [$]350 million total economic impact."

High-profile sport events are not the only economically beneficial ones. National championships for youth sports illustrate how low-profile events also can generate a significant economic impact relative to the funds expended. These events attract athletes, coaches, officials, and their families, and fans that pay their own way, stay in hotel rooms, eat in restaurants, and spend money on other essentials. The

Amateur Athletic Union (AAU) national Junior Olympic Games, for example, attracts approximately 15,000 athletes, not counting their entourages, making an estimated $40 million impact on the host community. Chris Green, a youth volleyball coach who frequently travels with her team exclaims:

> The biggest problem with youth volleyball tournaments is that event organizers do not communicate with the host community. We often play in small towns, and when 20 to 40 teams of 10 players each, not counting significant others, ascend on local restaurants they typically are not ready for the crowd and run out of food.

ORGANIZING A SPORTS COMMISSION

As the competition to attract sport events to a community increases, the need also rises to provide a central organization, a one-stop point of contact, where event organizers can go for assistance in hosting local events, bid requests can be reviewed and pursued, and private and public funds can be raised. Most sport commissions are housed within the Convention and Visitor Bureau or Chamber of Commerce, although some are independent for-profit or not-for-profit organizations. Many have a staff of one, while others have 10 or more employees, depending on the size of the area and number of events directly produced by the commission. Representatives from the sport, hospitality, entertainment, tourism, and transportation sectors, as well as corporate, media, and government officials should be included on an advisory board or on the board of directors, as each contributes to a successful sport event. Refer to the National Association of Sports Commissions Web site for additional information at www.sportscommission.org.

ASSESSING YOUR COMMUNITY

Utilizing the SWOT analysis approach, the first step a community should take is to assess their physical, financial, and human resources. This involves a facility inventory to determine exactly what venues are available to host sport events (e.g., gymnasiums, swimming pools, convention centers). It also requires a polling of the corporate community to determine if they will support sport events hosted in the community through sponsorships and ticket purchases. Finally, an evaluation should be conducted that analyzes the type of sports that are widely practiced and popular in your community (in other words, in what events will citizens participate as spectators or participants), as well as the expertise of the community in hosting sport events and their willingness to volunteer.

Following is a checklist to determine if your community is appropriate for the sport event:

Does your county/city have

- the appropriate facilities?
- a local sport club/organization to support the event?
- corporate and public interest in the event?
- expertise and time to successfully produce the event?
- space on the "big picture" calendar to schedule the event?

At the same time, the goals and objectives of hosting sport events should be determined. Is the community pursing events for economic gain, media exposure, business development, or quality-of-life enhancement? High-profile events are not necessarily money winners, because of the expense of hosting them, but they do create an enormous amount of media exposure and excitement within a community.

For sport events that offer little opportunity for local people to attend, it is most important for the organizers to offer an entertainment alternative. Local citizens may otherwise feel as though someone were having a party in their backyard and using their barbecue and swimming pool, but forgot to invite them. Such dismay in the long term may hurt future bid campaigns if public support is low.

This is why the NFL created the NFL Experience around the Super Bowl and the NBA created the NBA Fan Jam around the All-Star Game. Each of these events brings the sights, sounds, and feel of the NFL and NBA closer to all fans and local citizens unable to attend the game.

Once you have decided on the type of sport event that your community is interested in and capable of hosting, the next step is to approach the sports organizations or event property rights-holder.

BIDDING FOR EVENTS

Most sport organizations will be able to send you a bid document (also referred to as a "bid guide," "bid booklet," or "bid handbook"). This document should not only provide historical and demographic information about the organization and sport but details about the type and dates of events available to host, the rights and responsibilities of all parties involved, and the benefits associated with each event. A number of organizations also have this information posted on their Web site.

More specifically, the bid document should include the dates and locations of past events, along with the number of participants, officials, and spectators; the number of room nights booked; an estimated direct economic impact; the type and amount of media coverage; and a contact person. Furthermore, for future events, specific information should be provided regarding the minimum competition site dimensions (i.e., height, width) and other facility requirements such as spectator and media seating, parking, and restrooms; floor surface; light level; food service; locker rooms, storage, media, officials, and medical areas; practice facilities; and air conditioning. Additional information pertaining to the acceptable type and average cost of accommodations for athletes, spectators, media, and VIPs; the preferred time frame for hosting the events; and the bid deadline for each event should also be outlined. If this information is not provided, be sure to ask the appropriate questions.

Other items that need to be clarified in the bid document or through correspondence include the rights and responsibilities of the host committee and of the event rights-holder (e.g., the National Governing Body [NGB]). The host committee or promoter is generally responsible for the following:

- Collecting and accounting for all event-related money (e.g., entry fees, local sponsorships, program advertisements and sales, food and beverage concessions, and parking fees)
- Providing the competition venue and transportation service for all staff and participants from airport to hotels and to competition sites
- Making accommodation arrangements and covering the room and board for a specific number of officials and participants

- Hosting hospitality suites and VIP receptions
- Supplying office equipment (photocopying machine, fax, telephones, and computers with printers), event T-shirts, musical entertainment, meeting rooms, space for merchandise sales, electronic scoring/timing system, and complimentary tickets with preferential seating and parking for the sport organization
- Securing all management, volunteer, and medical support staff, designing and implementing a marketing plan, and paying a monetary bid fee or percent of gate receipts

Typically, the sport organization is responsible for sanctioning the event, providing insurance, securing and assigning officials and athletes, providing mailing labels, and providing athlete biographies and photos for promotional purposes. Other areas of responsibilities such as photography, public-address announcer, securing television coverage, designing and ordering awards, sponsor banners, and transportation costs to the event for officials and athletes are often delegated based on the resources and structure of each party.

In addition, to avoid any confusion in the marketplace, bid documents should define the sponsor product categories not available to the local host committee and the manner in which the local host committee can use the name and logo of the event and sport organization. Similarly, the property rights-holder should ask for a list of permanent corporate signage in the proposed facility; who has pouring, concession, and parking rights; if the facility workforce is unionized; and who controls the box office. Figure 12-1 lists the components of a bid proposal that need to be completed by the community interested in hosting an event.

For most events, a selection committee will simply review the submitted bid and make a decision. For other events, a site selection committee may conduct a site visit, and for major events such as the World Cup, the bidding organization will be asked to make a multimedia presentation. Although never included in any formal documentation, extra amenities and creativity in preparing and delivering bids never hurt. When the New York Knicks bid for the 1998 NBA All-Star Game, they sent their bid in a locked safe. The only way to obtain the combination to access the contents of the safe was to look at a five-minute videotape that was an audiovisual representation of their bid

Figure 12-1

Components of a Bid Proposal

Venue Specifications

Facilities
Dimensions
Light level
Prevailing winds
Age of floor surface
Seating (temporary/permanent)
Press box seating
Parking
Storage/meeting facilities
Food service availability
Locker room
Practice sites
Construction required

Business and Environment

Metropolitan population
Major industries
Colleges/universities
Pro teams
Foundations
Weather (highs, lows, precipitation)
Altitude
Public transportation
Accommodations (total bed capacity, average price per room)
Media outlets
Medical facilities
Tourist attractions
Bookend events
Family program
Agency Information

- Structure (e.g., 501-C-3)
- Experience
- Calendar of events

with the combination at the end. This obviously caught the attention of the selection committee.

As far as bid fees, the amounts listed in bid documents are negotiable based on the number of cities bidding and the overall package a community presents. For some NGBs, cash talks, and for others, the decision depends more on historical and technical factors.

Establishing an operationally and financially successful reputation is critical, explains Mark McCullers, general manager of the Crew Soccer Stadium, LLC. The sports world is small, and word spreads as to who can and cannot host a successful event. Frank Supovitz, group vice president, Events and Entertainment, for the National Hockey League, believes the major difference between what makes an event good and what makes an event great is how invested the local community is in the event. This was definitely proven by the success of the 2000 Sydney Olympic Games. The volunteers and citizens of Sydney were extremely hospitable and genuinely excited to host the Games. Whatever you do, don't be too anxious to attract an event and overbid. A good rule of thumb suggested by Dennis Gann, executive director of the Sioux City Convention Center and Auditorium Tourism Bureau, is to make sure you can cover the amount of the bid fees through sponsorship. If in doubt, it would be wise to share the request for proposal with local businesses to see if there is interest in the community, and whenever possible, get letters of commitment before bidding for the event.

HOMEGROWN EVENTS

Not all events require a bid application, and with rising bid fees, more and more communities are seeking to create their own events or looking toward supporting local event entrepreneurs. Many times, sport events begin as one individual's dream and build into a national or international event. The *Des Moines Register* newspaper's Annual Great Bicycle Ride Across Iowa (RAGBRAI) is but one example. This event was first planned in 1971 by a cyclist enthusiast employed by the *Des Moines Register*. In 29 years, the number of participants has increased consistently from 6 to 13,000 (of the 13,000 riders, only 8,500 paid entry fees and are considered sanctioned participants), with an additional 300 support staff and volunteers per overnight city stop.

Large sport events such as the Tour de France and the RAGBRAI can bring favorable publicity to and have an enormous economic impact on a region. In 1999, the economic impact of RAGBRAI on the Sioux City area was $900,000. Because of the high visibility and interest in being a host city along the tours, a competitive bid process is implemented. The organizers of each of these cycling events provide prospective cities with a bid manual outlining all the needs of the committee and responsibilities of hosting the start, finish, or overnight stop. A committee reviews each proposal based on established criteria and special circumstances that may enhance the event (e.g., the 100th anniversary of a city or special festival). Dennis Gann states that

> the RAGBRAI route is often planned for a specific reason and that an attitude of a city is very important in the selection process. It's amazing how many towns of two to three thousand want to host an event consisting of 13,000 participants. Surprisingly, it is these small towns that tend to do a better job.

Registration fees of $95 for the RAGBRAI are paid directly to the State of Iowa. Each host city is then reimbursed (e.g., Sioux City received $86,000 to offset some costs). Additional funds are raised through concessions. During the RAGBRAI, 10-foot × 10-foot concession booths are rented at a flat fee ($250 to $350), and the organizers take 10 percent of the gross sales.

Keep in mind that when looking at most sport events purely from a bottom-line perspective, typically not much profit is shown. The intangible and trickle-down economic impact, however, is what makes sport events worth the effort.

MARKETING YOUR CITY AS A SPORTS CENTER

To attract more events, many sport commissions produce quarterly newsletters; create attractive Web sites; produce a sports facilities guide or CD-ROM; advertise in trade publications such as *SportsTravel* magazine; and attend, exhibit, and network at sport conferences like the TEAMS (for Travel, Events, And Management in Sports conference) or the Sport Summit. In addition, it is important to build a reputation through hosting small to large events. Remember, the sport community is a tight circle, and word travels quickly concerning successes and failures.

Finally, within your community it is helpful to host a sport tourism/marketing seminar, like those conducted by Lisa Delpy Neirotti, to educate local hospitality providers, sport venue managers, coaches, government representatives, and other businesses about the process of bidding for events as well as the requirements to host events, including marketing, sponsorship, and logistics. This way, all local stakeholders understand what it takes to achieve the goals and objectives of the sport commission or the group promoting sport tourism in the community.

One of the fastest ways to build internal support for sport events is to measure their impact on the community.

MEASURING THE ECONOMIC IMPACT

Whether it is a national croquet tournament that attracts 300 visitors, a major youth soccer tournament that attracts 5,000 visitors, or the Olympic Games that attracts over a million visitors, measuring your economic impact as well as other success indicators is vital to the continued growth and support of the event and the organizing committee.

These studies are commissioned by organizing bodies as well as supportive governmental and sponsoring officials. Unfortunately, because of the complexity of economic impact research, many such studies are flawed, resulting in false conclusions about the economic effect an event has on a community. Therefore, it is important for sport event managers to understand how to conduct, interpret, and evaluate economic impact studies for sport events.

To begin with, sport event managers must decide whether they are interested in taking a conservative or liberal approach. For the most accurate and conservative estimate, expenditures of nonresident participants and spectators only should be included in the study, as this represents new dollars to the area. A narrow definition of a nonresident—also referred to as a visitor or tourist—is one who travels a minimum of 100 miles away from home or stays one or more nights in paid accommodations regardless of distance from home. A broad definition is anyone who travels outside of his or her residence.

Often, however, study organizers prefer a more liberal estimate of "economic activity" or "economic surge," including all expenditures associated with an event irrespective of whether they derive from residents or visitors. Obviously, such an estimate will produce a larger economic impact figure.

Likewise, the size and makeup of the impact area under study will influence results. The larger and more urban the jurisdiction, the less likelihood of leakage (money leaving the area) and the higher the multiplier coefficient (the number used to estimate indirect economic impact), if a multiplier is used.

To increase the accuracy of the study (and further complicate the selection process) only qualified visitors who would not otherwise be in the area except for the purpose of the sport event should be included in the sample. This eliminates expenditures from "casual attendees" and "time switchers"—those who are either visiting for another reason and happened to attend or participate in the sporting event or who had planned to visit the area anyway but switch dates in order to attend the sport event. Completely eliminating the casual attendees or time switchers, however, means not counting the extra money that these visitors may spend in a city because of the event (such as additional hotel nights).

Once you've decided whom to study and within what area, you must decide what data to collect and how. The data collected should include the amount of daily visitor spending on lodging, food and beverage, entertainment, transportation, retail shopping, and the number of nights stayed. A sample survey is provided in Figure 12-2. For large events such as the Olympic Games when plans begin six years in advance, operational expenses of the organizing committee should also be collected and included in the final economic impact. The chosen methodology will depend on how exact you want your numbers, as well as what resources you have available. In general, there are two ways to estimate the magnitude of economic impact: the survey method (primary data collection) and the nonsurvey method (secondary data collection).

The Survey Method

With the survey method, you collect data from a sample of people (such as event participants and spectators) through interviews, in person or over the phone; self-administered surveys filled out and returned by mail, in a drop box or to designated survey collectors; or expenditure logs/diaries, which the visitors use to keep track of what they spend and then mail back after they get home. Each survey method has its merits and shortcomings (see Figure 12-3).

In addition to the points listed in Figure 12-3, other factors related to the survey methodology may affect results, such as recall bias,

Figure 12-2

Sporting Events Economic Impact Survey

Have you traveled 100 miles or more to attend this event OR are you spending the night in (local) County? YES NO

Please list your RESIDENTIAL ZIP CODE ________________

(You must have traveled 100 miles or are spending the night to proceed with the survey. Thank you.)

1. Is this event the primary reason you traveled to the area? YES NO

   If no, what is your primary reason for traveling to this area?
   a. Business
   b. Visit friends/relatives
   c. Vacation
   d. Other _______

2. How many nights are you planning to stay in the area? _______
   (if none, proceed to number 6)

3. What type of accommodations are you staying in while in the area?
   a. Hotel/Motel (please check the specific property)
      ____ Holiday Inn
      ____ Hilton
      ____ Marriott
      ____ Hampton Inn
      ____ Other ______________________
   b. Staying with friends/relatives
   c. Other ____________________________

4. How did you find out about the accommodations?
   a. Convention and Visitor Bureau Web site
   b. Travel agency
   c. Tournament organizer
   d. Tourism advertisement
   e. Other ______________________

5. What are your individual expenditures on accommodations per day?

   $___________

6. How many people, including yourself, are traveling in your party?

   ____

6a. If applicable, how many hotel (motel) rooms is your travel party renting?

   ____

Based on a typical day during your visit, what are your individual expenditures on:

7. Food and beverage
   $_________

continued on next page

Figure 12-2 *continued*

8. Local entertainment (e.g., amusement parks, movie theaters, golf, etc.)
   $__________
9. Local transportation (e.g., rental car, metro, bus, taxi, gas, etc.)
   $__________
10. What type of transportation did you use to arrive to the area?
    a. Personal car (own or borrowed)
    b. Rental car
    c. Bus
    d. Train
    e. Commercial airline
    f. Other (specify) ______________

10b. If applicable, what was the cost of your air/bus/train ticket? $____________

What is your individual expected total expenditure on:

11. Event merchandise (excludes food and beverage)? $__________

11b. Other shopping (nonfood) in area? $__________

12. What is your individual expected total expenditure for this trip, excluding cost of air/bus/train transportation to area? $_______________

Demographics

13. Gender
    Male Female
14. Age
    - Between 18 and 24
    - Between 25 and 34
    - Between 35 and 44
    - Between 45 and 54
    - Between 55 and 64
    - Between 65 and 74
    - 75 or older
15. Marital status
    - Single (never married)
    - Married
    - Divorced/separated/widow
16. Highest level of education completed
    - High school (grade 12)
    - Some college
    - College or university
    - Advanced or postgraduate degree (Master or Ph.D.)
    - Technical school
17. Occupation
    - Executive

continued on next page

Figure 12-2 *continued*

- Professional
- Laborer/Service worker
- Retired
- Student
- Other ______________

18. How many members of your household contribute to your gross annual household income?

 1 3

 2 4 or more

19. What was your annual household income before taxes in (year) in U.S. dollars?
 - less than $50,000 U.S.
 - between $50,000 and $74,999 U.S.
 - between $75,000 and $99,999 U.S.
 - between 100,000 and $124,999 U.S.
 - between $125,000 and $149,999 U.S.
 - more than $150,000 U.S.
 - don't know/refused

Thank you very much for your time.

To be completed by interviewer

Interviewer Name: ______________________________

Location of Interview: ___________________________

Date of interview: ___/___/__ Interview Number: _______

response bias, and level of instruction. *Recall bias* generally occurs when subjects are not asked about their expenditures until a considerable time after their visit, which usually results in an underestimation of expenditures; it is recommended to survey visitors within 24 hours of their visit and certainly no later than one week afterward. Recall bias may be a factor for people on package tours or for corporate guests who do not know the exact cost of the trip and can only estimate.

Response bias may occur if the response rate is low, the sample is self-selected, or responses are projected. If the response rate is low, the question arises as to whether the nonrespondents differ from the respondents. One solution is to randomly select a small subsample of nonrespondents and interview them, either by telephone or mail follow-up, to see whether their responses are significantly different.

Figure 12-3

Summary of the Merits and Shortcomings of Various Survey Methods*

Survey Methods	Merits	Shortcomings
Interview		
On-site interview	Opportunities for feedback	Cost
	High participation	Labor-intensive
	High completion of survey	Projection bias
Telephone interview	Opportunities for feedback	Cost
	Absence of face-to-face contact	Sample bias
		Recall and response bias
Self-Administered Survey		
On-site self-drop-off	Low labor intensity	Low return rate
survey	No interviewer bias	Sample bias
Mail survey	Low labor intensity	Low return rate
	Interviewer's absence	Recall and response bias
	A representative sample	Cost
Expenditure logs or diaries	Most reliable and accurate	High mortality rate Low response rate

* This table is modified from the one developed by D. W. Turco in "Measuring the Economic Impact of a Sporting Event," a paper presented at the 1995 North American Society for Sport Management Annual Conference, Athens, Georgia.

The appropriate sample size depends on the size of the visitor population and the acceptable variability for the study. A mathematical formula is available, but for most sport events, a sample size of 300 to 400 would be appropriate. The issue of self-selected samples occurs when visitor addresses or telephone numbers are obtained mainly from lists of prepurchased tickets. The use of such lists automatically limits the sample to individuals who have the interest and resources to plan ahead; they may not represent the average visitor.

An alternative is to randomly or systematically (i.e., every nth patron entering the event) ask individuals at the event if they would be willing to answer questions in a follow-up telephone or mail survey. This approach not only allows for a more random sample but also helps to increase response rates. The obvious drawback is the cost of on-site staffing and the possibility of recall bias if the survey administrator does not contact the subject immediately after the event, whether by mail or telephone. Another method is to distribute the surveys at the sports event with instructions to complete and return them immediately upon returning home. The risk with this method is that subjects could lose the survey before filling it out and returning it, resulting in a low response rate.

Another option is to conduct the surveys on-site. Unfortunately, on-site surveys require the visitor to project their expenditure; those projections are typically underestimated. Daily expenditures often depend on the outcome of a competition. Early elimination may cause a spectator or participant to go home early and spend less; good results may encourage the spectator or participant to celebrate and thus spend more. The weather could also affect how long fans stay in the area.

To rely less on projections, the recommended method is to sample visitors daily and ask what they spent in the area in the previous 24 hours, as well as how long they expect to stay; for one-day events, interview visitors as they are leaving. The response rate of exit interviews, however, will likely be low, as most visitors are eager to depart.

Surveys can also be distributed in registration packets or programs if they are provided to all participants and spectators. Again, low response rates will likely bias the results. Overall, the diary or log appears to be the most reliable data collection methodology, eliminating the "projection" factor and recall bias. Response rates tend to be low, however, ranging from 5 to 30 percent depending on follow-up efforts and incentives. Incentives range from a complimentary program, beverage, or event souvenir to entry drawings for saving bonds or free tickets/registration to the next event.

Attention to where and when surveys are distributed and collected may also help to make the results more reliable. This is particularly true for multi-event and multivenue research. At the Olympic Games, for example, spectators at a tennis or gymnastic event may differ dramatically from the wrestling or track-and-field ticket holder, just as those who attend qualifying matches may differ from those at the finals. Likewise, specific-level ticket holders utilize certain venue entrances and exits.

The clarity and consistency of instruction to the subject, whether written or presented orally, will particularly affect the validity of the data. When asking subjects to record expenditures, they should be instructed to include only those expenses that were purchased in the impact area and paid for personally, whether for themselves or for others. Obviously, if a wife includes a meal that her husband paid for and the husband also reports this expense, an error in double counting will occur.

The Nonsurvey Method

The nonsurvey method is the most economical and convenient way to estimate economic impact of sporting events, so it is used most often. With this method, convention and visitors bureaus or economic development agencies develop per capita expenditure figures from past data, and those figures are multiplied by the number of visitors and the number of nights spent in the area. The result is an estimate of total direct visitor impact. One of the most significant problems with using existing per capita figures is that one must rely on the methods by which the initial data were gathered in the primary study. Spectators and participants at different types of sporting events spend differently. For example, differences exist between youth and adult competition, between regional and international events, between participant-dominant events and spectator-dominant events, and between individual events. Also, many per capita figures are based on business travel, where hotel occupancy is one per room, unlike sport travel, where the average is over two per room.

The best approach is to first conduct primary research at different sport events to determine a sport event per capita that can then be plugged into a formula for future events. Even so, a number of factors unique to each event influence their economic impact, which is why the economic impact reported for an event in one city should not be assumed to be the same for another city. Those factors include the distance of the participating teams from the host site, the novelty of the destination for spectators and participants, the size of the sport venue, the distance from the venue to the business district, the level of supporting infrastructure in the host community, the format of the event (i.e., single-elimination, day of rest between matches), and the time between qualifying tournaments and the championship tournament (i.e., the shorter the time, the less opportunity for sport tourists to plan their trips). The amount of positive or negative media attention, the promotional budget, the weather, and accessibility are also factors. For international events, the strength of the local currency, language barrier, and the ease of entry to a country may impact the number of foreign visitors to an event.

Once all of the direct economic impact figures have been determined through survey and nonsurvey methods, the next step is to determine if a multiplier should be used to calculate indirect (or induced) impact. Most researchers utilize a multiplier in order to estimate the total economic impact of an event, yet there is much discussion about the appropriateness of multipliers especially for short-term, one-time-only events (Direct + Indirect = Total Economic Impact).

The Use of Multipliers

Researchers who measure the total economic impact should decide what type of multiplier to use. Researchers who want to determine the total net economic change in a host community attributable to a sporting event usually apply an output or sales multiplier. Determining the total net economic change in residents' income or wealth because of a sport event calls for an *employment multiplier* or an *income multiplier*. Most economists believe that the most useful and conservative approach is the latter, as most residents are concerned with the impact of sales on household income and employment, not with the value of the sales themselves, which has no effect on their standard of living.

Others believe that the use of employment and income multipliers should depend on the potential of the event or establishment to generate new jobs and the durability of such jobs. For example, when studying the economic impact of sport facilities or businesses, an employment multiplier would be appropriate because the establishment is expected to be around for a long time.

The household income multiplier or a wage income multiplier is most appropriate in the case of short-term sporting events, as current local employees work more hours during the event, though the number of employees usually does not increase. The increase in household earnings can thus be estimated by multiplying total local expenditure by the average regional earnings multiplier. That multiplier is provided in terms of a number of annualized jobs for each million dollars in local expenditures. Remember that sales and earning impacts are simply different ways of looking at the effects of an event or establishment and should not be added together.

Furthermore, for each type of multiplier, there are different multiplier coefficients per industry category as calculated through one of the input-output models available. The most common models include the U.S. Department of Commerce's Regional Input-Output Modeling System (RIMS II), the U.S. Department of Agriculture Forest Service IMPLAN (Impact Analysis for Planning) model, and REMI (the Regional Economic Models, Inc.). Although it is beyond the scope of this book to provide in-depth information on the differences between each of these models, suffice it to say the RIMS II is most often used in economic impact analysis.

Finally, once a model is selected, to calculate the most accurate estimate of indirect impact, the direct expenditures per industry should be applied to the multiplier for that specific industry category (transportation expenditures x the multiplier of the transportation industry). Most commonly, however, an aggregated multiplier or the multiplier from the most relevant industry category (e.g., amusements) is used in the determination of the total economic impact. The Florida Department of Commerce, for example, suggests using the average regional amusements output multiplier.

Another type of impact to add to the analysis is fiscal impact. *Fiscal impact* refers to the government revenue generated by an event (e.g., sales tax, transient lodging tax, food service tax, amusement tax, auto rental tax, gasoline excise tax, and parking fee/fines). Estimates of fiscal impact are measured by applying the appropriate-category tax rates to the total spending for that category (e.g., hotel tax rate × hotel receipts). Fiscal impact should be calculated separately from direct economic impact because government revenue is not immediately recirculated through the impact area. A true net estimate of fiscal impact must also subtract government subsidies from the total revenue generated. (e.g., direct + indirect = total economic impact + fiscal impact − government subsidies).

Government subsidies include money spent by local government to attract the event or establishment and the cost of additional public services required by the event or establishment (e.g., traffic control, security; debt service on a publicly owned facility; and operating losses on a publicly owned facility if that facility was built to attract the event). If the facility is a multipurpose one, the debt service and operating loss should be prorated over various uses. Also, before subtracting all government subsidies, consideration needs to be given as to whether or not the area would have received these government funds without the event—that is, was money simply redirected from another project within your area or was it reallocated to your area?

Ways of Reporting

In addition to the use of different methodologies and multipliers, the way in which results are reported may also alter the overall picture of the economic impact and cause problems in comparing studies. Some researchers report the median versus the mean results or the expenditures per group versus individual. Some studies may report only visitor expenditures yet state that they have calculated the total economic impact. Others include local spectator and participant spending and claim that the economic impact is generated from new dollars to the community. These are just a few of the inconsistencies found in reports.

When it comes to employment impact, the number of jobs generated is best stated in full-time equivalents, or FTEs, but it is not always done this way. Because many of the jobs associated with stadium and event management are part-time, the total work hours related to part-time jobs should be aggregated and then divided by the number of hours in a full-time work year to derive the FTE measure. In reality, there will be a greater number of people employed than the FTE measure indicates, but some of them on a part-time basis. For example, for a typical Washington Redskins game day, there would be an estimated 1,800 part-time employees.

Other factors to consider in the reporting of a study are the information not included or additional impacts not accounted for. Most often, the return on investment (ROI) and/or net economic impact are missing from economic impact studies. Return on investment can be calculated by adding event revenue and tax revenue generated and dividing by the event expenses. Such calculations are particularly important when significant public investment (e.g., extra police, waste disposal, road maintenance, fire protection) is made, as government officials are interested in knowing if the investment was worth making or if there was an opportunity cost (could the money have provided a greater ROI if invested elsewhere). These measurements are also helpful for event organizers working toward the economic development of a community. "The host committee of a Super Bowl, for example, spends approximately $7.5 million," explains Jim Steeg, vice president of Special Events for the NFL.

Montgomery County in Maryland estimated a $100 million total economic impact from the 1997 Kemper Open and U.S. Open, which were held within a two-week time period. The cost to the county was estimated at $123,000, of which $50,000 was spent on traffic control and signs, $30,000 on extra police, and $43,000 on hospitality of representatives from current and potential companies conducting business in the county.

Overlooked Items

There are also a number of areas of significant activity that are often left out of economic impact studies because of the difficulty in collecting data or accurately attributing the impact. These include pre-event activities and training days; expenditures of nonspectator visitors traveling with ticket holders; air transportation; induced development and construction expenditures; off-site private parking; increased economic activity by local fans who are not ticket buyers; event product extensions such as youth sport clinics, educational training programs, and philanthropic/social causes; additional trade and business development; and property value increases.

Nontangible effects—those that cannot be definitively measured—should also be considered for inclusion in economic impact studies. These include long-term tourism promotional benefits, civic pride, increased community interest in sport, community development in terms of skills and facilities, and heightened media attention.

Finally, nontangible costs should be considered in an economic impact study to fully understand the net value of a sport event or establishment to a community. These include increased traffic congestion, crime, vandalism, litter, noise, and disruption to existing residents' lifestyles; the creation of a poor reputation if facilities and services are inadequate; inflation and increased hedonistic businesses; resident exodus; and interruption of normal business.

The economic impact of a sport event should be measured above and beyond the short term. It should be measured based on its impact on the area's long-term development plan and include the perceptions of residents within the impact area. Adopting a conservative methodology will limit the overestimation of an event's true economic impact and avoid possible disappointments.

ADDITIONAL RESEARCH

In addition to economic impact, exit studies of customers should be conducted to determine the customers' level of satisfaction with parking, admissions, advertising, facilities, and other important planning details of your event. Members of the community should also be surveyed to determine their psychographic reactions to the sport event and its contributions to community lifestyle. Finally, if a charity is a beneficiary of the sport event, survey the leadership, board, and staff to gain their perspective on whether this sport event was a success. Additional suggestions on how to successfully work with a charitable organization are provided in Chapter 13.

GAME HIGHLIGHTS

- Conduct a facility, financial, and human resource audit to determine the opportunities your city has to host sport organizations.
- Determine why you want to host events, and bid for those that meet these objectives.
- Market your city as a sport haven through advertisements, networking, and hosting well-organized and profitable events.
- Conduct research studies to determine the economic and social impacts of the event.
- Don't be overanxious to host events; make sure it is a good match for your community.

13

CHAPTER

CHARITABLE EVENTS

No matter how far you look and no matter how far you go, the greatest athletes in this world are these special athletes.

The late Lyle Alzado, Denver Broncos defensive lineman, on the Special Olympics

WHY DO CHARITIES ALIGN THEMSELVES with sport events and what are the benefits for each?

The Race for the Cure, the March of Dimes WalkAmerica, and the Dinah Shore Golf Tournament are familiar events because of the annual publicity they receive through television, radio, and newspapers. Each of these highly popular sport events also provides an opportunity to help others through sport.

In a charitable sport event, the proceeds—loosely defined as the funds remaining after all the expenses have been paid—are donated to a worthwhile cause such as AIDS research. Each year thousands of sport events benefiting charities take place throughout the United States and around the world.

Why the popular connection between sport and fund-raising? One reason is the enormous universal popularity of sport events. Whether you are selling tickets to a benefit basketball game where a local radio station's personalities are battling the Harlem Globetrotters or creating your own fun-run to benefit cancer research, you will find widespread support for your sport event program.

Another reason is that charitable events are spectator-friendly. The fans do not need to wear an evening gown or a black tie and tailcoat. Casual dress allows them to relax. Some individuals view the participation in the exercise (e.g., bicycling, running) as an added value for their charitable donation.

Perhaps the most important reason for this linkage is that sport represents health and many charities are concerned with illnesses that have no cure. An excellent example is the Susan G. Komen Race for the Cure. The event started in Dallas, Texas, with 800 participants and grew to a national series of 109 races with more than a million participants in 2000. Similarly, a field of 1,600 pedaled from North Carolina to Washington, D.C., as part of the AIDS Ride 2000. Each rider had to raise $2,000 to enter.

WHO BENEFITS?

The charity ultimately benefits from the proceeds of the sport event, but the linkage with a charity might also bring about greater fan interest in the sport. In the best of worlds, three interrelated groups will benefit:

1. The charitable organization will benefit from new monies to aid its cause and from greater visibility for the organization. Because sport events are highly public spectacles, the charitable organization has an opportunity to obtain a wider public through a well-planned public relations campaign tied to the sport event.
2. The participants benefit not only from the knowledge that their entry fees and concession dollars are benefiting a worthwhile cause but also because they are attending a healthy activity in cycling, bowling, golf, tennis, and so on.
3. The greater business community will benefit from the residual revenue that may be brought in a result of the sport event. As discussed earlier, hotels, restaurants, retailers, and parking lot operators will benefit from this activity.

FINDING THE RIGHT CHARITABLE ORGANIZATION

One of the most difficult tasks for a sport event professional is to identify a well-organized and reputable charitable organization to participate in a sport event. This task may be made easier by following the simple instructions in Figure 13-1. One key element to consider is how the charity's mission will appeal to your target audience. Some sport events attract primarily a male audience; therefore, a charity such as ovarian cancer research may have limited appeal to this audience. However, you can possibly broaden the appeal of the charity by introducing a famous soap opera actor or actress who will attract the wives and significant others of the primarily male audience.

Once you have identified your target audience, the next essential step is to begin discussions with the charity whose constituents will support your sport event. Find an opportunity for the charity's leadership to witness one of your sport events. Invite leaders of the arena, park, or bowling alley to see your sport event in action. It will be easier to enlist their support and full participation following this positive experience.

Organize the important planning meeting with the charity well in advance. Speak with the executive director of the charity and get his or her agreement on the agenda. This planning meeting is critical to your overall success, and therefore, it must be well organized. Figure 13-2 suggests a sample agenda for this meeting.

Figure 13-1

How to Find a Suitable Charity

1. Ask the National Society of Fund Raising Executives to recommend names of reputable charitable organizations in your community.
2. Determine the type of charity that is a complementary match to your sport event. Drag car racing is probably an inappropriate match for Mothers Against Drunk Driving (MADD), while tennis, golf, or basketball might be fine.
3. Interview the charity's executive director and find out what his or her strategic plan is. How does your sport event activity fit in?
4. Ask what the charity's leadership will contribute in terms of mailing lists, volunteers, and other contributions in exchange for being designated the official beneficiary of your event.

Figure 13-2

Sample Agenda: Planning the Charitable Sport Event

1. Welcome and introduction of committee members
2. History of sport event and charity
3. Goals and objectives of sport event and charity
4. Strategies for achieving goals and objectives
5. Public relations, marketing, and advertising
6. Financial goals
7. Role and scope of individual responsibilities
8. Discussion
9. Establishment of next meeting date
10. Adjournment

WHAT DOES THE CHARITY BRING TO THE SPORT EVENT?

Athletes Against Drugs, a Chicago-based charity, provides a detailed proposal to event organizers and asks that promoters do the same. "Once, during a golf tournament, we discovered that the promoter was unscrupulous. Had we done our homework, we could have avoided this awkward and potentially embarrassing situation," says Stedman Graham, its executive director.

The charity may possess numerous resources that will contribute to the success of the sport event. Figure 13-3 indicates the range of resource possibilities, although you will not necessarily require all of them. These are only a few of the possible resources. Most major charities such as the United Way will have a detailed planning guide for staging your live event that will make the implementation of these resources easier to accomplish.

LEGAL CONSIDERATIONS

Nonprofit organizations are required by federal, state, and local law to report their activities on a regular basis. As a fund-raising activity, your sport event may be required to document its activities. Therefore, good financial records are essential. In setting up your ledger, seek the advice of an accountant who specializes in not-for-

Figure 13-3

Possible Charitable Resources

Volunteers for:
- Mailing
- Telemarketing of tickets
- Staffing the event such as ushers, ticket takers, and officials

Concession suppliers and operators for:
- Programs
- Food and beverage
- Merchandise

Transportation for:
- VIPs
- Entertainers
- Game officials
- Spectator parking shuttles
- Media

Entertainment for:
- Pregame
- Halftime
- Postgame
- Private hospitality tents
- Contacts with major-name stars supporting the charity

Guest and mailing lists for:
- Major donors
- Corporate donors to purchase skyboxes
- General admission sales
- Participants

Name identity (charity's official name) for:
- Credibility
- Merchandising
- Publicity
- Recognition

Prospective sponsors for:
- Credibility
- Merchandising
- Publicity
- Recognition

Prospective sponsors for:
- Corporate in-kind support such as food, beverage, seats
- Directed giving such as underwriting the cost of tents

Nonprofit postage rate for:
- Direct mail
- Invitations

profit organizations. You are not allowed to show a profit but must reinvest in the charity's operations and distribute profit to those who benefit, such as the elderly or children.

During your first meeting with the charity's leadership, identify the financial goals for the event and establish your fees for planning and managing it. A standard rule of thumb for planners and managers of charitable events is to charge fixed and direct expenses plus a management fee. This limits the earning of the sport management organization, but it also establishes a secure margin of potential retained earning for the charity. The donors will want to know prior to their investment how much of their financial gift will be received by the beneficiaries and how much will be used for overhead. Figure 13-4 demonstrates a simple way to state the donation so that charitable donors understand and accept your invitation to contribute.

The actual percentage that the charities receive as a result of the sport event may vary according to your agreement. Some charities may require a minimum guaranteed donation in the contract. Some event owners may include a maximum cap on the earnings to be awarded to a beneficiary. Take, for instance, a successful 3-on-3-basketball tournament in which the Multiple Sclerosis Society of Washington, D.C., provided volunteers who assisted with mailings and recruited teams. The event organizer specified that the charitable contribution be calculated solely on the entrance fees, with a minimum guarantee of $300 and a maximum $2 per registered team. At this point, the charity must calculate its potential income to see whether participation in this event is worthwhile.

Figure 13-4

Sample Donor Language Describing Charitable Gifts

According to the National Society of Fund Raising Executives, the Federal Omnibus Reconciliation Act of 1993 requires that charitable organizations soliciting for events where the cost to purchaser/donor is $75 or greater must disclose in writing to the purchaser /donor the actual monies that are directly benefiting the charity and are therefore deductible by law. The amount that is not deductible is the fair market value of the goods or services used to produce the event. Sample language to notify donors might state: "$50 of your $75 is tax deductible as a charitable donation."

One standard used in measuring the validity of charitable events is less than 20 percent gross revenues should be allocated for fixed and direct expenses. The remainder should be used for direct support of charitable services. This standard may be difficult to achieve when staging a sport event because of the large up-front costs, but it can be achieved through sponsorship. Another legal consideration is the Unrelated Business Income Tax (UBIT) law that the Internal Revenue Service has recently been enforcing. This law spells out the difference between a purely corporate donation to a charity and a corporation giving money to a not-for-profit organization for specific purposes such as advertising (e.g., sponsorship contracts for college bowl games).

To guarantee a return on their investment, corporations have included specific requirements that a bowl committee must provide a sponsor *x* minutes of TV exposure, *x* number of signs, and *x* number of mentions. The IRS considers this to be a taxable service contract between the sponsor and the nonprofit bowl committee acting as an advertising agency, not simply a charitable contribution between a sponsor and an educational arm of a university, which would not be taxed. After numerous hearings, the ruling now stands that such agreements are acceptable under the tax-exempt clause as long as there is no direct endorsement of the product by the organizing committee (e.g., "The Orange Bowl encourages you to drink Coke") and no language in the contract requiring that such services be rendered in order to keep the donation.

Two examples of successful sport events that benefit charities are golf tournaments and various "athons" (e.g., walk, ride, swim). Half of all proceeds from major golf tournaments are usually designated to a charity. In addition, a pro-am golf tournament typically precedes the event that generates additional revenue for the charity. Pro-am tournaments provide an opportunity for local residents to play golf with professional golfers and other celebrities for a specified charitable contribution.

The most common sport-related fund-raiser among charities is the walkathon or bike-a-thon where participants pay an entrance fee and solicit sponsors for a certain amount of money per mile completed. Barry Glassman, formerly program director for the Muscular Dystrophy Association, created the "Tour de Bud" event, which is basically a glorified bike-a-thon.

Why an "athon" versus a race? Glassman explains that "it all comes down to the bottom line." By staging a "tour," you can avoid the expense of a timing system (approximately $6,000) and the hassle of officials, awards, and so forth. The target audience also consists of fund-raisers versus competitors. You want to attract individuals who will bring in a minimum of $65 worth of pledges; not those interested in becoming Olympic medallists.

SEEKING SPONSORS

Through their networks, charitable organization can be very helpful in steering you toward prospective corporate donors. The leaders of not-for-profit boards are often successful business professionals with extensive contacts in the world of commerce. See Chapter 9 for more information on seeking sponsors.

THE CHARITY SPOKESPERSON

At some point, a check may be presented to the charity that benefited from the sport event. Therefore, it is important to designate a spokesperson. Many charities have official national or, in the case of UNICEF, international ambassadors who promote their cause.

During your exploratory meetings with the charity, find out whether it has an official spokesperson and if this person is a celebrity. If the spokesperson is a well-known celebrity, determine if the "star" will appear in a public service announcement (PSA) to promote the event. A televised or radio PSA is extremely effective in generating excitement about the forthcoming sport event. You may also wish to invite the celebrity to appear at the sport event to throw out the first ball, fire the starting pistol, or make brief remarks. Be sure that the celebrity's role and fees (if there are any) are spelled out clearly in writing when you develop your agreement with the charity (see Chapter 7 on sport celebrities).

POTENTIAL LIABILITIES

In any relationship, there is always the potential for liabilities caused by either or both parties. Figure 13-5 lists some threats you should

Figure 13-5

Charity Threats

- Lack of organization by the charity's permanent staff
- Inability of the charity's staff and volunteers to focus on your event until late in the planning
- Limited or no commitment from the charity's volunteers
- Too many legal problems in establishing the relationship
- Inability of the charity to market the event effectively to its constituents
- Lack of sponsorship prospects on the part of the charity
- Inability to focus on the sport event because of other responsibilities
- Limitation of staff that can be dedicated to this sport event

recognize early in your planning and monitor throughout the development of the sport event.

MEASURING YOUR SUCCESS

Long-Term Success

Charitable golf tournaments, especially in states with warmer climates, walkathons, and bike-a-thons have successfully provided a source of funds to nonprofit organizations and will continue to do so. The key to long-term success is to keep your sponsors and charitable committees and board members happy.

Despite the founder's death, the Dinah Shore Golf Tournament continues to benefit charities. This 26-year-old tournament prospers not only because of the commitment of its organizers and charitable beneficiaries, but most importantly, because it has been organized to achieve long-term success.

To establish your own long-term success, consider planning not merely in terms of years but of eras. Planning in 5- or 10-year blocks will help you focus your sights on a long-term future for the development of your sport event. Granted, things change. You may decide to award the proceeds to a new charity, the location may shift, or other significant changes may take place, but with the proper planning, this recurring event will endure.

One major advantage of long-term planning is your ability to attract sponsors who wish to amortize the cost of their event over several years.

Whether you are negotiating long-term deals with bottlers or other brand-name products, the marketing decision makers will appreciate and possibly support your long-term vision. In golf, for example, the baby boomers are expected to flood the fairways in the next decade. Therefore, it is a smart move for a sponsor or a city to get in on the action early and enjoy the ride as the interest in the sport accelerates.

How to Measure Your Success

The charity will measure success primarily in one way: the total net proceeds that benefit its constituents. Based on experts in the field, a minimum standard to achieve is 50 percent over and above costs. Additional measurement scales include positive public relations, new volunteer involvement, expanded mailing list, and opportunities to reward and recognize volunteer leaders.

You, as the sport event planner and marketer, will measure success by your ability to recover your investment, earn a fair profit (although this would be less than if this were a strictly commercial venture), develop new fans for your sport, and generate new business.

These goals and objectives are not mutually exclusive. In fact, they are quite similar. When both the sport event management and marketing executive and the charitable organization's executive director mutually respect these common goals, a win-win scenario is developed. You could say that a win-win opportunity exists!

Opportunities are infinite to help the greater community through planning, managing, and marketing a successful charitable sport event. The next time you are presented with the opportunity to develop a sporting event, why not ask your team, "Whom might we help, together?"

As we enter the final turn or approach the 18th hole, we refuse to end this game of learning and instead choose to go into overtime with some additional advice. Remember Yogi Berra's remark, "It ain't over till it's over"? Yogi was right, and it's just the beginning, as you will see in the pages that follow.

GAME HIGHLIGHTS

- Determine if a charity tie-in is appropriate for your sport event.
- Contact the National Association of Fund Raising Executives for sources of reputable charitable organizations.

- Organize a planning meeting between your organization and the charity's leadership.
- Develop mutually acceptable goals and objectives, especially financial.
- Establish what resources the charity can bring to your event.
- Create a measurement and evaluation program to identify areas for improvement.

14
CHAPTER

CLOSING CEREMONIES: ADVICE TO NEW SPORT EVENT MANAGEMENT AND MARKETING PROFESSIONALS

I don't get my kicks from flirting with death. I flirt with life. It's not that I enjoy the risks, the dangers, and the challenge of the race. I enjoy the life it gives me. When I finish a race, the sky looks bluer, the grass looks greener, and the air feels fresher. It's so much better to be alive.

Jackie Stewart, race car driver

GET UP AT DAWN: THE FUTURE IS YOURS

Golfer Ben Hogan was famous for having a brusque manner. A young golfer called him one morning and asked for some free advice.

Hogan answered crisply, "Got an alarm clock?"

"Yes," the young golfer answered in a shy and somewhat confused voice.

He started to ask why when Hogan interrupted, "Tonight, before you go to bed set it for dawn and go out on the green tomorrow and start hitting until dark. Do that every day for a year and I'll be asking you for pointers." With that, Hogan hung up!

We don't know what happened to that young golfer. If statistics can be trusted, he probably failed to heed "professor" Hogan's advice, as do many students. A professor of writing once told his class of budding authors, "You signed up for a class on How to Write a Book, but what most of you really want to learn is how to 'sell' a book." The embarrassed adults in the classroom nodded affirmatively.

Succeeding in the competitive world of sport event management and marketing requires a combination of talent, hard work, training, and persistence. Most executives in sport made it to the top of their profession because they were prepared to do something they loved so much that they would have done it for nothing. Through training and experience, they mastered their craft and are now financially rewarded for it.

When asked what he liked most about his job, Chicago Bulls executive Steve Schanwald replied:

> Knowing that you have given the fans a good show and good value for their entertainment dollar. That is really what we are here to do. We are here to provide a diversion from the drudgery of everyday life, a little bit of an escape, a minivacation for the people who come to the games. If we accomplish that, then we can feel good about ourselves. But also you get a lot of satisfaction out of seeing the growth of the individuals within the company—seeing them grow as people and professionals. I think for the most part, people get into it because they enjoy it, even though they can make more money doing other things.

In terms of breaking into the field, Lisa Delpy Neirotti, associate professor of sport and event management at The George Washington University, advises her students to "see and be seen." Delpy Neirotti, who regularly attends major sport events such as the Super Bowl, the Olympic Games, and other hallmark events, says:

> I am constantly making contacts that will increase my students' chances for landing an important job. Knowing the major sport executives on a first-name basis is essential for networking. I feel as though I am building a network for the students not unlike a series of bridges that they must elect to cross as they move from academia into industry.

Delpy Neirotti realizes, however, that for her students to take full advantage of these contacts they must understand the sport business and possess the necessary skills for achievement in the field.

Susan Roane, author of *How to Work a Room*, recommends that job seekers develop a brief introduction of themselves that can be given easily during social encounters such as a reception. She also advocates collecting as many business cards as possible and following up later with a brief written thank-you note with your business card enclosed. This technique allows you to collect contact cards for later reference and to send your own card directly to the offices of people you met. In this way, the chances of their misplacing your card are much less likely. More important, the personal written note reminds them of the meeting; you have begun to weave your net to include them in your contact group (see Figure 14-1 on networking tips).

No matter how the introduction is made, relationships require care and feeding. You must extend a hand, take advice, and put it to good use. Do not waste their time or yours. It is also wise to select a variety of mentors from different professional and political backgrounds. Avoid being pigeonholed into any social circle early in your career.

READY, SET, GO!

Set your alarm for dawn. Go out on the green on cloudy as well as sunny days. But don't stop there. As golf legend Ben Hogan advised, stay later, practice longer, and one day you will not only be producing award-winning sport events but also the next generation of pros will seek you out for advice. When they ask, be generous with your knowledge because there is so much to learn. You are helping to

Figure 14-1

Networking Tips

- If possible, have someone else introduce you to a key person you wish to meet. It is always better to have a referral than to make a cold call.
- Always find out the dress code for any function that you attend. Dress conservatively but memorably. Develop a personal style that sets you apart from the other contenders. When in doubt, overdress slightly.
- When introduced to someone say, "It is a pleasure meeting you." Then flatter them in a straightforward manner. For example, "Joan says that you are enjoying great success this season with your new radio promotion strategy. Tell me about it."
- Encourage others to talk about themselves and listen intently. Showing keen interest in others will create interest in you.
- Before you end the brief encounter, ask the contact for help. Briefly explain what you are trying to accomplish and then ask for suggestions. At this point, it is extremely important that you take a deep breath and listen carefully because your contact is likely to open up and share some golden information with you.
- At the conclusion of all encounters, thank the contacts for their time, tell them it was a great pleasure to meet them, and ask for their card. When they ask for your card, tell them you do not have cards with you but will mail one to them.
- Always follow up promptly. Within 72 hours, write a personal note and enclose your business card. Refer in your note to particular comments made by the contacts and thank them again for their suggestions.

sculpt a new profession. Use your talents to create a masterpiece of design that will be a tribute to the champions who brought you this rich opportunity that you now recognize as sport event management and marketing.

A FINAL WORD

"Like you, I am a student of this emerging profession of sport event management and marketing. It is my hope that you will use your talents to research, plan, manage, and measure sport events in a way others never dreamed.

"Your talent is needed in this field, but even more crucial to the field's continued growth is your commitment to raise the level of professionalism to one of consistent quality. As you pursue your dreams in this exciting field, don't let small defeats prevent you from winning your game.

"In sport, as in politics, it only takes one point to emerge victorious. Put in the extra effort that will help you score the extra point, not only for yourself but for the entire profession of sport event management and marketing."

—Stedman Graham

3

P A R T

APPENDIXES

Appendix One

Sample Agreements

A. INDEPENDENT CONTRACTOR AGREEMENT

INDEPENDENT CONTRACTOR AGREEMENT

This Independent Contractor Agreement ("Agreement") is entered into this ________ day of ________, ________ by and between [Company Name and State Corporate Status if applicable], ("Company"), and [Contractor Name], ("Contractor").

RECITALS

A. The Company is engaged in the business of, among other things, sport event management and sport event marketing.

B. Contractor represents that he/she is experienced in the areas of public relations, event management, TV production, or sports and entertainment marketing.

C. The Company desires to engage Contractor to provide his/her services to the Company, and the Contractor desires to provide such services, all on the terms, and subject to the conditions, contained in this Agreement.

AGREEMENTS

NOW, THEREFORE, the parties hereto agree as follows:

1. *Term of Engagement.* Subject to the terms and conditions set forth herein, the Company will engage Contractor, and Contractor will provide services for the Company, as a Contractor of the Company, for a period commencing on the date hereof and, unless terminated sooner as provided herein, terminating upon thirty (30) days advance written notice by either party (the "Term of Engagement"). Also, the parties agree to renegotiate the Agreement if the Company desires Contractor to become an employee of the Company.

2. *Duties.* During the term of Engagement, as a Contractor, Contractor will have the duties and responsibilities as determined by, and at the direction and control of, the President of the Company. Contractor is being contracted to do the work associated with the job title of [Job Title of Contractor]. A job description is attached to this document. Contractor will, during the Term of Engagement, serve the Company faithfully, diligently, competently, and to the best of his/her ability. Contractor will devote his/her full business time during the hours of [Beginning Time] to [Ending Time], Monday through Friday and at other times and at such places as designated by the Company and give his/her best efforts and skill, to perform the duties with respect to the business, affairs, and operations of the Company.

3. *Independent Contractor.* Contractor and Company hereby acknowledge that (i) Contractor shall be solely responsible for and shall pay all taxes in respect of Contractor's income and engagements hereunder, (ii) Contractor has requested that the Company not withhold taxes and other amounts from any payments of compensation to Contractor hereunder, and (iii) Contractor shall be solely responsible for his/her retirement and disability protection, subject to paragraph 5 below, and all other so-called "fringe benefits" and the Company shall not in any way be responsible therefore. Nothing in this Agreement shall be construed as giving Contractor any rights as a partner in or owner of the business of the Company or entitling Contractor to control in any manner the conduct of the Company's business.

4. *Compensation.* During Contractor's engagement, he/she shall be paid $________ per month. Of this $________, $________ shall be paid on the 1st day and $________ on the 15th day of each month. Contractor shall be entitled to ________ percent of the net profits from any project that is designated the "Contractor's Project" by the Company. These projects will be named in writing by the Company, will be signed and dated by both parties, and will include the payment terms of the percentage of net profits. This document will become an addendum to this agreement.

5. *Expenses and Other Benefits.* Reasonable business expenses incident to the rendering of services by Contractor hereunder will be paid or reimbursed by the Company, subject to the approval of the Company in advance, and the submission of appropriate vouchers and receipts in accordance with the Company's policy from to time in effect.

6. *Death or Disability.* This Agreement shall be terminated by the death of the Contractor. If Contractor becomes permanently disabled during the Term of Engagement, this Agreement shall terminate as of the date such permanent disability is determined. Contractor's right to his/her compensation, if any, provided for under Section 4 shall cease upon his/her death or permanent disability, it being understood that Contractor shall be entitled to his/her compensation, if any, for services performed as of the date of termination of this Agreement.

7. *Disclosure of Information.* Contractor will promptly disclose to the Company all processes, concepts, techniques, inventions, methods, designs, developments, improvements, discoveries, and other ideas and information that may be of benefit to the Company, whether or not patentable (collectively, the "Developments"), conceived, developed, or acquired by him/her alone or with others during the Term of Engagement, or within six (6) months after termination of his/her engagement, or during his/her earlier engagement by the Company or any of its predecessors whether or not during regular working hours wherever such Developments relate to, would be useful in, or arise out of any part of the business of the Company or incorporate or make use of information relating to the Company's business which he/she shall have acquired during any past or present period of engagement with the Company or which were developed using materials or facilities of the Company. All such Developments made within the scope of engagement shall automatically be the sole and exclusive property of the

Company. In the event the Company does not request such an assignment of rights in any such Developments, the Company shall have a nonexclusive right to use such Developments and make and sell items embodying the Developments, without obligation to make any payment for such usage. At the Company's request, whether during or after the Term of Engagement, Contractor (or in the event of Contractor's death, his/her personal representative) shall, at the expense of the Company execute and deliver to the Company such assignments and other documents, including without limitation all drawings, sketches, models, and other data and records relating to such Developments, and perform or cause to be performed such other lawful acts, and give such testimony, as the Company deems necessary or desirable to obtain patents on, or otherwise perfect its ownership interest in, any Developments. The Company shall automatically own as a "work for hire" within the meaning of the U.S. Copyright Act, all copyrights in any drawings, reports, software, notes, customer lists, work papers, correspondence, and other tangible things, including but not limited to any which embody a Development, which Contractor creates, in whole or in part, within the scope of his/her engagement.

8. *Certain Definitions.*

(a) for the purpose of this Section 8:

(i) "Competing Business" means any person or entity which is engaged or making plans to engage, in whole or in part, in public relations, TV production, event management and/or sports and entertainment marketing, design, development, manufacture and/or offering of any product(s) or service(s) that compete with any product(s) or service(s) which the Company is then marketing or preparing to market in any market of the Company.

(ii) "Confidential Information" means all information, and all documents and other tangible things which record it, relating to or useful in connection with the Company's businesses, which at the time or times concerned is protectable as a trade secret under applicable law, and which has been or is from time to time disclosed to or developed by Contractor as a result of his/her engagement with the Company or any of its predecessors in interest. Confidential Information includes, but is not limited to, the following especially sensitive types of information: (*a*) the Company's product development and marketing plans and strategies; (*b*) the Company's unpublished drawings, manuals, know-how, laboratory books, production techniques, proprietary formulas, research in progress, and the like; (*c*) the Company's finances; (*d*) the identity, purchase and payment patterns of, and special relations with, the Company's customers; (*e*) the identity, net prices and credit terms of, and special relations with, the Company's suppliers; (*f*) the Company's proprietary software and business records; (*g*) the Developments, and (*h*) any other information or documents which Contractor is told or reasonably ought to know the Company regards as confidential. Confidential Information does not, however, include general business knowledge acquired from published sources or experience in dealing with the public; nor does it include information which Contractor establishes as of the time concerned is available from published sources, was known to him/her prior to his/her first engagement by the Company or any of its predecessors in interest, or was publicly disclosed by the Company.

(b) *Restrictive Covenants.* Contractor agrees that for so long as he/she is engaged by the Company, he/she will faithfully and to the best of his/her ability perform and render such services and duties for the Company as the Company directs. He/she shall not:

(i) While so engaged, engage in any other business activity (except passive personal investments and real estate holdings in a non-Competing Business), whether or not such business activity is pursued for gain, profit or other pecuniary advantage, unless the Company gives its prior written consent, understanding such written consent will not be unreasonably withheld; or

(ii) While so engaged, and for a period of one (1) year after the termination of such engagement, with or without cause, directly or indirectly, own any interest in any Competing Business, or be employed by or be associated in any way with any of the Company's past or active clients at the time of termination or potential clients who are in negotiation with the Company at the time of termination.

(c) *Confidentiality.* Contractor shall hold Confidential Information in the strictest confidence, as a fiduciary. Without limiting this obligation, he/she shall comply with all of the Company's instructions (whether oral or written) for preserving the confidentiality of Confidential Information, and shall use Confidential Information only at places designated by the Company, in furtherance of the Company's businesses, and pursuant to the Company's directions. In addition, he/she shall not, except as the Company otherwise directs

(i) Copy Confidential Information;

(ii) Directly or indirectly sell, give, loan, or otherwise transfer any copy of Confidential Information to any person who is not an employee or a signed independent Contractor of the Company;

(iii) Publish, lecture on, display, or otherwise disclose Confidential Information to any third party; or

(iv) Use Confidential Information for his/her personal benefit or the benefit of any third party. The obligations of Contractor as set forth in this Section 8(c) shall survive termination of this Agreement and remain in effect with respect to particular information for so long as that information continues to fall within the definition of Confidential Information or until the fifth anniversary of the termination of this Agreement, whichever shall occur first.

(d) *Return of Documents.* Promptly on the termination of his/her engagement with the Company for any reason, Contractor (or, in the event of his/her death, his/her personal representative) shall surrender to the Company without retaining copies, all tangible things that are or contain Confidential Information. Such person shall also surrender all computer print-outs, laboratory books, floppy disks, and other media for storing software and information, work papers, files, client lists, telephone and/or address books, Rolodex cards, internal memoranda, appointment books, calendars, keys, and other tangible things entrusted to him/her by the Company, or authored in whole or in part by him/her within the scope of his/her engagement by the Company, even if such things do not contain Confidential Information. Contractor acknowledges that he/she does not have, nor can he/she acquire, any property rights or claims to any of such materials or the underlying data.

(e) Contractor acknowledges that the restrictions contained in the Agreement are reasonable and necessary to protect the company's interest and that the compensation being paid to Contractor reflects additional consideration for these restrictions.

(f) During the term of this Agreement and for a period of one year thereafter, Contractor agrees not to solicit, or encourage any other person, firm, or entity to solicit, the customers of the Company. For the purpose of this Agreement, "Customer" means any person or entity to which Company provided services to prior to the date of this Agreement and such Customer which Company is responsible for bringing to the Company during the term of this Agreement.

9. *Remedies.* Contractor acknowledges that irreparable damage would result to the Company if the provisions of Sections 7 and 8 were breached by Contractor, and the Company would not have an adequate remedy by law for such a breach or threatened breach. In the event of such a breach or threatened breach, Contractor agrees that the Company may, notwithstanding anything to the contrary herein contained, and in addition to the other remedies which may be available to it, enjoin Contractor, together with all those persons associated with him/her, from the breach or threatened breach of such covenants.

10. *Termination for Cause.* Contractor's engagement with the Company may be terminated immediately by the President for cause which shall include (i) Contractor's conviction for, or plea of nolo contendere to, a felony or crime involving moral turpitude, (ii) Contractor's commission of an act of personal dishonesty or fraud involving personal profit in connection with Contractor's engagement by the Company, (iii) Contractor's commission of an act which the President of the Company shall have found to have involved willful misconduct or gross negligence on the part of the Contractor in the conduct of his/her duties hereunder, (iv) habitual absenteeism, chronic alcoholism, or any other form of addiction on the part of the Contractor, (v) Contractor's material and continued failure, after reasonable notice and opportunity to cure, to satisfactorily perform his/her duties hereunder as determined by the President of the Company, or (vi) Contractor's breach of any material provision of this Independent Contractor Agreement including without limitation, Sections 7 and 8 hereof. In the event of termination under this Section 10, the Company's obligations under this Agreement shall cease and Contractor shall forfeit all right to receive any future compensation under this Agreement except that Contractor shall be entitled to his/her compensation for services already performed as of the date of termination of this Agreement.

11. *Waiver of Breach.* Any waiver or any breach of this Agreement shall not be construed to be a continuing waiver or consent to any subsequent breach on the part of either Contractor or the Company.

12. *Assignment.* Neither party hereto may assign his/her/its rights or delegate his/her/its duties under this Agreement without the prior written consent of the other party; *provided, however,* that this Agreement shall inure to the benefit of and be binding upon the successors and assigns of the Company.

13. *Severability.* In the event that any provision of this Agreement, including any territorial or time limitation, shall be held to be unreasonable, invalid, or unenforceable for any reason whatsoever, the Company and Contractor agree that (i) such invalidity or unenforceability shall not affect any other provisions and provisions hereof shall remain in full force and effect and (ii) any court of competent jurisdiction may so modify the objectionable provision as to make it valid, reasonable, and enforceable and that such provision as so modified, shall be valid and binding as though the invalid, unreasonable, or unenforceable portion thereof had not been included therein.

14. *Notices.* All notices required or permitted to be given hereunder shall be in writing and shall be deemed given when delivered in person, or two (2) business days after being deposited in the United States mail, postage prepaid, registered or certified mail address to the Contractor's last known address:

[Contractor Address]

and if to the Company:

[Company Address]

and/or to such other respective addresses and/or addressees as may be designated by notice given with the provisions of this Section 14.

15. *General.* The terms and provisions of this Agreement shall be construed and enforced in accordance with the laws of the State of [Company State Name], and any disputes regarding this Agreement shall be settled in the Circuit Court of [Company County Name]. This Agreement shall constitute the entire agreement by the Company and Contractor with respect to the subject matter hereof, and shall supersede any and all prior agreements or understanding between Contractor and Company, whether written or oral. This Agreement may be amended or modified only by a written instrument executed by Contractor and the Company.

IN WITNESS WHEREOF, the parties have executed this Agreement as of the day and year first above written.

CONTRACTOR	[Company Name]
______________________________	BY:______________________________
	PRESIDENT

B. SPONSORSHIP AGREEMENT

SAMPLE EXCLUSIVE SPONSORSHIP AGREEMENT

The following will confirm the agreement between [Name] ("Company") and XYZ Productions ("Contractor") for the services of the [Name] ("Attraction") in connection with Company's products all collectively referred to herein as "Company's Products."

1. Company shall be the exclusive sponsor of the Attraction tentatively scheduled for [dates]. Without limiting the generality of the foregoing, no other party may be listed or mentioned as a sponsor or presenter of the Attraction.

2. As full compensation for the rights and services granted herein, Company shall pay Contractor the sum of [amount] payable in three (3) equal installments: [specify dates].

3. In connection with said Attraction, Company will receive seventy-five (75) free tickets at each performance. Such tickets shall be for favorable seats in the highest price range locations. In addition, Company shall have the right to purchase, at the face value ticket price, up to ten percent (10%) of tickets at each venue, said tickets to be favorable seats in the highest price range locations and to be made available to Company at the earliest date(s) possible.

4. (a) An official logo and identification phraseology shall be developed for the Attraction by Contractor which shall be subject to the approval of Company and which shall refer to Company (in first position), Attraction and XYZ Productions (e.g., COMPANY presents an XYZ production"). Said logo and/or identification phraseology, as applicable, shall be prominently included in all promotional and advertising references that relate to the Attraction and are disseminated throughout any media (e.g., print, radio, television, and point of sale) by Company or Contractor announcing the Attraction. Nothing herein contained shall constitute an obligation on Company's part to advertise or promote the Attraction, it being understood that Company may do so at its option or may refrain therefrom.

5. (a) Company's sponsorship of the Attraction shall be prominently featured and/or displayed in connection with the Attraction and all aspects thereof, including but not limited to, references on tickets, passes, handbills, inflatables (if any), indoor and outdoor venue signage (if any), venue marquee, stationery (if any), press releases, the stage (and curtain, if any) and a sponsor reference on the front cover of the Official Program. The form of such sponsorship references shall be subject to the mutual approval of Company and Contractor. Company shall also receive a full-page advertisement in the Official Program on the inside back cover. Company shall be responsible for providing: banners with its name and/or logos of Company's Products and/or references to its sponsorship of the Attraction to be prominently displayed in the venues, graphic layouts, and any other materials deemed necessary or desirable by both shall appear on the backside of all T-shirts and on all of the clothing items sold (the manner and location of such sponsorship reference on such other clothing to be determined by Contractor and approved by Company); provided, however if Contractor feels it advisable, up to twenty-five percent (25%) of such T-shirts and up to twenty-five

percent (25%) of such other clothing items offered for sale need not include such sponsorship reference. Company sponsorship reference on T-shirts and clothing shall be at least one inch in diameter and comparable in size to any reference to XYZ Productions references, and Contractor will use its best efforts to satisfy Company's reasonable requirements with respect to such sponsorship reference. All such Company sponsorship reference shall refer to XYZ Productions in a manner mutually agreeable to Contractor and Company. The official logo and/or identification phraseology shall be included on the posters offered for sale by or under the auspices of Contractor or Attraction or their respective agents or licensees.

(b) Company's Products will be the only such products provided in the backstage area and none of the products of Company's competitors shall be publicly consumed at the venue or otherwise during the term hereof.

6. Contractor shall use its best efforts to provide Company with exclusive venue signage and to permit Company to sell or distribute its Products at all venues; subject, however, to each venue's rules, regulations, and contractual obligations.

7. Contractor shall hold a Press Conference regarding the Attraction on or about [date], and, unless Company otherwise agrees, the only reference to Company shall be Company's sponsorship of the Attraction.

8. Company shall have the right to offer a single poster, T-shirts, and other items as premium merchandise for sale to the public, which features the identification of one or more of Company's Products and Attraction's name and/or likeness; provided such items shall be subject to Contractor's prior approval of quality, design, appropriateness, and consumer value. Company recognizes that Contractor and Attraction shall be exploiting merchandising rights in connection with the Attraction and that the Company's premium items shall in some manner differ in design from those offered in connection with Contractor's exploitation of its merchandise rights so as to minimize direct competition between Company's and Contractor's respective items. The poster and other items shall be offered on a free or self-liquidating basis.

9. Company shall use its best efforts to promote to the public Contractor's licensed merchandise during the term of this Agreement, provided such material is acceptable to the Company with respect to quality, appropriateness, design, and consumer value. Company will use its best efforts to assist Contractor to develop licensed merchandise items that meet Company's reasonable criteria as provided herein. Contractor shall indemnify Company for any liability in connection with its licensed merchandise. Company shall similarly indemnify Contractor and Attraction for any liability from Company's premium merchandise offer, exclusive of product liability relating to the materials provided by Contractor.

10. Attraction grants the Company the right to use the Attraction's name and likeness for advertising and promotional materials during the term of this Agreement in connection with Company's Products on the following terms and conditions:

(a) Attraction shall be available and shall cooperate in pre-production consultation. Attraction shall provide Company with five (5) consecutive full days of its services, tentatively scheduled for the first week in [month], to produce and record such advertising and promotional materials. All such workdays shall otherwise be at mutually agreeable times.

(b) From the results of the services rendered pursuant to subparagraph (*a*) above, the Company may produce two (2) television commercials with two (2) local TV tag formats, two (2) radio commercials, with two (2) local radio tag formats, two (2) print advertising designs, two (2) outdoor billboard advertising designs, and one (1) point-of-sale design, all for use from January 1, [year] through December 31, [year] to promote Company's products separately and/or in connection with the Attraction. Print advertising, outdoor billboards, and the point-of-sale pieces can be appropriately modified as to size and other minor modifications, provided such modifications do not change the basic concept.

(c) The commercial materials produced hereunder may be used throughout the United States, Canada, and Mexico from January 1, [year] until December 31, [year].

(d) Attraction shall neither endorse nor render any promotion, publicity, or advertising services for any other product or service during the term of this Agreement, nor grant any other licenses for name or likeness in connection therewith.

11. The term of this Agreement shall commence with the execution hereof by Contractor, Attraction, and Company and shall continue until [Date].

12. Company shall be given the right of first negotiation and first refusal with respect to the comparable television material, whether on free, pay, or cable television, prominently featuring Attraction, which is substantially filmed, taped, and/or produced during the negotiation and refusal shall not apply to materials substantially produced, taped, or filmed prior to the effective date of this Agreement.

13. All trademarks, photos, transparencies, and similar production materials produced hereunder shall be the exclusive property of the Attraction and shall be returned promptly after expiration of this Agreement, provided that any underlying music and lyrics provided by Company shall be owned by Company. Further, following expiration or termination of this Agreement, no further uses whatsoever may be made of official logo by Company, Contractor, or Attraction, but the official logo may be used by Contractor or Attraction without a reference to Company or Company's Product.

14. Contractor and Attraction shall secure and maintain throughout the term of this Agreement all insurance customarily secured for events of this stature and size, subject to mutual approval of the type of insurance and amount of coverage, which policies may, at Company's option, name Company as an additional named insured. If Company is so named, Company will bear a proportional cost of the premium.

15. If Contractor is prevented from fully performing this Agreement due to a Force Majeure as customarily defined in the entertainment industry, Contractor and/or Company may suspend and/or terminate this Agreement in accordance with standard industry provisions for such occurrences, provided in no event

shall Contractor be obligated to return sums advanced, loaned, or paid hereunder. The parties will attempt in good faith to negotiate a more detailed Force Majeure clause as provided below.

16. Company, Contractor, and Attraction agree that the terms and conditions of this Agreement are confidential and cannot be disclosed to any third party except as expressly provided herein.

17. Company shall have no liability whatsoever with respect to any commissions due agents of Contractor in connection with the securing of this Agreement, all of which obligations shall be Contractor's sole liability, and Company shall likewise be solely responsible for any commissions due its agents.

18. Company shall have the right to hold receptions and other social affairs in association with the Attraction for the purpose of entertaining clients, retailers, contest winners, etc. Attraction shall have the obligation to participate in these receptions.

19. Attraction, Contractor, and Company warrant and represent they have the right and authority to enter into this Agreement and their performance hereunder shall not conflict with rights granted any other party. Contractor and Attraction agree to be jointly and severally liable for the performance of their obligations under this Agreement.

This Agreement is intended to be fully binding on the parties hereunder provided this Agreement shall not become effective until formally approved by Attraction, which approval must occur within seven (7) business days from the date hereto and executed by all other parties listed. It is contemplated that this Agreement shall be supplemented by a more detailed Agreement between parties containing additional terms and conditions customarily contained in agreements of this type (e.g., rights to secure life insurance, indemnities, conduct clause, protection of trademark, reasonable notice and cure provisions, where appropriate, etc.), all of which shall be negotiated in good faith. Provided, however, that until such more detailed Agreement is executed, this Agreement will remain in full force and effect after approval of Attraction.

Agreed to this date as evidenced by the signatures below.

______________________________ _______

Contractor Date

______________________________ _______

Attraction Date

Source: Courtesy Ron Bergin, *Sponsorship Principles and Practices*.

C. LICENSING AGREEMENT

STANDARD LICENSE AGREEMENT

This agreement, effective this ________ day of ________, ______, is made by and between (organization), having offices at ____________________ (hereinafter referred to as "LICENSOR"), and ____________________ having its principal place of business at ____________________ (hereinafter referred to as "LICENSEE").

RECITALS

WHEREAS, LICENSOR has established and desires to preserve, protect, enhance, and promote the national and international reputation and prestige of the (organization), as a (state nature of organization), and LICENSEE acknowledges and recognizes this reputation and prestige; and whereas, the (organization) is the exclusive owner of various trademarks, trade names, logos, initials and other symbols/devices associated with the (organization); and

WHEREAS, LICENSOR possesses valid Federal and/or State Registrations for TRADEMARKS, and (if applicable) State/Local Law provides further protection under Statute/Code, etc., and

WHEREAS, LICENSEE desires a License to use certain of LICENSOR's TRADEMARKS on and in connection with the products and in the geographic areas specified below, and LICENSOR is willing, subject to certain conditions, to grant such a license;

NOW, THEREFORE, for and in consideration of the mutual covenants and undertakings hereinafter set forth, and other good and valuable consideration hereby acknowledged, it is agreed as follows:

1. DEFINITIONS

1.1 The term "LICENSED MARKS" shall mean the LICENSOR's TRADEMARKS and any other trademark, service mark, mark, logo, insignia, seal, design, or other symbol/device used by the LICENSOR and associated with or referring to the (organization) or any of its facilities, and such LICENSED MARKS are shown in Exhibit A, attached hereto and made a part hereof.

1.2 The term "LICENSED PRODUCTS" shall mean any product or part thereof bearing a LICENSED MARK and listed in the attached Exhibit B, attached hereto and made a part hereof.

1.3 The term "TERRITORY" shall mean the United States of America and its territories.

1.4 The term "PARTIES" and/or "PARTY" shall mean LICENSOR and/or LICENSEE.

1.5 The term "NET SALES PRICE" shall mean the final selling price of the LICENSED PRODUCTS to any and all customers by LICENSEE, after deducting any credits for returns actually made or allowed. In computing NET SALES PRICE, no direct or indirect expenses incurred in manufacturing, selling, distributing, or advertising (including cooperative and other advertising and promotion allowances) the LICENSED PRODUCTS shall be deducted, nor shall any deduction be made for uncollectible accounts. NET SALES PRICE must include the royalty amount. Any taxes actually paid and any universally offered published discount actually applied may be deducted. Sales to any party directly or indirectly related to or affiliated with LICENSEE shall be computed based on the NET SALES PRICE.

1.6 The term "NET SALES" shall refer to the total of all sales by LICENSEE of LICENSED PRODUCTS at NET SALES PRICE.

1.7 The term "AGREEMENT" shall mean this License Agreement between LICENSOR and LICENSEE.

2. GRANTS

2.1 Subject to the terms of the AGREEMENT and to the extent permitted by law, LICENSOR hereby grants LICENSEE a non-exclusive License to use the LICENSED TRADEMARKS on the LICENSED PRODUCTS in the TERRITORY.

2.2 LICENSEE may not export LICENSED PRODUCTS from the TERRITORY or otherwise use LICENSED TRADEMARKS outside the TERRITORY, and any such right is expressly withheld from this AGREEMENT.

2.3 LICENSEE may not assign its rights or sublicense the use of the LICENSED MARKS to third parties, and any such right is expressly withheld from this AGREEMENT. LICENSEE may use a sub-contractor to manufacture LICENSED PRODUCTS but must require said third party to be bound to the same terms and conditions as is LICENSOR relating to this AGREEMENT.

3. QUALITY ASSURANCE

3.1 LICENSEE agrees to submit samples of all LICENSED PRODUCTS to LICENSOR at no cost for review and approval prior to any use, sale, or other distribution to the public. LICENSEE agrees not to distribute any LICENSED PRODUCTS until such approvals of final samples are received in writing from LICENSOR. LICENSEE further agrees to submit all examples of LICENSED MARK use on LICENSED PRODUCTS to LICENSOR prior to any use, sale, or other distribution.

3.2 LICENSEE agrees the LICENSED PRODUCTS it manufactures and sells meet or exceed the quality and specifications of the final samples approved by LICENSOR. LICENSEE agrees to remove from public sale or distribution any previously approved LICENSED PRODUCT to which LICENSOR rescinds approval.

3.3 LICENSEE agrees that any proposed change to LICENSED PRODUCT, involving the graphic or any change in the use of LICENSED MARKS, or any alteration in the product structure, design, or quality of the LICENSED PRODUCT shall be submitted to LICENSOR for approval prior to any use, sale, or other distribution of the LICENSED PRODUCT.

3.4 LICENSEE agrees to maintain such reasonable manufacturing, servicing, and quality standards as may, from time to time, be requested by LICENSOR.

3.5 LICENSEE agrees that LICENSOR, or its duly authorized representatives, may inspect the manufacturing premises and LICENSED PRODUCTS of LICENSEE during all reasonable hours of operation upon reasonable notice during the term of this AGREEMENT to assure that LICENSED PRODUCTS are being produced in accordance with this AGREEMENT.

4. TRADEMARK USE AND OWNERSHIP

4.1 LICENSEE agrees to use the LICENSED MARKS only in the form and manner with appropriate legends as prescribed from time to time by LICENSOR, and not to use any other trademark in combination with any of said LICENSED MARKS without the prior written approval of LICENSOR. LICENSEE agrees it will not alter, modify, dilute, or otherwise misuse the LICENSED MARKS.

4.2 LICENSEE agrees that upon request it shall cause to appear on or within each LICENSED PRODUCT by means of a tag, label, imprint, or other appropriate device, such copyright, trademark, or service mark notices as LICENSOR may from time to time, upon reasonable notice, designate. LICENSEE agrees that all LICENSED PRODUCTS will bear an "Official Licensed Product" label or identification on the product or packaging in a form and manner that LICENSOR may from time to time, upon reasonable notice, designate.

4.3 LICENSEE agrees to submit to LICENSOR for approval samples of all tags, labels, and packaging to be used in connection with any LICENSED PRODUCT, and to remove therefrom or add thereto any element LICENSOR may from time to time, upon reasonable notice, designate.

4.4 LICENSEE agrees to submit to LICENSOR copies of any advertisement or promotional materials containing LICENSED MARKS for LICENSOR's approval prior to any use thereof, and to remove therefrom either any reference to LICENSED MARKS or any element which LICENSOR may from time to time, upon reasonable notice, designate.

4.5 LICENSEE acknowledges the ownership of LICENSED MARKS in LICENSOR, and LICENSEE agrees that it will do nothing inconsistent with such ownership, and that use of the LICENSED MARKS by LICENSEE shall inure to the benefit of LICENSOR. LICENSEE agrees that it shall not apply for registration or seek to obtain ownership of any (organization) TRADEMARK in any nation.

4.6 LICENSEE agrees that it will not state or imply, either directly or indirectly, that the LICENSEE or the LICENSEE's activities, other than those permitted by this AGREEMENT, are supported, endorsed, or sponsored by LICENSOR and upon the direction of LICENSOR, shall issue express disclaimers to that effect. LICENSEE agrees not to use the name of (organization) in business or affairs except for the use of the LICENSED MARKS as authorized herein or as may be incidental to its financial and internal reports.

4.7 LICENSEE agrees it will use the LICENSED MARKS only in a fashion authorized by the AGREEMENT and will comply with all appropriate local and national laws in the United States.

4.8 LICENSEE recognizes the goodwill associated with the LICENSED MARKS and acknowledges that said goodwill belongs to the LICENSOR.

5. ROYALTIES

5.1 LICENSEE agrees to pay LICENSOR a royalty of ________ percent (%) of NET SALES of all LICENSED PRODUCTS sold by LICENSEE at NET SALES PRICE during the term of this AGREEMENT. LICENSED PRODUCTS shall be deemed to have been sold when invoiced, or if not invoiced, then when delivered, shipped, or paid for, whichever occurs first.

5.2 Royalty payment shall be made in April, July, October, and January for the preceding calendar quarter's sales, and no later than thirty (30) days following the end of each quarter.

5.3 (If exemptions permitted) LICENSEE shall not include any amount for royalties in the NET SALES PRICE for sales of LICENSED PRODUCTS to the ________________ (e.g., university book store), or for sales of LICENSED PRODUCTS to any department or organization of the LICENSOR when said purchaser states the sale is for their own consumption and not for resale. But if LICENSEE does charge royalties for such sales, the royalties are also owed to LICENSOR.

5.4 LICENSEE shall pay LICENSOR an annual minimum payment of $__________ ($_____) for each calendar year in which this AGREEMENT is in effect. Upon signing the AGREEMENT, LICENSEE shall pay as an advance a prorated share of the annual minimum guarantee due for the first year of the License. LICENSEE may then credit quarterly royalties owed in the first year to that advance. In succeeding years, no advance will be required but LICENSEE will be expected to meet the annual minimum requirement within the Calendar/Fiscal Year. Failure to meet the annual minimum guarantee is cause for cancellation of the AGREEMENT. Upon termination of this AGREEMENT, the annual minimum royalty payable shall also be prorated for the period of the year in which the license was in effect.

5.5 In the event the royalty payment is not received by LICENSOR when due, LICENSEE agrees to pay LICENSOR interest charges at an annual rate of either (*a*) ten percent (10%), or (*b*) five percent (5%) plus the rate of interest that was charged by the (location) Federal Reserve Bank to member banks twenty-five (25) days prior to the date the payment was due, whichever is greater. Such interest shall be calculated from the date payment was due until actually received by LICENSOR.

6. ACCOUNTING AND REPORTING

6.1 LICENSEE shall submit to LICENSOR quarterly reports of its NET SALES of LICENSED PRODUCTS. Said reports shall be prepared in a format agreeable to LICENSOR and shall itemize all sales of LICENSED PRODUCTS by product category, style, units, dollars, and customer numbers. Reports of sales made in each calendar quarter shall be submitted within thirty (30) days following the end of each quarter, in April, July, October, and January. Each quarterly report shall be accompanied by a statement from a chief financial officer of LICENSEE acceptable to LICENSOR certifying that the report is correct and complete and prepared in accordance and in compliance with this AGREEMENT. If no sales or other use of the LICENSED PRODUCTS are made during any reporting period, a statement to that effect shall be provided to LICENSOR.

6.2 LICENSEE shall keep account books, records, and duplicates of all invoices to customers showing the manufacture, sales, and other distribution of LICENSED PRODUCTS. These books, records, and invoices shall be maintained for a period of at least three (3) years after the payment of the corresponding royalty. Such records shall be available for inspection and copying by duly authorized representatives of LICENSOR during regular business hours upon reasonable prior notice. LICENSEE shall cooperate fully with LICENSOR in making the inspection.

6.3 Once during each calendar year in which this AGREEMENT is in effect, and once after expiration or termination of this AGREEMENT, LICENSOR shall be entitled to an independent audit of LICENSEE's account books, records, invoices, and other pertinent data by a certified public accountant or qualified auditor to be designated by LICENSOR, to determine LICENSEE's sales of LICENSED PRODUCTS. The audit shall be limited to the determination of LICENSEE's sales of LICENSED PRODUCTS, and shall be conducted during normal business hours at LICENSEE's home office. The costs of the audit shall be paid by LICENSOR unless the audit shows the LICENSEE understated sales of LICENSED PRODUCTS by more than ten percent (10%), in which case the LICENSEE shall pay all of the LICENSOR's costs of the audit.

7. LIFE OF THE AGREEMENT

7.1 This AGREEMENT shall be in full force and effect from the date first herein written and shall remain in effect for [number of years] (_____) years unless terminated by operation of law or by the acts of the PARTIES in accordance with the terms of this AGREEMENT.

8. INFRINGEMENT

8.1 LICENSEE agrees to notify LICENSOR promptly of any known use of LICENSED MARKS by others not duly authorized by LICENSOR. Notification of such infringement shall include all details known by LICENSEE that would enable or aid LICENSOR to investigate such infringement.

8.2 Upon learning of any infringement, LICENSOR shall at its sole discretion take all such action as may be necessary or appropriate to enforce its rights or suppress or eliminate such infringement. LICENSEE agrees to fully cooperate with LICENSOR in the prosecution of any action against an infringer but LICENSEE shall not be liable for any legal fees or other expenses unless agreed upon in advance.

9. TERMINATION BY LICENSEE

9.1 LICENSEE shall have the right to terminate this AGREEMENT at any time upon ninety (90) days' written notice to LICENSOR provided, however, that such termination shall not impair or affect any accrued rights of LICENSOR.

10. TERMINATION BY LICENSOR

10.1 LICENSOR shall have the right to terminate this AGREEMENT at any time upon ninety (90) days' written notice to LICENSEE provided, however, that such termination shall not impair or affect any accrued rights of LICENSOR.

10.2 It is expressly agreed that, notwithstanding the provisions of paragraph 5.5 herein concerning late payments, if LICENSEE should fail to materially perform any act required by this AGREEMENT, or otherwise breach any covenant or agreement herein, LICENSOR shall give written notice of default to LICENSEE. If LICENSEE should fail to repair such default within thirty (30) days, LICENSOR shall have the right to terminate this AGREEMENT by sending to LICENSEE a notice of termination. This AGREEMENT shall automatically terminate on the date indicated in the notice. However, such termination shall not impair or affect any accrued rights to LICENSOR. Any of the following may be considered curable defaults by LICENSEE; (1) fails to commence production of LICENSED PRODUCTS with one hundred twenty (120) days from the effective date of this AGREEMENT; or (2) fails to commence selling LICENSED PRODUCTS in commercial reasonably quantities within one hundred eighty (180) days from the effective date of this AGREEMENT; or (3) after having commenced sale, fails to continuously sell LICENSED PRODUCTS for three (3) consecutive quarters. (4) fails to maintain required quality of product. (5) fails to obtain or maintain insurance of the amount and type required by this AGREEMENT. (6) is more than fifteen (15) days late in making its royalty payments or providing sales and royalty reports more than once in any calendar year; (7) fails to file a sales and royalty report for two consecutive quarters; or (8) fails to apply appropriate trademark designations, or fails to use proper licensed markings.

10.3 LICENSOR shall have the right to immediatley terminate this AGREEMENT by giving written notice to LICENSEE if LICENSSE does any of the following:

(1) files a petition of bankruptcy or is adjudicated as bankrupt or insolvent, or makes an assignment for the benefit of creditors, or an arrangement pursuant to any bankruptcy law, or if the LICENSEE discontinues its business or a receiver is appointed for the LICENSEE for the LICENSEE's business and such receiver is not discharged within sixty (60) days; or (2) if the LICENSED PRODUCTS become the subject of a recall by the Consumer Product Safety Commission or any corresponding state or federal agency and LICENSEE fails to take immediate action to recall such products; or (3) ceases to operate as a business; or (4) undergoes a change of more than fifty percent (50%) of its ownership or sells or disposes of more than fifty percent (50%) of its stock.

10.4 In no event shall LICENSOR's termination or this AGREEMENT for any of the reasons recited above relieve LICENSEE of its obligations to pay royalties for the actual sales of the LICENSED PRODUCTS.

10.5 LICENSEE acknowledges that money damages alone are inadequate to compensate LICENSOR for any breach by LICENSEE of any provision of this AGREEMENT. Therefore, in the event of a breach or threatened breach of any provision of this AGREEMENT by LICENSEE, LICENSOR may, in addition to all other remedies, immediately obtain and enforce injunctive relief prohibiting the breach or compelling specific performance.

11. EFFECT OF TERMINATION

11.1 Upon termination of this AGREEMENT, LICENSEE agrees to: (1) immediately discontinue the manufacture of all LICENSED PRODUCTS and the use of all LICENSED MARKS. (2) immediately destroy all dies, molds and screens used to apply the LICENSED TRADEMARKS to the LICENSED PRODUCTS, or their packaging or advertising, and to certify their destruction to LICENSOR specifying the type and number of each destroyed. These items may also be returned to LICENSOR. (3) immediatley return to LICENSOR at LICENSEE's cost all materials relating to the LICENSED TRADEMARK including, but not limited to, all artwork, color separations, prototypes and the like. (4) within thirty (30) days LICENSEE shall provide LICENSOR with a written inventory of all LICENSED PRODUCTS currently in its stock at the time of termination or expiration.

11.2 Notwithstanding the provisions of 11.1 above, LICENSEE shall have the privilege of disposing of all approved LICENSED PRODUCTS within said stock at its normal wholesale price within three (3) months after said termination or expiration; provided that such disposal is not allowed where the basis for termination is LICENSEE's failure to comply with the quality requirements of Section 3, and/or the Trademark Use requirements of Section 4.

11.3 All such disposition shall be subject to the terms of this AGREEMENT, including the requirement to pay royalty. After the three-month (3) period, LICENSEE agrees to destroy all remaining unsold LICENSED PRODUCTS and to report to LICENSOR the number of each destroyed.

11.4 In no event shall LICENSEE sell such inventory to wholesalers, diverters, jobbers, or any other entity which does not sell exclusively at wholesale.

11.5 LICENSEE agrees that all legal rights and goodwill associated with the (organization) TRADEMARKS shall remain the property of the LICENSOR and LICENSEE shall make no claim to them.

12. INDEMNIFICATION

12.1 LICENSEE shall defend, indemnify, and hold harmless LICENSOR, its officers, employees, and agents from and against any losses and expenses (including attorneys' fees), claims, suits, or other liability, including product liability, resulting from injury to or death of any person, or damage to property arising out of or in any way connected with the exercise of the license granted by this AGREEMENT, provided such injuries to persons or damage to property are due to the acts of commissions or omissions of LICENSEE, its officers, employees, or agents, or the products manufactured or sold by them.

13. INSURANCE

13.1 During the term of this AGREEMENT, LICENSEE shall maintain in effect insurance for both bodily injury and property damage liability, including product liability, in per occurrence limits of not less than One Million U.S. Dollars (US $1,000,000) for personal injury and not less than One Million U.S. Dollars (US $1,000,000) for property damage. The policy(ies) shall include an endorsement naming LICENSOR as an additional insured insofar as this AGREEMENT is concerned and provide that notice shall be given to LICENSOR at least thirty (30) days prior to cancellation or material change in the form of such policy(ies). LICENSEE shall furnish LICENSOR, prior to commencing any performance hereunder, certificates of insurance with the endorsements required herein. LICENSOR shall have the right to inspect the original policies of such insurance.

14. SEVERABILITY

14.1 Should any provision of this AGREEMENT be held unenforceable or in conflict with the law of any jurisdiction, then the validity of the remaining provisions shall be affected by such a holding.

15. NEGATION OF AGENCY

15.1 LICENSEE is an independent contractor. Nothing contained herein shall be deemed to create an agency, joint venture, franchise, or partnership relation between the PARTIES, and neither PARTY shall so hold itself out. LICENSEE shall have no right to obligate or bind LICENSOR in any manner whatsoever, and nothing contained in this AGREEMENT shall give or is intended to give any rights of any kind to third persons.

16. MODIFICATION AND WAIVER

16.1 The PARTIES agree that *Exhibits A* and *B* of this AGREEMENT may be modified from time to time in a writing signed by both PARTIES for the purpose of adding or deleting items therefrom.

16.2 It is agreed that no waiver by either PARTY hereto of any breach or default of any of the provisions herein set forth shall be deemed a waiver as to any subsequent and/or similar breach or default.

17. LICENSE RESTRICTIONS

17.1 It is agreed that the rights and privileges granted to LICENSEE are each and all expressly conditioned upon the faithful performance on the part of LICENSEE of every requirement herein contained, and that each of such conditions and requirements may be and the same are specific license restrictions.

18. LIMITED WARRANTY

18.1 LICENSOR warrants it has the lawful capacity to execute this AGREEMENT, but does not warrant and shall not be held to have warranted the validity or scope of all TRADEMARKS licensed under this AGREEMENT.

18.2 LICENSOR makes no warranty, express or implied, that LICENSED PRODUCTS will be commercially successful.

18.3 LICENSOR makes no representations or warranties with respect to the products manufactured or sold by LICENSEE and disclaims any liability arising out of the sale of LICENSED PRODUCTS sold or service rendered under the LICENSED MARKS.

18.4 LICENSEE warrants that the products manufactured or sold by LICENSEE under this AGREEMENT will be suitable for the purpose for which they are intended to be used.

19. ASSIGNABILITY

19.1 This AGREEMENT shall inure to the benefit of LICENSOR, its successors and assigns, but will be personal to LICENSEE and shall be assignable by LICENSEE only with the prior written consent of LICENSOR, except to a wholly owned subsidiary or as a result of a sales, consolidation, reorganization, or other transfer involving substantially all of the LICENSEE's business and assets.

20. GOVERNING LAW

20.1 This AGREEMENT shall be construed in accordance with and all disputes hereunder shall be governed by the laws of the State of ______________________________. The PARTIES hereto consent to the jurisdiction of the courts of competent jurisdiction, federal or state, situated in the State of ____________________ for the bringing of any and all actions hereunder.

21. HEADINGS

21.1 The headings herein are for reference purposes only and shall not constitute a part hereof or be deemed to limit or expand the scope of any provision of this AGREEMENT.

22. NOTICES AND PAYMENTS

22.1 Any notice required by this AGREEMENT shall be deemed to have been properly received when delivered in person or when mailed by registered first-class mail, return receipt requested, to the address as given herein, or such addresses as may be designated from time to time during the term of this AGREEMENT.

To Licensee:	To Licensor:
____________________	____________________
____________________	____________________
____________________	____________________
____________________	____________________

23. COMPLETE AGREEMENT

23.1 It is understood and agreed between the PARTIES that this AGREEMENT constitutes the entire agreement between them, both oral and written, and that all prior agreements or representations respecting the subject matter hereof, whether written or oral, expressed or implied, shall be abrogated, cancelled, and are null and void and are of no effect.

IN WITNESS WHEREOF, the PARTIES have caused this AGREEMENT to be executed by their duly authorized representatives and to become effective as of the day and year first above written.

____________________	____________________
LICENSEE Date	LICENSOR Date
____________________	____________________
____________________	____________________

EXHIBIT A

LICENSED MARKS

1. ____________________	6. ____________________
2. ____________________	7. ____________________
3. ____________________	8. ____________________
4. ____________________	9. ____________________
5. ____________________	10. ____________________

EXHIBIT B

LICENSED PRODUCTS

1. ____________________	6. ____________________
2. ____________________	7. ____________________
3. ____________________	8. ____________________
4. ____________________	9. ____________________
5. ____________________	10. ____________________

Source: Revoyr, J. *A Primer on Licensing* (1994) GB Press: Stamford, Connecticut.

In addition to the sample agreements and resources contained in this appendix, the following additional agreements and resources are available for purchase from The George Washington University Sports Management Program in Washington, D.C. Please write or fax your request to:

Lisa Delpy Neirotti, Ph.D.
The GWU Sports Management Program
600 21st Street NW
Washington, DC 20037

(202) 994-1630 (Facsimile)

Available resources

1. Arena Lease Agreement: A sample of the legal terminology exhibited in a traditional lease agreement used by sport event management.

2. Endorsement Agreement: The agreement used by sport event marketers to identify endorsement policies and procedures.

3. Insurance Application: A sample of a typical application for comprehensive general liability insurance in regular use in the sport event field.

Appendix Two

Useful Resources

A. CAREER OPPORTUNITIES IN SPORT EVENT MANAGEMENT AND MARKETING

1. *Not-for-profit charitable organizations* produce walks, runs, cycling, and other fund-raising, sport-related activities (e.g.,Special Olympics, multiple sclerosis, muscular dystrophy).
2. *Secondary and collegiate sport programs* require special event coordination for promotions, fund-raisers, halftime shows, media- and marketing-related activities, and tournaments. For example, the importance of events in sports led The George Washington University to hire a promotions manager to assist the marketing and sport information directors.
3. *Corporate or association sport event marketing* with a focus on developing sports-related events such as golf tournaments. One example is the *New York Times* sports marketing division; another is Xerox Corporation's Olympic Games team.
4. *National sport organizations* responsible for producing events such as national championships, state games, Olympic trials, and others that require experienced special event managers to coordinate production companies and handle hospitality, catering, transportation, media, cultural, and other highly detailed tasks (e.g., United States Olympic Committee, United States Track and Field governing body).
5. *Professional minor league sports organizations* that rely on promotions often driven by special events to boost attendance.
6. *Professional major league sports organizations* that often have an entire special events department, which may produce hundreds of events annually especially for marketing and public relations purposes.
7. *International and hallmark events* such as the Olympic Games and the Goodwill Games, which require highly experienced special event management personnel to design and organize these visible and increasingly complex activities.
8. *Independent or freelance consulting opportunities* are increasing because more and more corporations, including sports organizations, are relying on project managers rather than full-time employees in order to reduce costs.
9. *High-level consulting with corporate executives* to produce feasibility studies and other data to determine the viability of staging a sport event. Management expertise might be provided if the project is given a green light.

More and more opportunities are generated as companies downsize and hire consultants to work on a contract basis.

10. *Entrepreneurial opportunities* abound. Dozens of new sport management and marketing firms are launched each year. If you identify the right market for your services, you may find a lucrative way to use your talents.
11. *Sport manufacturers and retail stores* such as Nike, Adidas, Wilson, and Footlocker offer marketing and management opportunities. Consider how you would guide thousands of qualified buyers through the aisles straight to your booth at The Super Show, the fourth largest trade show in the United States. In addition to buyer previews, ad packages, and fashion shows, some exhibitors spend over $1 million annually to have celebrity athletes appear at their booths.
12. *Representation and management* is another major field to consider. The development of athletes as full-fledged superstar sports celebrities is a major field dominated by three firms: International Management Group (IMG), SFX, and Octagon. In 1999, IMG had annual earnings in excess of $1 billion. With 2,500 full-time employees, IMG dominates the field and makes entry difficult to all but the best-funded and most aggressive of competitors.
13. *New opportunities in Europe, the Pacific Rim, and the rest of the world.* Individuals with a specific interest in other cultures and international business, and who have a strong second or even third language ability, may wish to consider international marketing through sport and event management. This field is literally wide open, especially in Eastern Europe and the Pacific Rim. The National Basketball Association (NBA) raised over $14 million through exhibition games in 1999 and is looking beyond the possible 250 million U.S. NBA fans to 5 billion international fans.
14. *Sports museums, halls of fame, and venues* are staging special events, primarily in response to increased financial pressures. Owners now use sports arenas and stadia for events such as tractor pulls, rodeos, concerts, trade shows, flea markets, and professional wrestling exhibitions to provide new revenue streams.

B. TYPES OF SPORT EVENTS

Acrobatics
Aerobics
Aikido
Air hockey
Air sports
Archery
Arm wrestling
Auto sports
Badminton
Backgammon
Ballooning
Bandy
Baseball
Basketball
Beach volleyball
Beach soccer
Biathlon
Bicycling
Billiards
Boardsailing
Boating
Bobsledding
Bocce
Bodyboarding
Bodybuilding
Bowling
Boxing
Bridge
Canoeing
Chess

Climbing
Cricket
Crew
Croquet
Curling
Cycling
Darts
Diving
Dog racing
Equestrian events
Exercise/fitness
Fastball
Fencing
Field hockey
Figure skating
Fishing
Flag football
Foosball
Football
Frisbee/ultimate
Golf
Greyhound racing
Gymnastics
Handball
Hang gliding
Hockey
Horse racing
Horseshoes
Hunting
Hydroplaning
Ice hockey
Ice racing
Ice skating
In-line skating
Jai alai
Jousting
Judo
Karate
Kayaking
Kiting
Korfball
Lacrosse
Lawn bowling
Lifesaving
Luge
Martial arts
Military sports
Motorboating
Motorcycling
Motorsports
Netball
Orienteering
Paddle sports
Paddle tennis
Parachuting
Pentathlon
Platform tennis
Polo
Power lifting
Racquetball
Rodeo
Roller hockey
Roller skating
Rowing/crew
Rugby
Running
Sailing
Scuba diving
Shooting
Shuffleboard
Skateboarding
Skeet shooting
Skiing
Skimboarding
Skydiving
Sled dog racing
Snowboarding
Snowmobiling
Snowshoeing
Soaring
Soccer
Softball
Speed skating
Squash
Stickball
Street hockey
Surfing
Swimming
Synchronized swimming
Table tennis
Taekwondo
Team handball
Tennis
Track-and-field
Trampoline
Triathlon
Tug-of-war
Underwater hockey
Volleyball
Water Polo
Waterskiing
Weight lifting
Wrestling
Yachting

C. SPORT AWARDS BANQUET: SAMPLE SCRIPT

Note: This script may be adapted for individual team sports by using decor, music, and analogous sport stories in the text to match the sport being showcased.

[ ] = Stage directions and cues

6:00 P.M. Registration area. Guests receive name badges and place cards.
6:25 P.M. Preset salad placed at each place setting.
6:30 P.M. Doors open to banquet. [*Prerecorded march music is playing*]
6:45 P.M. Guests are seated.
6:46 P.M. *Announcer/emcee:* Ladies and gentlemen, please rise for the presentation of colors and our national anthem.

(Note: When many international athletes are present you may wish to display flags of each country and substitute the United Nations prayer for peace in place of the anthems.)

[*Guests rise for patriotic opening. Color guard enters from rear and marches to front of head table. Colors are presented and placed. Pledge is recited. Guard exits right. Audiotape of "Star Spangled Banner" is played and audience sings. Vocalist may lead.*]

6:50 P.M. *Announcer/emcee*: Please remain standing for our invocation. (Note: delete this activity when event is sponsored by a public school system.) (Reverend, Rabbi, Mr. or Ms.) ____________________ will lead us in prayer.

6:51 P.M. *Invocation* [*Minister or private individual walks to lectern and speaks. Dim lights to 50 percent.*]

Let us pray. We are grateful for this opportunity to gather together and celebrate the achievement of these athletes and enjoy this fellowship. Please grant them and all of us the strength to compete as best we can and the humility to accept our victories with grace as well as to understand that our defeats are only temporary and with courage may be overcome. Thank you for this unique opportunity to recognize and reward achievement and grant peace to all who are assembled here. Amen. Please enjoy your dinner. Our program will continue in a few moments.

6:53 P.M. Minister is seated. [*Raise lights to 100 percent*]
7:00 P.M. Clearing of salads begins.
7:15 P.M. Entree is served.
7:45 P.M. Clearing of entree begins.
7:46 P.M. *Emcee*:

In honor of our athletes and coaches, we have prepared a spectacular dessert. Please welcome your servers with a taste of victory!

7:47 P.M. [*Play audiotape of football march. Cheerleaders lead in servers who parade the dessert to the head table. Music fades.*]
7:50 P.M. Coffee is served.

8:00 P.M. Servers leave the room. [*Dim lights to 50 percent.*]

8:01 P.M. *Emcee*: I hope you enjoyed your dinner. [*Lead applause*] Let's thank those who organized this fine event [*List names*]. Join me in giving all of them a well-deserved round of applause! [*Lead applause*]

It is time to recognize our heroes and heroines of sport. During both practice and actual play, these individuals have distinguished themselves as outstanding competitors and teammates. As I call their names and present their awards, please join in enthusiastically recognizing their achievements. [*Name individuals in either alphabetical order by team or by sport. Each recipient walks to the head table, receives award, poses for pictures, and remains standing in a straight line behind emcee. Once all are assembled emcee speaks.*]

Emcee:

Here they are. The best and the brightest. Now, once again join me in saluting them! [*Lead applause. Those assembled behind emcee exit left and right and return to their seats.*]

8:30 P.M. In honor of these individuals we have invited Coach___________ from ____________________ to speak to us tonight. [*Read introduction of coach*] Please join me in welcoming Coach____________________.

Note: An alternative to a speaker is to show slides or a video of the season's highlights. Some organizations prefer to first show a bloopers program, which is a humorous look back at the season, followed by an inspirational review of the season's triumphs. The blooper tape is particularly useful when staging a golf awards banquet for corporate executives. Some resorts such as Innisbrook Hilton Resort in Tarpon Springs, Florida, feature a bloopers videotape as part of the golf package offered to individual groups. Bonus: Mail a copy of the videotape to each corporate executive. [*Raise house lights to 100 percent*]

8:33 P.M. Coach speaks or video/slide program is shown.

8:58 P.M. Conclusion of coach's speech or video slide program.

8:59 P.M. *Emcee*:

Thank you Coach for that inspiring and motivational program. Let's thank Coach____________________ once more. [*Lead applause*]

9:00 P.M. *Emcee*:

Thank you for joining us this evening. We look forward to your continued support and an even more successful season next year. Thanks and good night! [*Audiotape of marching music plays as guests depart*]

D. PRODUCTION SCHEDULE DESIGNED BY ROBERT W. HULSMEYER AND ADAPTED FOR BASKETBALL BY DYLAN ARAMIAN

Basketball Game Halftime Show on November 9

Time	Activity	Location	Responsibility
November 8			
3:00 P.M.	Site inspection of facility	Arena	Venue manager, event manager
4:00 P.M.	Meet with venue manager. Discuss needs and limitations including loading dock, door width, parking information, electrical and sound limitations, and necessary licenses and insurance certificates.	Arena	Venue manager, event manager
4:30 P.M.	Find storage area accessible to center court. Oversee loading in of equipment to storage area. Make sure all equipment has arrived: stage, microphone, podium, signs, table, chair, and gobos.	Arena	Venue manager, event manager
5:00 P.M.	Meet with lighting, sound, and moving crew supervisors. Discuss needs and time availability. Require crew to be on hand for entire performance, not just setup and breakdown. Determine responsibility for feeding the crew.	Arena	Crew supervisors, venue manager, event manager
6:00 P.M.	Meet with dancers/cheerleaders, choreographer. Discuss expectations and needs.	Arena	Choreographer, event manager, sound manager
7:00 P.M.	Meet with celebrity/agent. Discuss needs and speech, including time and equipment.	Arena	Celebrity, agent, event manager
November 9			
8:00 A.M.	Meet with venue manager and crew supervisors to discuss risk management and start setup.	Arena	Venue manager, crew, crew managers, event manager
8:30 A.M.	Check equipment. Decide on best lighting and sound support. Use gobos of stars for the dance section.	Arena	Sound and lighting crew, event manager

Time	Activity	Location	Responsibility
	Decide where the celebrity will sit during the game—preferably in the front row with easy access to center court.	Stands	Venue manager, event manager
9:00 A.M.	Rehearse the setup and breakdown time of stage and equipment. Make sure all cables are taped down and secure, and that signs are posted.	Arena	Crew, event manager
10:00 A.M.	Take pictures of risk management areas.	Arena	Assistant
10:20 A.M.	Rehearse performance with stand-ins and time each segment.	Arena	Event manager, assistants, crew
11:00 A.M.	Dress rehearsal. Make sure everyone has arrived, including client.	Arena	Event manager, celebrity, cheerleaders, choreographer
11:10 A.M.	Lights dim. Set up temporary stage, podium, and microphone.	Center court	Sound and light crew
	Announcer introduces celebrity.	Arena	Sound crew, announcer
	Cue celebrity.	Arena	Event manager
11:12 A.M.	Celebrity enters stage right, walks to podium.	Center court	Celebrity
11:15 A.M.	Celebrity gives speech.	Center court	Celebrity
11:25 A.M.	Celebrity exits stage left.	Center court	Celebrity
	Lights dim, stage is removed.	Center court	Crew
	Cheerleaders move to center court.	Center court	Cheerleaders
	Announcer introduces cheerleaders.	Arena	Announcer
11:28 A.M.	Music starts, lights up, gobos of stars projected on audience.	Stands	Lighting crew
	Cheerleaders start performance.	Center court	Choreographer, cheerleaders
11:35 A.M.	Cheerleaders end performance.	Center court	Cheerleaders
	Lights up full. Performance ends.	Arena	Lighting crew
11:36 A.M.	Announcement thanking cheerleaders.	Arena	Announcer
12:00 P.M.	Lunch	Breakout room	Caterer

Time	Activity	Location	Responsibility
1:00 P.M.	Extra rehearsal time. Final changes.	Arena	As appropriate
2:00 P.M.	Clean up area. Allow for venue crew to prepare for game.	Arena	Venue crew
2:30 P.M.	Announcer introduces players.	Arena	Announcer
2:40 P.M.	Game begins.	Arena	Players
All times hereafter depend on the game. Times are approximate. Time frame is needed for each segment.			
3:30 P.M. (5 min.)	Halftime starts. Players clear the field.	Arena	Players
3:35 P.M. (3 min.)	Lights dim. Temporary stage, podium, and microphone is set up.	Center stage	Venue crew, lighting and sound crew
	Cue celebrity.	Stands	Event manager
	Announcer introduces celebrity.	Arena	Announcer
3:38 P.M. (1 min.)	Celebrity walks to stage.	Center court	Celebrity
3:39 P.M. (10 min.)	Celebrity gives speech.	Center court	Celebrity
3:49 P.M. (1 min.)	Celebrity walks off stage.	Court	Celebrity
3:50 P.M. (3 min.)	Lights dim, stage is removed.	Arena	Lighting and sound crew
	Cheerleaders move into position on center court.	Center court	Cheerleaders
	Announcer introduces cheerleaders.	Arena	Announcer
3:53 P.M. (5 min.)	Music starts, lights up, gobos of stars projected on audience. Performance starts.	Arena/ stands	Lighting crew
	Cheerleaders end performance.	Center court	Cheerleaders
	Lights up full.	Arena	Lighting crew
	Announcement thanking cheerleaders.	Arena	Announcer
	Performance ends. Cheerleaders exit center court.	Court	Cheerleaders
3:58 P.M. (2 min.)	Players return to the court.	Arena	Players
4:00 P.M.	Game restarts.	Arena	Players
4:30 P.M.	Table is set up outside exit area. Signs posted to show where autographs will be signed.	Outside arena	Venue crew

Time	Activity	Location	Responsibility
5:15 P.M.	5 minutes before end of game, celebrity is taken by security to sign autographs. Security is stationed around the celebrity.	Arena	Security/celebrity
5:20 P.M.	Game ends. Announcement made that celebrity will sign autographs.	Arena	Announcer
	Celebrity signs autographs.	Outside arena	Celebrity/security
6:00 P.M.	Event ends, celebrity stops signing.	Arena	Celebrity/ security/event manager
	Provide for signs and gobos to be shipped back to office.	Storage area	Event manager
	Make sure storage area is clean and inspected. Make sure podium, stage, and microphone are ready to be shipped back to the rental company.	Storage area	Venue crew, event manager
	Thank and release crew and security.	Arena	Event manager
	Take celebrity out to dinner.	Arena	Celebrity, event manager

Logistics

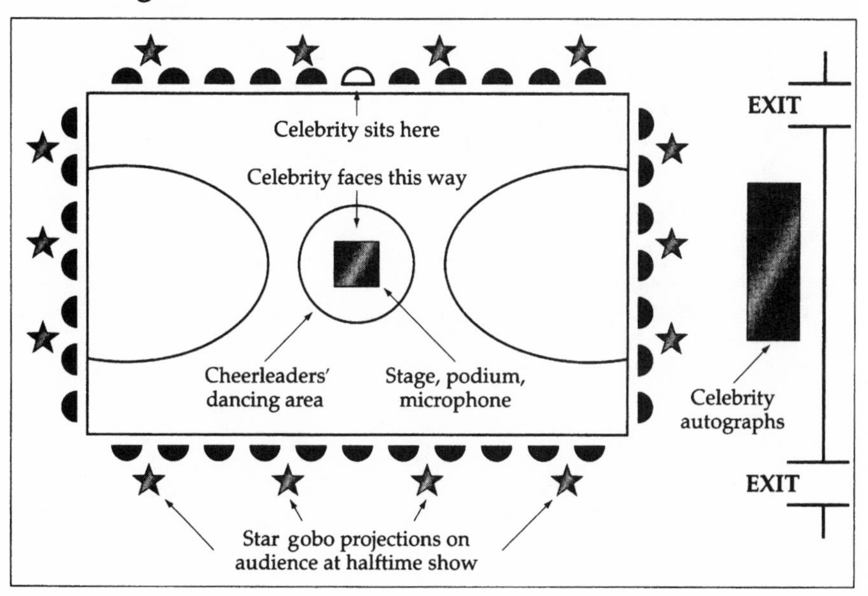

E. OLYMPIC GAMES OFFICIAL OPENING/ CLOSING CEREMONIES

The opening and closing ceremonies shall be held in accordance with the protocol decided by the International Olympic Committee (IOC). The detailed program of such ceremonies shall be put forward by the Organizing Committee of the Olympic Games (OCOG) and submitted to the approval of the IOC Executive Board.

The Opening Ceremony shall take place not earlier than one day before the competitions of the Games of the Olympiad and of the Olympic Winter Games. The Closing Ceremony shall take place on the last day of the competitions of the Games of the Olympiad and of the Olylmpic Winter Games.

1. Opening Ceremony
   - 1.1 The Olympic Games shall be proclaimed open by the head of state of the host country.
   - 1.2 The head of state is received at the entrance of the stadium by the president of the IOC and by the president of the OCOG. The two presidents then show the head of state into his or her box in the official stand.
   - 1.3 The parade of the participants then follows. Each delegation, dressed in its official uniform, must be preceded by a nameboard bearing its name and must be accompanied by its flag, to be carried by a member of the delegation. The flags of the participating delegations, as well as the nameboards, shall be provided by the OCOG and shall all be of equal size. The nameboard bearers shall be designated by the OCOG.
   - 1.4 No participant in the parade is permitted to carry flags, banners, banderoles, cameras, or other visible accessories or objects that are not part of his or her uniform.
   - 1.5 The delegations parade in alphabetical order according to the language of the host country, except for Greece, which leads the parade, and for the host country, which brings up the rear. Only those athletes participating in the Olympic Games with the right to accommodation in the Olympic Village may take part in the parade, led by a maximum of six officials per delegation.
   - 1.6 The delegations salute the head of state and the president of the IOC as they walk past their box. Each delegation, after completing its march, proceeds to the seats which have been reserved for it in order to watch the ceremony, with the exception of its flag bearer who remains in the field.
   - 1.7 The president of the IOC, accompanied by the president of the OCOG, proceeds to the rostrum positioned on the field in front of the official stand. The president of the OCOG gives an address lasting a maximum of three minutes, then adds these words: "I have the honor of inviting

____________________, president of the International Olympic Committee, to speak."

1.8 The president of the IOC then gives a speech, adding: "I have the honor of inviting ____________________, (the head of state) to proclaim open the Games of the ____ Olympiad of the modern era (or the ____ Olympic Winter Games)."

1.9 The head of state proclaims the Games open by saying: "I declare open the Games of ________________ (name of city) celebrating the _____ Olympiad of the modern era (or the ____ Olympic Winter Games)."

1.10 While the Olympic anthem is being played, the Olympic flag, unfurled horizontally, is brought into the stadium and hoisted on the flagpole erected in the area.

1.11 The Olympic torch is brought into the stadium by runners relaying each other. The last runner circles the track before lighting the Olympic flame, which shall not be extinguished until the closing of the Olympic Games. The lighting of the Olympic flame shall be followed by a symbolic release of pigeons.

1.12 The flag bearers of all the delegations form a semicircle around the rostrum. A competitor of the host country mounts the rostrum. Holding a corner of the Olympic flag in his or her left hand, and raising the right hand, the competing athlete takes the following solemn oath: "In the name of all the competitors I promise that we shall take part in these Olympic Games, respecting and abiding by the rules which govern them, in the true spirit of sportsmanship, for the glory of sport and the honor of our teams."

1.13 Immediately afterward, a judge from the host country mounts the rostrum and, in the same manner, takes the following oath: "In the name of all the judges and officials, I promise that we shall officiate in these Olympic Games with complete impartiality, respecting and abiding by the rules which govern them, in the true spirit of sportsmanship.

1.14 The national anthem of the host country is then played or sung. The flag bearers then proceed to the seats that have been reserved to enable them to attend the artistic program.

1.15 In the event that the IOC authorizes a secondary opening ceremony to take place at another Olympic venue, the IOC Executive Board shall determine its protocol, upon the proposal of the OCOG.

2. Closing Ceremony

2.1 The closing ceremony must take place in the stadium after the end of all the events. The participants in the Olympic Games having the right to accommodation in the Olympic Village take the seats reserved for them in the stands. The flag bearers of the participating delegations and the nameboard bearers enter the stadium in single file in the same order and take up the same positions as they did at the opening ceremony of the Olympic Games. Behind them march the athletes, without distinction of nationality.

2.2 The flag bearers then form a semicircle behind the rostrum.

2.3 The president of the IOC and the president of the OCOG mount the rostrum. At the sounds of the Greek national anthem, the Greek flag is hoisted on the flagpole that stands to the right of the central flagpole used for the winners' flags. The flag of the host country is then hoisted on the central flagpole, while the host country's anthem is played. Finally, the flag of the host country of the next Olympic Games is hoisted on the left-hand flagpole to the strains of its anthem.

2.4 The mayor of the host city joins the president of the IOC on the rostrum and hands the president, for the Games of the Olympiad, the flag donated in 1920 by the Belgian Olympic Committee, and for the Olympic Winter Games, the flag donated in 1952 by the city of Oslo. The president of the IOC hands it on to the mayor of the host city of the following Olympic Games. This flag must be displayed until the following Olympic Games in the latter city's main municipal building.

2.5 After an address by the president of the OCOG, the president of the IOC gives the closing speech of the Olympic Games, which ends with these words: "I declare the Games of the ____ Olympiad (or the ____ Olympic Winter Games) closed and, in accordance with tradition, I call upon the youth of the world to assemble four years from now at ____ (in case the city has not yet been chosen, the name of the city is replaced by the words: "the place to be chosen"), to celebrate with us there the Games of the ____ Olympiad (or the ____ Olympic Winter Games)."

2.6 A fanfare then sounds, the Olympic flame is extinguished, and while the Olympic anthem is being played, the Olympic flag is slowly lowered from the flagpole and, unfurled horizontally, carried out of the arena, followed by the flag bearers. A farewell song resounds.

Source: International Olympic Charter, International Olympic Committee.

F. RULES FOR ESTABLISHING PRECEDENCE (PROTOCOL) FOR YOUR SPORT EVENT

Edited by Hugh Wakeham
Protocol by the Book

Ceremony Script Development

- Preshow
- Arrival of VIPs
- Flag raising/national anthem
- VIP introductions
- Speeches
- Performance
- Official announcement
- Performance/grand finale

Script: Energy/Time

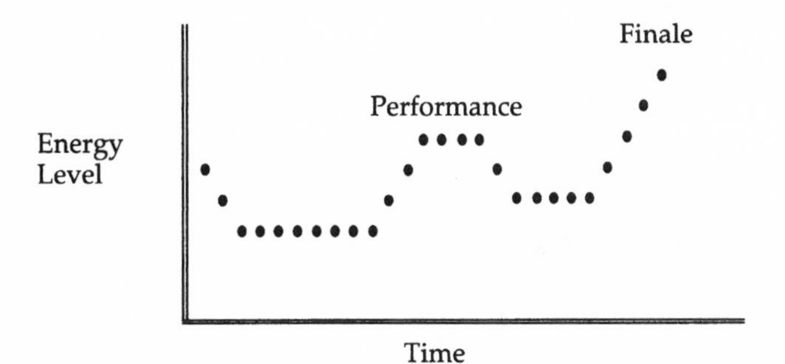

Precedence of Political Order in the United States

- President of the United States
- Vice President of the United States
  Governor of a state (when in his or her own state)
- Speaker of the House of Representatives
  Chief Justice of the U.S. Supreme Court
  Former presidents of the United States
  American ambassadors (when at post)
- Secretary of State
- Ambassadors of foreign powers accredited to the United States (in order of presentation of their credentials)
- Widows of former presidents of the United States

- Ministers and envoys of foreign powers accredited to the United States (in order of presentation of their credentials)
- Associate justices of the Supreme Court
  Retired chief justices
  Retired associate justices (associate justices who resign and have no rank)
- Cabinet officers (other than Secretary of State, ranked according to the date of establishment of department)
- President of the Senate
  Senators (according to length of continuous service; if the same, arrange alphabetically)
- Governors of states (when outside their own state). Precedence in this case is determined by the state's date of admission into the Union (see state precedence) or alphabetically by state
  Acting heads of executive departments (e.g., acting secretary of defence)
- Former vice presidents of the United States
- Members of the House of Representatives (according to length of continuous service; if the same, arrange by their state's date of admission into the Union or alphabetically by state)
  Delegates from the District of Columbia, Guam, Virgin Islands, American Samoa, and resident commissioner from Puerto Rico to the House of Representatives (nonvoting members)
- Charge d'affaires of foreign powers
- Former secretaries of state
- Other federal officials
- State officials
- Local officials

Precedence of the Order of States

(Determined by date of admission into the Union)

1.	Delaware	December 7, 1787
2.	Pennsylvania	December 12, 1787
3.	New Jersey	December 18, 1787
4.	Georgia	January 2, 1788
5.	Connecticut	January 9, 1788
6.	Massachusetts	February 6, 1788
7.	Maryland	April 28, 1788
8.	South Carolina	May 23, 1788
9.	New Hampshire	June 21, 1788
10.	Virginia	June 26, 1788
11.	New York	July 26, 1788

12.	North Carolina	November 21, 1789
13.	Rhode Island	May 29, 1790
14.	Vermont	March 4, 1791
15.	Kentucky	June 1, 1792
16.	Tennessee	June 1, 1796
17.	Ohio	March 1, 1803
18.	Louisiana	April 30, 1812
19.	Indiana	December 11, 1816
20.	Mississippi	December 10, 1817
21.	Illinois	December 3, 1818
22.	Alabama	December 14, 1819
23.	Maine	March 15, 1820
24.	Missouri	August 10, 1821
25.	Arkansas	June 15, 1836
26.	Michigan	January 26, 1837
27.	Florida	March 3, 1845
28.	Texas	December 29, 1845
29.	Iowa	December 28, 1846
30.	Wisconsin	May 29, 1848
31.	California	September 9, 1850
32.	Minnesota	May 11, 1858
33.	Oregon	February 14, 1859
34.	Kansas	January 29, 1861
35.	West Virginia	June 20, 1863
36.	Nevada	October 31, 1864
37.	Nebraska	March 1, 1867
38.	Colorado	August 1, 1876
39.	North Dakota	November 2, 1889
40.	South Dakota	November 2, 1889
41.	Montana	November 8, 1889
42.	Washington	November 11, 1889
43.	Idaho	July 3, 1890
44.	Wyoming	July 10, 1890
45.	Utah	January 4, 1896
46.	Oklahoma	November 16, 1907
47.	New Mexico	January 6, 1912
48.	Arizona	February 14, 1912
49.	Alaska	January 3, 1959
50.	Hawaii	August 21, 1959

Precedence Positions

Arriving:
1. Host
2. 8th most important person
3. 7th most important person
4. 6th most important person
5. 5th most important person
6. 4th most important person
7. 3rd most important person
8. 2nd most important person
9. Most important person

Entering a room:
1. Host
2. Most important person
3. 2nd most important person
4. 3rd most important person
5. 4th most important person
6. 5th most important person
7. 6th most important person
8. 7th most important person
9. 8th most important person

Entering a theater and seating position:
1. 8th most important person
2. 6th most important person
3. 4th most important person
4. 2nd most important person
5. Host
6. Most important person
7. 3rd most important person
8. 5th most important person
9. 7th most important person

Speaking:
Most Common Speaking Arrangement
1. Host
2. Most important person
3. 2nd most important person
4. 3rd most important person
5. 4th most important person
6. 5th most important person
7. 6th most important person
8. 7th most important person
9. 8th most important person

When a president is the most important person
1. Most important person
2. Host
3. 2nd most important person
4. 3rd most important person
5. 4th most important person
6. 5th most important person
7. 6th most important person
8. 7th most important person
9. 8th most important person

Saving the best for last
1. 8th most important person
2. 7th most important person
3. 6th most important person
4. 5th most important person
5. 4th most important person
6. 3rd most important person
7. 2nd most important person
8. Host
9. Most important person

Departing:
For pictures
1. Host
2. Most important person
3. 2nd most important person
4. 3rd most important person
5. 4th most important person
6. 5th most important person
7. 6th most important person
8. 7th most important person
9. 8th most important person

No pictures
1. Most important person
2. 2nd most important person
3. 3rd most important person
4. 4th most important person
5. 5th most important person
6. 6th most important person
7. 7th most important person
8. 8th most important person
9. Host

REFERENCES

BOOKS

American Sport Education Program. *Event Management for Sport Directors*. Champaign, IL: Human Kinetics, 1996.

Bergin, R. *Sponsorship Principles and Practices*. Nashville, TN: Amusement Business, 1989.

Berlonghi, Alexander. *The Special Event Risk Management Handbook*. Distributed by BookMasters, Mansfield, OH, phone: 800-537-6727.

Bridges, F., and L. Roquemore. *Management for Athletic/Sport Administration*. Decatur, GA: ESM Books, 2000.

Brooks, C. *Sports Marketing: Competitive Business Strategies for Sports*, Upper Saddle River, NJ: Prentice-Hall, 1994.

Byl, J. *Organizing Successful Tournaments*. Champaign, IL: Human Kinetics, 1999.

Carter, D. *Keeping Score*. Grants Pass, OR: Oasis Press, 1996.

Chelladurai, P. *Human Resource Management in Sport and Recreation*. Champaign, IL: Human Kinetics, 1999.

Crompton, J. *Measuring the Economic Impact*. Ashburn, VA: Division of Professional Services, National Recreation and Park Association, 1999.

Flannery, T., and M. Swank. *Personnel Management for Sport Directors*. Champaign, IL: Human Kinetics, 1999.

Goldblatt, J., and F. Supovitz. *Dollars and Events*. New York: John Wiley & Sons, Inc., 1999.

Helitzer, M. *The Dream Job: Sports, Publicity, Promotion, and Public Relations*. 3d ed. Athens, OH: University Sports Press, 1992.

Howard, D., and J. Crompton. *Financing Sport*. Morgantown, WV: Fitness Information Technology, 1995.

International Events Group. *IEG Legal Guide to Sponsorship, IEG Directory, and Special Event Report*. Chicago, IL: International Events Group (phone: 312/244-1727).

Johnson, J. *Promotions for Sport Directors*. Champaign, IL: Human Kinetics, 1996.

Jozsa, F., and J. Guthrie. *How the Major Leagues Respond to Market Conditions*. Westport, CT: Greenwood Publishing Group, Inc. 1999.

Kestner, J. *Program Evaluation for Sport Directors*. Champaign, IL: Human Kinetics, 1996.

Mackenzie, J. *It's Show Time!* Homewood, IL: Dow Jones-Irwin, 1989.

McCormack, M. *What They Don't Teach You at Harvard Business School*. New York: Bantam, 1985.

Milne, G., and M. McDonald. *Sport Marketing*. Amherst, MA: University of Massachusetts, 1999.

Milne, G., and M. McDonald. *Cases in Sport Marketing*. Amherst, MA: University of Massachusetts, 1999.

Mullin, B., S. Hardy, and W. Sutton. *Sport Marketing*. 2d ed. Champaign, IL: Human Kinetics, 1999.

Olson, J. *Facility and Equipment Management for Sport Directors*. Champaign, IL: Human Kinetics, 1997.

Pemberton, K. *Sports Marketing: The Money Side of Sports*. Marina Del Rey, CA: Sports Services of America Publishing, 1997.

Pitts, B., and D. Stotlar. *Fundamentals of Sport Marketing*. Morgantown, WV: FIT, 1996.

Quirk, J., and R. Fort. *Pay Dirt*. Princeton, NJ: Princeton University Press, 1997.

Sport Market Place Directory. Chandler, AZ: Franklin Covey Sports Division (published annually).

The Sports Sponsor Factbook. Chicago, IL: Team Marketing Report (published annually; phone: 312-829-7060).

Sport Summit Sports Business Directory. Bethesda, MD: EJ Krause (published annually).

Standeven, J., and P. DeKnop. *Sport Tourism*. Champaign, IL: Human Kinetics, 1999.

Stier, W. *Fundraising for Sport and Recreation*. Champaign, IL: Human Kinetics, 1994.

Stier, W. *More Fantastic Fundraisers for Sport and Recreation*. Champaign, IL: Human Kinetics, 1997.

Stotlar, D. *Successful Sport Marketing*. Madison, WI: WCB Brown and Benchmark Publishers, 1993.

Wilkinson, D. *Sport Marketing Institute Resource Manual*. Sunnydale, CA: The Event Management and Marketing Institute, 1986.

SELECT PERIODICALS

2000 Sports Business Market Research Handbook. Sports Business Market Research, Inc., Norcross, GA.

Advertising Age. Crain Communications, Inc., 740 Rush St. Chicago, IL 60611-2590

The American Spectator. PO Box 549, Arlington, VA 22216-0549

Amusement Business. 49 Music Square West, Nashville, TN 37203.

Around the Rings. Ed Hula, Atlanta, GA.

Journal of Sport Management. Human Kinetics Publishing, Champaign, IL.

Marquette Sports Law Journal. Marquette University Law School.

Revenues from Sport Ventures (RSV Fax). Mediaventures, Milwaukee, WI.

Sponsorship Newsletter. BDS Sponsorship Ltd., London, UK.

Sport Business: The Magazine for the International Business of Sport. SportBusiness Limited, London, England.

Sport Marketing Newsletter. Westport, CT (phone: 203/255-1787).

Sport Marketing Quarterly. Fitness Information Technology, Morgantown, WV.

Sports Business Journal. Street & Smith, Charlotte, NC.

Sports on the Road. Net Works Communications, Englewood, CO.

SportsTravel Magazine. Schneider Publishing Company, Los Angeles, CA.

Stadia. Broadcast Publishing Ltd., Phoenix House, Brighton, UK.

Stadium Insider. Mediaventures, Milwaukee, WI.

Team Market Report. Chicago, IL (phone: 312-829-7060).

Television Sports Rights 2000. Gould Media, Anna Maris, FL.

SOFTWARE

Sport Director: Professional Edition. Human Kinetics Software, Champaign, IL, 2000.

Sport Director: Volunteer Edition. Human Kinetics Software, Champaign, IL, 2000.

Youth Sport Director Guide and Software, Rainer Martens, American Sport Education Program, Champaign, IL.

INDEX

ABOUT THE AUTHORS

Stedman Graham is president of Graham and Associates, a leading sports marketing firm that has played a role in events including the Volvo Tennis Tournament and the NBA Legends Pride Classic. An adjunct professor at Northwestern University's Kellogg Graduate School of Management, Graham is the best-selling author of *You Can Make It Happen* and *Teens Can Make It Happen*. He also writes a popular column for *Inside Sports*.

Lisa Delpy Neirotti, Ph.D., is director of the sports management program at The George Washington University. Dr. Neirotti consults with corporate sponsors and sports commissions around the world and is a frequent contributor to academic and industry publications.

Joe Jeff Goldblatt is director of the event management program at The George Washington University. The author of *Special Events: The Art and Science of Celebration*, Goldblatt has produced corporate events for Marriott, Xerox, and dozens of other Fortune 500 companies.